EYEWITNESS 👁 *HANDBOOKS*

ROCKS
AND
MINERALS

ROCKS
— AND —
MINERALS

CHRIS PELLANT

HELEN PELLANT
Editorial Consultant

Photography by
HARRY TAYLOR
(Natural History Museum)

A DK PUBLISHING BOOK

Editors Stella Vayne, James Harrison
Art Editor Clive Hayball
Editorial Authenticator Dr Robert Symes
(Natural History Museum, London)
Production·Controller Caroline Webber
U.S. Consultant Joseph J. Peters
Senior Scientific Assistant
(Department of Mineral Science,
American Museum of Natural History)
U.S. Editor Charles A. Wills

First American Edition, 1992
10 9

Published in the United States by DK Publishing, Inc.
95 Madison Avenue, New York, NY 10016

Pellant, Chris
     The eyewitness handbook of rocks and minerals / by Chris Pellant. —
1st American ed.
     p. cm.
     Includes index
     ISBN 1–56458–033–4 hardcover: $29.95
     ISBN 1–56458–061–X flexibound: $17.95
     1. Rocks—Handbooks, manuals, etc. 2. Minerals—Handbooks,
manuals, etc. 3. Rocks—Identification—Handbooks, manuals, etc.
4. Minerals—Identification—Handbooks, manuals, etc. I. Title.
QE431.2.P45 1992
549—dc20   91–58222

Computer page makeup by
The Cooling Brown Partnership, Great Britain

Text film output by Creative Ace and
The Right Type, Great Britain

Reproduced by
Colourscan, Singapore

Printed and bound by
Kyodo Printing Co., Singapore

CONTENTS

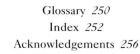

COLLECTING ROCKS AND MINERALS

Rocks and minerals are a fundamental part of the earth's crust. Collecting and studying them can be both a rewarding and an absorbing hobby. This can involve traveling to wild and exciting places, much research, and some time spent cataloging and displaying finds. As your collection grows, you can exchange material with other collectors and purchase rare or exceptional specimens from mineral dealers.

A COLLECTING TRIP may take you to a site a few miles away, or to the other side of the world. Wherever your exact destination is, you may find rock faces in sea or river cliffs, or in man-made exposures such as quarries, road or rail cuttings, and building excavations. Seek permission to collect when on private, state, or federally owned land, and collect specimens in moderation. Always treat natural exposures with care, and don't chip away natural rock faces. Collectors can also be conservationists.

FIELD SPECIMENS

You may come to explore an area where, millions of years ago, hot fluids – possibly associated with molten magma beneath the earth's surface – have deposited minerals in overlying strata. In such an area, you can find many different specimens: Rocks like granite and limestone, and minerals such as fluorite, occuring within a short distance of each other.

SEASIDE CLIFF EXPOSURE
Search the shore below the cliffs for rocks and minerals. The dumps of abandoned mines, as on the cliff top here, are an excellent area to hunt for minerals.

CRINOIDAL LIMESTONE

GRANITE

CRYSTALLINE FLUORITE

crystalline fluorite often found in old mine dumps

granite is often found in disused quarries

crinoidal limestone occurs on limestone cliffs

GEOLOGICAL MAPS

Geological maps display the surface distribution of rocks, their age relationships, and structural features. The colored patterns of a geologic map show individual rock formations. Dip symbols provide clues to predict the structure, indicating the angle that a rock strata makes with the horizontal. Interpreting a geologic map is a matter of experience and common sense. For instance, note that the crystallized mineral shown below occurs near a metamorphic contact zone. Geologic maps can be found in libraries throughout the country, or purchased from the U.S. Geological Survey, or your State's Geological Survey.

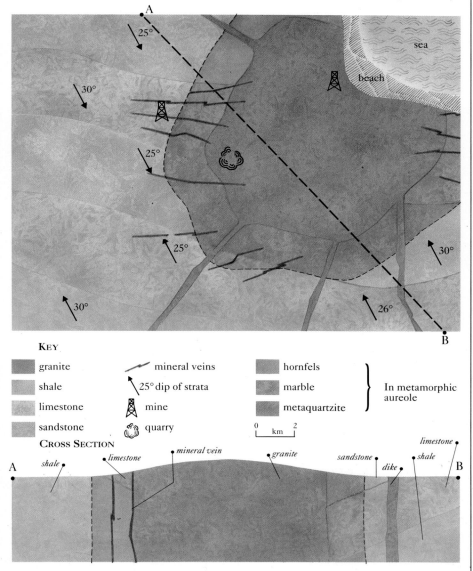

KEY

granite		mineral veins		hornfels		
shale		25° dip of strata		marble		In metamorphic aureole
limestone		mine		metaquartzite		
sandstone		quarry				

CROSS SECTION

FIELD EQUIPMENT

DO YOUR HOMEWORK before your field work: check your locality reference material, such as guide books and detailed maps, before setting out on any field trip. Geological maps are a great asset (see page 7) but, because overprinted colors may obscure features such as roads and quarries, you should also take a detailed, large-scale map to pinpoint the actual site. Take a compass for areas with few topographical features on the ground, so that you can locate sites. Protective clothing is essential. When working below a high cliff or quarry face, a hard hat is a must. Put on goggles to shield your eyes from chips of rock flying off as you use your hammer, and wear strong gloves to protect your hands. Take a geological hammer to break up blocks of material already on the ground, but use it sparingly. Several hardened steel chisels are handy for extracting different minerals or for splitting rocks. Write notes, take pictures, or make a videotape of the location of your specimens. Without field notes, especially of a location, specimens are of little scientific value.

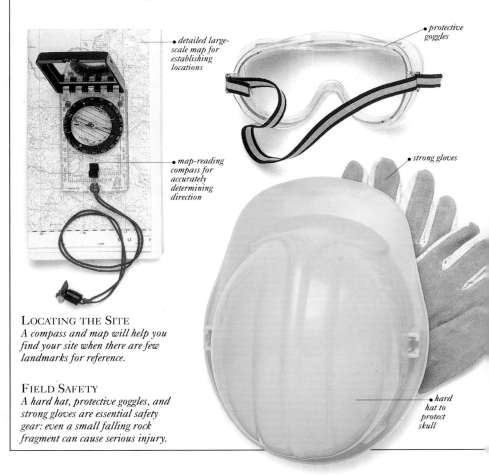

detailed large-scale map for establishing locations

map-reading compass for accurately determining direction

protective goggles

strong gloves

hard hat to protect skull

LOCATING THE SITE
A compass and map will help you find your site when there are few landmarks for reference.

FIELD SAFETY
A hard hat, protective goggles, and strong gloves are essential safety gear: even a small falling rock fragment can cause serious injury.

camera

notepad

pencil

spare film

ballpoint pen

RECORDING SPECIMENS

Mineral or rock samples are of little interest without detailed location information. Record the details at the site, not when you get home, since you are likely to forget the facts. Make notes and sketches in a small notebook, and take pictures of the strata, rock structures, and location. If you have access to a camcorder, use it to keep a detailed audiovisual record.

cloth bag to pack specimens

newspaper for wrapping

HAND LENS

A powerful hand lens enables you to see your rock and mineral specimens in far better detail, making on-the-spot identification possible.

geological hammer for breaking up larger rocks

utility knife to test hardness (see p.11)

bubble wrap

clear plastic bag with seal

wide-ended chisel

thin, sharp-pointed chisel

hard plastic container

PRYING AND PACKING

Use a geological hammer sparingly. Only break up rocks that are already on the ground. Do not use a hammer to quarry exposures. Collect in moderation, wrapping specimens safely in newspaper, cloth, or bubble wrap. Remember to label each item clearly.

HOME EQUIPMENT

YOU HAVE COLLECTED your specimens and brought them home. Now you should prepare them carefully for identification, and then for display or storage. Your home equipment should have the essential identification aids shown here. Many specimens will have soil and/or the rock matrix attached to them which you will have to clean off. Use a soft brush to remove very loose soil and other rock debris. Avoid hammering at specimens with heavy or sharp tools unless you want to reveal fresh surfaces. Hold the specimens in your hand while you brush away the loose material – a vice or metal clamp may cause damage.

If you are preparing a hard rock specimen, such as granite or gneiss, you can do very little damage, even with a fairly coarse brush and running water. For delicate minerals, such as calcite crystals, use distilled water (which doesn't contain reactive chemical additives) and a very fine brush. For minerals that dissolve in water (the cubes of halite lose their sharp edges), use other liquids. Alcohol cleans nitrates, sulfates, and borates, and weak hydrochloric acid is a good cleaner for silicates, but will dissolve carbonates. Soaking silicates overnight in acid will remove coatings of carbonate debris.

SCRAPING AND PRYING TOOLS
Clean off loose debris from some specimens with sharp metal implements. A pointed tool like a bradawl is useful for prying material off, but take great care not to damage the underlying rock. This is a preliminary stage of specimen preparation.

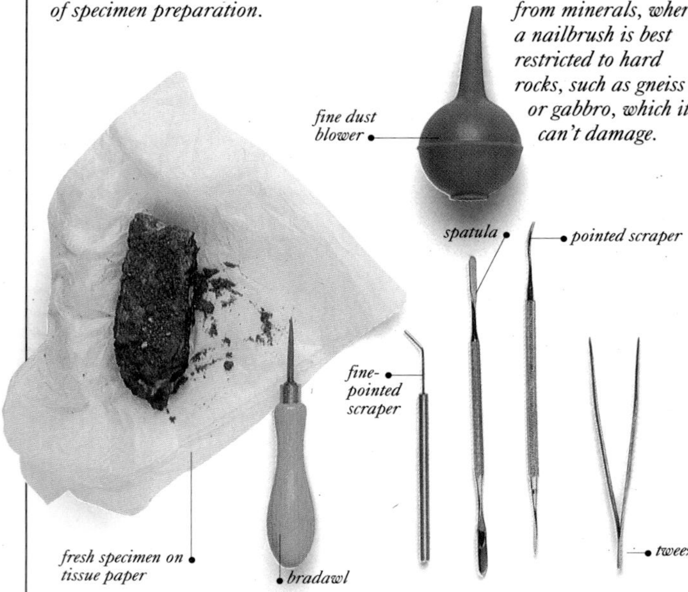

CLEANING BRUSHES
You can clean rocks and minerals using brushes of various sizes – from a soft paintbrush to a nailbrush – depending on the fragility of the specimen. A soft sable brush is best for removal of tiny sediment grains from minerals, whereas a nailbrush is best restricted to hard rocks, such as gneiss or gabbro, which it can't damage.

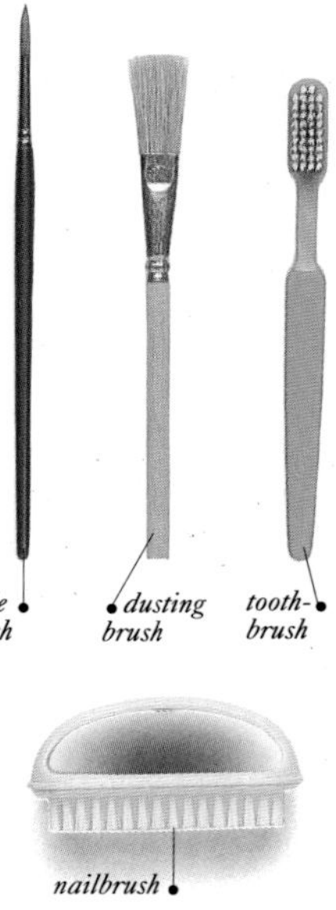

fine dust blower •

spatula •

• pointed scraper

fine-pointed scraper

sable brush •

• dusting brush

tooth-brush •

fresh specimen on tissue paper •

• bradawl

• tweezers

nailbrush •

• *distilled water*

CLEANING LIQUIDS
Use distilled water, if possible, for cleaning, because tap water contains various chemicals that may react with minerals. Diluted hydrochloric acid will dissolve carbonate matrix. This acid is safe to use.

weak hydrochloric acid

MINERAL TESTS
At home, basic chemistry tests are a good way of establishing a mineral's identity. Dilute acids will give consistent reactions on a given mineral: for example, carbonates effervesce in dilute hydrochloric acid. (Always wear gloves when working with acids.) A controlled flame is another test. Place a specimen on a charcoal block and concentrate a Bunsen flame onto it, using a blowpipe. The mineral may color the flame, indicating chemical composition, or it may fuse, forming a small, globular, beadlike mass, or give off odors.

• *soft tissue paper for absorbing cleaning liquids*

cotton swabs for reaching into cavities •

• *x10 hand lens for identifying specimens*

porcelain streak plate or tile •

IDENTIFICATION AIDS
A streak plate, hardness kit and hand lens are all indispensable identification aids. The properties of hardness and streak are explained on pages 25 and 26 respectively.

HARDNESS KIT
If you scratch a mineral with everyday objects in sequence – say a coin followed by a knife, followed by a piece of glass or quartz – you can determine the mineral's hardness (see page 25).

• *glass (hardness 6)*

• *quartz (hardness 7)*

• *specimen on bubble wrap*

• *hardness points (usually rated from 3 to 10)*

coin (hardness 3)

• *knife blade (hardness 5½)*

ORGANIZING YOUR COLLECTION

A COLLECTION OF ROCKS and minerals is of little scientific value unless it is sensibly organized. Once you have collected and cleaned your specimens, they should be organized for storage and display, as well as cataloged and labeled. You'll probably want to display the more attractive specimens and those which are fairly robust. Display these in a glass-fronted cabinet. Store delicate specimens in individual trays or boxes, slightly larger than the specimens themselves, in a cabinet. Add a specimen label to each tray, recording the specimen's name, locality, date of collection, and catalog number. Enter each specimen in your catalog – this can be a card file or computer-based system. Number the entries to correspond with the numbers on the labels in the specimen trays. There should also be room for more detailed information in the catalog than on the specimen tray. Write or key-in map references as well as any geological information such as other minerals or rocks at that location. Also record details of the rock structure, any large-scale formation, and field features you saw there – perhaps a mineral vein and the rock in which the vein was running. The source and value of exchanged or purchased specimens should also be recorded. Also note key identifying features, which you can refer to in the relevant rock or mineral entry in this book.

notepad and ballpoint pen •

NOTES AND RECORDS
Transfer field notes to an index card or a computer. Put a little typewriter correcting fluid or white paint on each specimen (in an unimportant area) and write a catalog number on this.

• floppy disks

mark for • numbering

• correcting fluid

COMPUTER RECORDS
A computer-based system is the most convenient way to store, add, and modify data.

• cards for cataloging

CARD FILE
A catalog on index cards is inexpensive, reliable, and quick to use. Enter the specimens alphabetically. There is space to transcribe field notes and even copy location sketches.

• card file box

well-sorted
drawer

STORING YOUR SPECIMENS

House your rocks and
minerals in trays
within a drawer.
You can easily make
the trays at home to fit
the drawer and the
specimens, or you can
buy them from specialist
suppliers. Pack the
more delicate items with
tissue paper to prevent them
from moving or rubbing
against each other. Small,
clear plastic boxes are also
useful for storage.

specimen labels

tissue-lined
cardboard trays

HOW THIS BOOK WORKS

THE BOOK IS ARRANGED in two parts: minerals, followed by rocks. The minerals, pages 46–179, are organized into eight main chemical groups (see pages 20–21 for an explanation). The mineral groups with the simplest chemistry come first, and are followed by the more complex varieties. Each separate group has a short introduction describing its general characteristics. The entries that follow give detailed information about the minerals found in the groups. The annotated example below shows how a typical entry is organized. The rocks, pages 180–249, are set out in the three large recognized classes (see pages 30–31). Typical annotated entries are shown opposite.

MINERALS

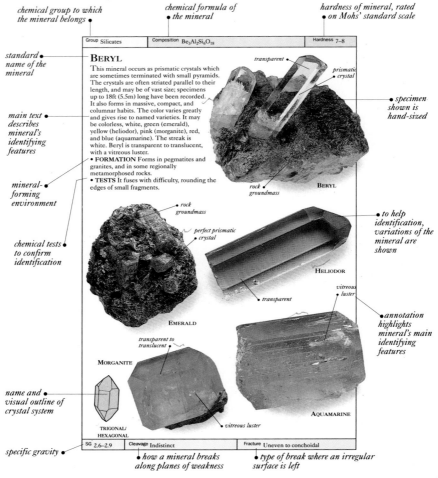

chemical group to which the mineral belongs

chemical formula of the mineral

hardness of mineral, rated on Mohs' standard scale

| Group Silicates | Composition Be₃Al₂Si₆O₁₈ | Hardness 7–8 |

standard name of the mineral

BERYL

This mineral occurs as prismatic crystals which are sometimes terminated with small pyramids. The crystals are often striated parallel to their length, and may be of vast size; specimens up to 18ft (5.5m) long have been recorded. It also forms in massive, compact, and columnar habits. The color varies greatly and gives rise to named varieties. It may be colorless, white, green (emerald), yellow (heliodor), pink (morganite), red, and blue (aquamarine). The streak is white. Beryl is transparent to translucent, with a vitreous luster.

main text describes mineral's identifying features

mineral-forming environment

• **FORMATION** Forms in pegmatites and granites, and in some regionally metamorphosed rocks.

• **TESTS** It fuses with difficulty, rounding the edges of small fragments.

chemical tests to confirm identification

transparent

prismatic crystal

specimen shown is hand-sized

rock groundmass

BERYL

rock groundmass

perfect prismatic crystal

to help identification, variations of the mineral are shown

HELIODOR

vitreous luster

transparent

annotation highlights mineral's main identifying features

EMERALD

transparent to translucent

MORGANITE

name and visual outline of crystal system

TRIGONAL/ HEXAGONAL

vitreous luster

AQUAMARINE

| SG 2.6–2.9 | Cleavage Indistinct | Fracture Uneven to conchoidal |

specific gravity

how a mineral breaks along planes of weakness

type of break where an irregular surface is left

IGNEOUS ROCKS

classification of the rock •

material from which rock has formed •

• *size of grains in rock*

crystal shape: euhedral is well formed, anhedral is poorly formed •

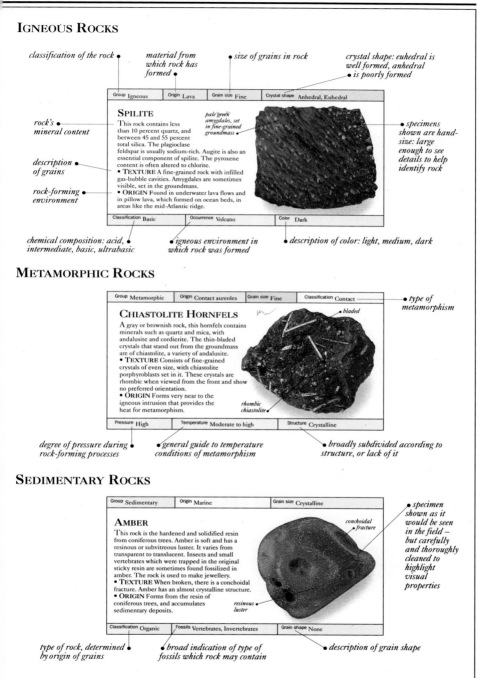

Group Igneous	Origin Lava	Grain size Fine	Crystal shape Anhedral, Euhedral

rock's •
mineral content

description •
of grains

rock-forming •
environment

SPILITE

pale green amygdales, set in fine-grained groundmass •

This rock contains less than 10 percent quartz, and between 45 and 55 percent total silica. The plagioclase feldspar is usually sodium-rich. Augite is also an essential component of spilite. The pyroxene content is often altered to chlorite.
• TEXTURE A fine-grained rock with infilled gas-bubble cavities. Amygdales are sometimes visible, set in the groundmass.
• ORIGIN Found in underwater lava flows and in pillow lava, which formed on ocean beds, in areas like the mid-Atlantic ridge.

• *specimens shown are hand-size: large enough to see details to help identify rock*

Classification Basic	Occurrence Volcano	Color Dark

chemical composition: acid, •
intermediate, basic, ultrabasic

• *igneous environment in which rock was formed*

• *description of color: light, medium, dark*

METAMORPHIC ROCKS

Group Metamorphic	Origin Contact aureoles	Grain size Fine	Classification Contact

• *type of metamorphism*

CHIASTOLITE HORNFELS

• *bladed*

A gray or brownish rock, this hornfels contains minerals such as quartz and mica, with andalusite and cordierite. The thin-bladed crystals that stand out from the groundmass are of chiastolite, a variety of andalusite.
• TEXTURE Consists of fine-grained crystals of even size, with chiastolite porphyroblasts set in it. These crystals are rhombic when viewed from the front and show no preferred orientation.
• ORIGIN Forms very near to the igneous intrusion that provides the heat for metamorphism.

rhombic chiastolite •

Pressure High	Temperature Moderate to high	Structure Crystalline

degree of pressure during •
rock-forming processes

• *general guide to temperature conditions of metamorphism*

• *broadly subdivided according to structure, or lack of it*

SEDIMENTARY ROCKS

Group Sedimentary	Origin Marine	Grain size Crystalline

• *specimen shown as it would be seen in the field – but carefully and thoroughly cleaned to highlight visual properties*

AMBER

conchoidal fracture •

This rock is the hardened and solidified resin from coniferous trees. Amber is soft and has a resinous or subvitreous luster. It varies from transparent to translucent. Insects and small vertebrates which were trapped in the original sticky resin are sometimes found fossilized in amber. The rock is used to make jewellery.
• TEXTURE When broken, there is a conchoidal fracture. Amber has an almost crystalline structure.
• ORIGIN Forms from the resin of coniferous trees, and accumulates sedimentary deposits.

resinous luster •

Classification Organic	Fossils Vertebrates, Invertebrates	Grain shape None

type of rock, determined •
by origin of grains

• *broad indication of type of fossils which rock may contain*

• *description of grain shape*

MINERAL OR ROCK?

ROCKS ARE aggregates of minerals – usually several, but sometimes only one or two. Similarly, minerals are either free, uncombined native elements, or elemental compounds. Gold, silver, and copper are metallic native elements. Feldspars, pyroxenes, amphiboles, and micas are rock-forming silicates – compounds in which metallic elements combine with linked Si-O tetrahedra.

WHAT IS A MINERAL?

With a few notable exceptions (water, mercury, opal), minerals are solid, inorganic elements or elemental compounds. They have definite atomic structures and chemical compositions which vary within fixed limits. Each and every quartz crystal, whether crystallized in a sandstone vein, or in volcanic lava, possesses the same chemical and physical properties.

*bubbles of carbon
dioxide*

PHYSICAL PROPERTY
*All specimens of the same
mineral will have a
similar atomic structure.*

*calcite always
effervesces with cold, dilute
hydrochloric acid*

*calcite cleaves into rhombs, proving its
consistent physical structure*

CHEMICAL PROPERTY
*Every mineral has a
definite composition
which varies within
fixed limits.*

cleaved calcite rhombs

cleavage plane

NATURAL
OCCURRENCE
*Minerals often crystallize
from fluids associated
with volcanic lava (left).
Crusts of minerals may
also form around the
volcano's vent as other
fluids dissipate.*

WHAT IS A ROCK?

Rocks are the essential components of our planet. They are classified into three major groups, determined by how they were formed: igneous, metamorphic, and sedimentary (see pages 30–31). Rocks are aggregates of many different mineral grains, which are fused, cemented, or bound together.

GRANITE

ROCK: A MINERAL AGGREGATE

Granite is a rock composed essentially of three minerals: quartz, mica, and feldspar. Their crystals interlock as a result of crystallization during the cooling of molten magma. The quartz is gray and glassy, the feldspar is light, often in prismatic crystals, and the mica is glittery, and dark or silvery.

mica

quartz

feldspar

QUARTZ
A common mineral in granite, quartz is light-colored and hard.

FELDSPAR
Two types of feldspar occur in granite. In the rock, they are often very well formed crystals.

MICA
Forming as small glittery crystals in granite, mica can be both dark biotite and light muscovite.

MICROSCOPIC CLOSE-UP
This granite is shown at about x30 magnification. Notice how the crystals making up the rock are interlocked.

quartz

mica

feldspar

MINERAL FORMATION

THE EARTH'S CRUST is made of rocks, which themselves are aggregates of minerals. The finest mineral specimens usually occur in hydrothermal veins. These are fractures in the earth's crust through which very hot fluids circulate. These fluids contain the elements from which many minerals form. Mineral specimens also occur in igneous rocks, crystallizing directly from cooling magma (molten rock beneath the earth's surface) or lava (molten rock ejected at the earth's surface). A range of minerals forms in metamorphic rocks when pre-existing rocks are crystallized. In some sedimentary rocks, such as limestones, evaporites, and ironstones, minerals will crystallize from low temperature solutions often very near the surface of the earth.

MINERAL VEINS

These are sheet-like areas of minerals which often cut through existing rock structures. Originally, they may have been faults where rocks have been broken, and one rock mass has moved in relation to another; or joints, where fractures occur without movement. In the vein there can be a complete mineral filling, or crystallization around fragmented masses (breccias).

CASSITERITE

• *typical mineral from a hydro-thermal vein*

common vein • mineral formed from hot chemical solutions beneath the earth's crust

MILKY QUARTZ

QUARTZ VEIN

A vein of white milky quartz (left), cutting through dark slates (far left). Originally formed at great depth, this has been exposed by both weathering and erosion.

IGNEOUS ROCKS

Minerals develop in igneous rocks (see page 32) when molten magma solidifies. The densest minerals, ferro-magnesian silicates like olivine and pyroxene, form at the highest temperatures, while less dense minerals, like feldspar and quartz, occur later in the cooling sequence. Minerals forming in molten rock often grow unrestricted, and can have a fine crystal form.

ORTHOCLASE FELDSPAR

• *silicate mineral commonly found in many igneous rocks*

GRANITE EXPOSURE

An exposure of the igneous rock, granite, showing large feldspar crystals set in the rock groundmass.

GARNET

• *almandine, a garnet commonly found in metamorphic rocks*

METAMORPHIC ROCKS

A range of minerals, including garnet, mica, and kyanite, develop in metamorphic rocks (see page 34). Temperature and pressure may re-arrange chemicals in the existing rocks to create new minerals; or chemically potent fluids circulating through the rock may add extra elements.

MUSCOVITE MICA

• *shiny mineral found in many metamorphic rocks, especially schist*

SCHIST OUTCROP

Schist forms where rocks have been folded deep in the earth's crust, due to intense pressures.

MINERAL COMPOSITION

MINERALS ARE free uncombined elements or elemental compounds. Their compositions are given as chemical formulae. The formula for fluorite is CaF_2. This indicates that calcium (Ca) atoms have combined with fluorine (F) atoms. The subscripted number ($_2$) shows there are twice as many fluorine atoms as there are of calcium. Minerals are arranged into groups according to their chemical composition and their crystal structure.

NATIVE ELEMENTS
These are free uncombined elements. This relatively small group consists of around 50 members, some of which (gold, silver) are very rare and commercially valuable.

SILVER

HALIDES
All minerals in this group contain one of the halogens: fluorine, chlorine, bromine, or iodine. Atoms of these elements combine with metallic atoms to form minerals like halite (sodium and chlorine) or fluorite (calcium and fluorine). This is a small group of minerals, with around 100 members in all.

HALITE

OXIDES AND HYDROXIDES
This is a large group of over 250 minerals. Oxides are compounds in which one, or two metallic elements combine with oxygen. A metallic element combining with water and hydroxl forms a hydroxide.

HEMATITE

SULFIDES
A common group of over 300 minerals, sulfides are chemical compounds in which sulfur has combined with metallic and semimetallic elements. Pyrite and realgar are examples of this group.

SULFUR

PYRITE

REALGAR

OPAL

CALCITE

CARBONATES

A group of 200 minerals, carbonates are compounds in which one or more metallic elements combine with the $(CO_3)^{-2}$ carbonate radical. Calcite, the commonest carbonate, forms when calcium combines with the carbonate radical.

SULFIDES

These are compounds in which one or more metallic elements combine with the sulfate $(SO_4)^{-2}$ radical.

GYPSUM

PYROMORPHITE

PHOSPHATES

A brightly colored group of minerals, phosphates are compounds in which one or more metallic elements combine with the phosphate $(PO_4)^{-3}$ radical. Arsenates and vanadates are associated with this group.

SILICATES

A significant and common group of over 500 minerals, silicates are compounds in which metallic elements combine with either single, or linked Si-O (silicon-oxygen) tetrahedra Si_{4+}. Silicates are divided into six structural classes.

HORNBLENDE

GROSSULAR GARNET

CHEMICAL ELEMENTS

Symbol	Name	Symbol	Name
Ac	Actinium	Mn	Manganese
Ag	Silver	Mo	Molybdenum
Al	Aluminum	N	Nitrogen
Am	Americium	Na	Sodium
Ar	Argon	Nb	Niobium
As	Arsenic	Nd	Neodymium
At	Astatine	Ne	Neon
Au	Gold	Ni	Nickel
B	Boron	No	Nobelium
Ba	Barium	Np	Neptinium
Be	Beryllium	O	Oxygen
Bi	Bismuth	Os	Osmium
Bk	Berkelium	P	Phosphorus
Br	Bromine	Pa	Protactinium
C	Carbon	Pb	Lead
Ca	Calcium	Pd	Palladium
Cd	Cadmium	Pm	Promathium
Ce	Cerium	Po	Polonium
Cf	Californium	Pr	Praseodymium
Cl	Chlorine	Pt	Platinum
Cm	Curium	Pu	Plutonium
Co	Cobalt	Ra	Radium
Cr	Chromium	Rb	Rubidium
Cs	Cesium	Re	Rhenium
Cu	Copper	Rh	Rhodium
Dy	Dysprosium	Rn	Radon
Er	Erbium	S	Sulfur
Es	Einsteinium	Sb	Antimony
F	Fluorine	Sc	Scandium
Fe	Iron	Se	Selenium
Fm	Fermium	Si	Silicon
Fr	Francium	Sm	Samarium
Ga	Gallium	Sn	Tin
Gd	Gadolinium	Sr	Strontium
Ge	Germanium	Ta	Tantalum
H	Hydrogen	Tb	Terbium
He	Helium	Tc	Technetium
Hf	Hafinium	Te	Tellurium
Hg	Mercury	Th	Thorium
Ho	Holmium	Ti	Titanium
I	Iodine	Tl	Thallium
In	Indium	Tu	Thulium
Ir	Iridium	U	Uranium
K	Potassium	V	Vanadium
Kr	Krypton	W	Tungsten
La	Lanthanum	Xe	Xenon
Li	Lithium	Y	Yttrium
Lu	Lutetium	Yb	Ytterbium
Lw	Lawrencium	Zn	Zinc
Md	Mendelevium	Zr	Zirconium
Mg	Magnesium		

MINERAL CHARACTERISTICS

MINERALS EXHIBIT a number of properties which are used for identification. It is essential to take a scientific approach when testing a mineral. First, observe the color (see page 26), luster (page 27), and habit (page 23). Then test for hardness (page 25), specific gravity (page 25), and streak (page 26). Fracture and cleavage (page 24) may be obvious, or you may have to break the mineral.

CRYSTAL SYSTEMS

The geometrical shapes in which minerals crystallize are organized, according to their symmetry, into six main groups called crystal systems. Within each of these systems, many different forms are possible, but all the shapes in a crystal system can be related to the symmetry of that system. From a study of mineral habits, it may be possible to say to which crystal system the mineral belongs. The small blue diagram which appears with each mineral represents its crystal system.

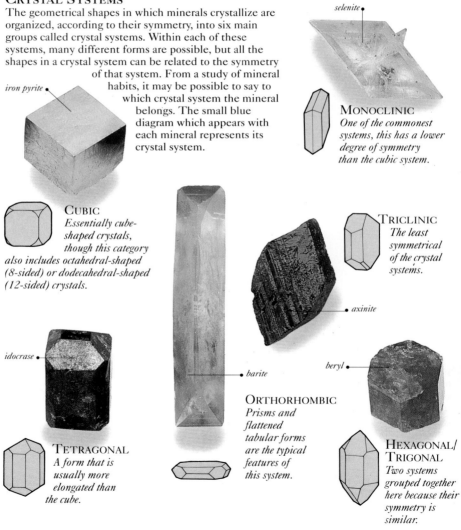

selenite

MONOCLINIC
One of the commonest systems, this has a lower degree of symmetry than the cubic system.

iron pyrite

CUBIC
Essentially cube-shaped crystals, though this category also includes octahedral-shaped (8-sided) or dodecahedral-shaped (12-sided) crystals.

TRICLINIC
The least symmetrical of the crystal systems.

axinite

idocrase

barite

beryl

TETRAGONAL
A form that is usually more elongated than the cube.

ORTHORHOMBIC
Prisms and flattened tabular forms are the typical features of this system.

HEXAGONAL/TRIGONAL
Two systems grouped together here because their symmetry is similar.

HABIT

The habit is the characteristic appearance of a crystal which has been determined by its predominate form. Several descriptive terms to identify a crystal's habit are listed below.

DENDRITIC
Plant-like shape

copper

beryl

PRISMATIC
Shows a uniform cross-section.

scolecite

ACICULAR
Slender needle-like masses.

actinolite

BLADED
Looks like the blade of a knife.

barite

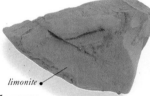

limonite

MASSIVE
Indicates no definitive shape.

hematite

PRISMATIC
Terminated prisms.

RENIFORM
Rounded kidney-shaped masses.

TWINNING

Twinning refers to a non-parallel, symmetrical intergrowth of two or more crystals of the same species. Twinning can occur by contact or interpenetration. Multiple and polysynthetic twins involve more than two individual crystals.

cerussite

staurolite

CONTACT TWIN
Radiating mass of touching, contact crystals.

PENETRATION TWIN
Showing two parts of a crystal intergrown.

CLEAVAGE

Cleavage is the way that a mineral breaks along well-defined planes of weakness. Often these planes are between layers of atoms or other places where the atomic bonding is weakest. Cleavage surfaces are not perfectly smooth like crystal faces, though they are very consistent and reflect light evenly. Cleavage is described as perfect, distinct, indistinct, or none.

PERFECT BASAL CLEAVAGE

• breaks parallel to base of lepidolite crystal

Iceland spar • displays perfect rhombohedral cleavage

PERFECT RHOMBIC CLEAVAGE

PERFECT CUBIC CLEAVAGE

• cube-shaped break in galena

PERFECT PRISMATIC CLEAVAGE

• surfaces parallel to a prism in cerussite

FRACTURE

If you strike a mineral with a geological hammer and it breaks, leaving surfaces which are rough and uneven, it is said to fracture. Cleavage surfaces are usually flat and exactly the same shape may be produced by repeated hammer blows. This is not so with a fracture. Most minerals fracture and cleave, but some will only fracture. Common fracture terms are uneven, conchoidal (shell-like), hackly (jagged), and splintery.

UNEVEN FRACTURE

• rough, uneven surfaces of rock crystal

CONCHOIDAL

curved fracture • in opal

HARDNESS

A useful aid for identifying a mineral is the hardness test. The hardness of a mineral is its resistance to being scratched. The scale of hardness from 1 (talc) to 10 (diamond) was devised by Friedrich Mohs. Minerals with higher Mohs' numbers will scratch those lower in the scale. Thus calcite will scratch gypsum, but not fluorite. Minerals can also be tested with everyday objects: a mineral scratched with a coin will have a hardness of less than 3½.

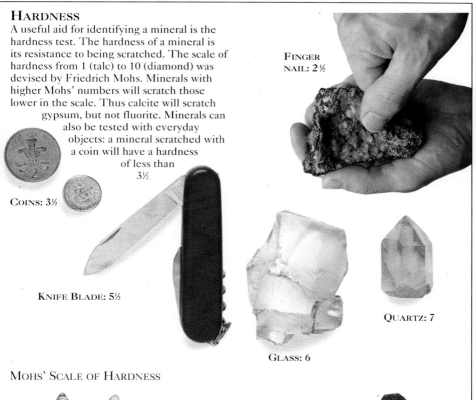

FINGER NAIL: 2½

COINS: 3½

KNIFE BLADE: 5½

GLASS: 6

QUARTZ: 7

MOHS' SCALE OF HARDNESS

TALC: 1 GYPSUM: 2 CALCITE: 3 FLUORITE: 4 APATITE: 5 ORTHOCLASE: 6 QUARTZ: 7 TOPAZ: 8 CORUNDUM: 9 DIAMOND: 10

SPECIFIC GRAVITY (SG)

Comparing the weight of a mineral with the weight of an equal volume of water gives a mineral's specific gravity. This is shown numerically: an SG of 2.5 indicates that the mineral is two-and-a half times as heavy as water. The quartz specimen (right) is larger than the galena but weighs less as it has a lower SG.

QUARTZ SG: 2.65

GALENA SG: 7.5

COLOR

The color of a mineral – as seen in natural light – is an obvious and useful identification feature. While it helps to identify those minerals with characteristic colors, there are pitfalls in relying solely on color. Many minerals – quartz, for example – occur in a variety of colors, while a large number of minerals are white or colorless. The selection of quartz minerals below, indicates the range of colors found in minerals.

ROSE
• *pink quartz*

• *milky quartz*

• *citrine*

COLORLESS
• *rock crystal*

WHITE – GRAY-WHITE

YELLOW – YELLOWISH BROWN

• *amethyst*

PURPLE-VIOLET

smoky quartz •

BROWN–BLACK

STREAK

The color of a mineral's powder is called streak. You obtain streak by rubbing the specimen across the surface of an unglazed porcelain tile. If testing a very hard mineral, crush a small amount of it with a geological hammer or rub it against a hard surface. Streak is a better diagnostic than color, because it is far more consistent.

crocoite

YELLOW

chalcopyrite

BLACK

orpiment

GOLDEN-YELLOW

cinnabar

RED

hematite

RED-BROWN

molybdenite

GRAY

TRANSPARENCY

Transparency refers to the way in which light passes through a mineral specimen. It depends on the way mineral atoms are bonded. Mineral specimens that allow objects to be seen through them are transparent. If light passes through, but the object cannot be clearly seen, then the specimen is translucent. When light does not pass through a specimen, even when cut very thin, it is opaque.

TRANSPARENT

objects seen through rhombohedral calcite appear twice due to double refraction

OPAQUE

gold allows no light to pass through it

TRANSLUCENT

aquamarine allows light to pass through it

LUSTER

Luster describes the way light is reflected off a mineral's surface. The type and intensity of luster vary according to the nature of the mineral surface and the amount of light absorbed. Well-recognized, mainly self-explanatory terms are used to describe luster. They include dull, metallic, pearly, vitreous (glassy), greasy, and silky.

VITREOUS

glass-like surface on quartz rock crystal

greasy luster on halite surface

GREASY

SILKY

metallic luster on galena surface

DULL, METALLIC

silky surface on "satin spar" gypsum

dull and metallic luster on hematite

METALLIC

MINERAL IDENTIFICATION

TO HELP with mineral identification, minerals are listed according to hardness. Obvious, reliable properties are included alongside each entry.

KEY TO ABBREVIATIONS:
av-average; con.-conchoidal; dis.-distinct; h-heavy; imp.-imperfect; ind.-indistinct; not det.-not determined; oct.-octahedral; per.-perfect; pin.-pinachoidal; prism.-prismatic; rhom.-rhombohedral; subcon.-subconchoidal; un.-uneven; vh-very heavy; vl-very light; <-less than or equal to; >-more than.

MINERAL	SG	CLEAVAGE	FRACTURE
HARDNESS <2½			
Acanthite	vh	none.	uneven
Annabergite	h	perfect	uneven
Artinite	av	perfect	uneven
Aurichalcite	h	perfect	uneven
Autunite	h	perfect basal	uneven
Bismuth	vh	perfect basal	uneven
Bismuthinite	vh	perfect	uneven
Borax	vl	perfect	con.
Brucite	av	perfect	uneven
Carnallite	vl	none	con.
Carnotite	h	perfect basal	uneven
Chalcanthite	av	imperfect	con.
Chlorargyrite	vh	none	un. - subcon.
Chrysotile	av	none	uneven
Cinnabar	vh	perfect prism.	con. - un.
Clinochlore	av	perfect	uneven
Covellite	h	perfect basal	uneven
Cryolite	av	none	uneven
Cyanotrichite	av	none	uneven
Epsomite	vl	perfect	con.
Erythrite	h	perfect	uneven
Galena	vh	perfect cubic	subcon.
Glauconite	av	perfect basal	uneven
Graphite	av	perfect basal	uneven
Gypsum	av	perfect	splintery
Halite	av	perfect cubic	un. - con.
Hydrozincite	h	perfect	uneven
Jamesonite	vh	good basal	un. - con.
Kaolinite	av	perfect basal	uneven
Linarite	vh	perfect	con.
Molybdenite	h	perfect basal	uneven
Muscovite	av	perfect basal	uneven
Nitratine	av	perfect rhom.	con.
Orpiment	h	perfect	uneven
Phlogopite	av	perfect basal	uneven
Proustite	vh	distinct rhom.	con. - un.
Pyrargyrite	vh	distinct rhom.	con. - un.
Pyrophyllite	av	perfect	uneven
Realgar	h	good	con.
Sepiolite	av	not det.	uneven
Stephanite	vh	imperfect	un. - subcon.
Stibnite	h	perfect	un. - subcon.
Sulfur	av	imp. basal	un. - con.
Sylvanite	vh	perfect	uneven
Sylvite	vl	perfect cubic	uneven
Talc	av	perfect	uneven
Torbernite	h	perfect basal	uneven
Tungstite	vh	perfect	uneven
Tyuyamunite	h	perfect basal	uneven
Ulexite	vl	perfect	uneven
Vermiculite	av	perfect	uneven
Vivianite	av	perfect	uneven
Wad	h	none	uneven
HARDNESS <3½			
Adamite	h	good	subcon. - un.
Anglesite	vh	good basal	con.
Anhydrite	av	perfect	un.- splintery
Antigorite	av	perfect basal	con. - splintery
Antimony	vh	perfect basal	uneven
Astrophyllite	h	perfect	uneven
Atacamite	h	perfect	con.

MINERAL	SG	CLEAVAGE	FRACTURE
Barite	h	perfect	uneven
Bauxite	av	none	uneven
Biotite	av/h	perfect basal	uneven
Boleite	vh	perfect	uneven
Bornite	vh	very poor	un. - con.
Boulangerite	vh	good	uneven
Bournonite	vh	imperfect	subcon - un.
Calcite	av	perfect	subcon.
Celestine	h	perfect	uneven
Cerussite	vh	dis. prismatic	con.
Chalcocite	vh	indistinct	con.
Chamosite	h	not det.	uneven
Clinoclase	h	perfect	uneven
Copiapite	av	perfect	uneven
Copper	vh	none	hackly
Crocoite	vh	dis. prismatic	con. - un.
Descloizite	vh	none	un. - con.
Enargite	h	perfect	uneven
Gibbsite	av/h	perfect	uneven
Glauberite	av	perfect	con.
Gold	vh	none	hackly
Greenockite	h	distinct	con.
Jarosite	av/h	distinct	uneven
Leadhillite	vh	perfect basal	con.
Lepidolite	av/h	perfect basal	uneven
Millerite	vh	perfect rhom.	uneven
Olivenite	h	indistinct	un. - con.
Polybasite	vh	imp. basal	uneven
Polyhalite	av	perfect	uneven
Silver	vh	none	hackly
Strontianite	h	per. prismatic	uneven
Thenardite	av	perfect	uneven
Trona	av	perfect	uneven
Vanadinite	vh	none	con. - un.
Volborthite	h	perfect basal	uneven
Witherite	h	distinct	uneven
Wulfenite	vh	dis. pyramidal	subcon.
HARDNESS <5½			
Alunite	av	distinct basal	con.
Analcime	av	very poor	subcon.
Ankerite	av	perfect rhom.	subcon.
Apatite	h	poor	con. - un.
Aragonite	av	distinct pin.	subcon.
Azurite	h	perfect	con.
Bayldonite	vh	none	uneven
Brochantite	h	perfect	con. - un.
Chabazite	av	indistinct	uneven
Chalcopyrite	h	poor	un. - con.
Chromite	h	none	uneven
Chrysocolla	av/h	none	uneven
Cobaltite	vh	perfect	uneven
Colemanite	av	perfect	un. - con.
Cuprite	vh	poor oct.	con. - un.
Datolite	av	none	un. - con.
Dioptase	h	perfect	un. - con.
Dolomite	av	per. rhom.	subcon.
Eudialyte	av	indistinct	uneven
Fluorapophyllite	av	perfect	uneven
Fluorite	h	per. oct.	uneven
Glaucodot	vh	perfect	uneven
Goethite	h	perfect	uneven
Gyrolite	av	perfect	uneven

MINERAL	SG	CLEAVAGE	FRACTURE
Harmotome	av	distinct	un. - subcon.
Hauerite	h	perfect	subcon. - un.
Hausmannite	h	good	uneven
Hemimorphite	h	perfect	un. - con.
Hydrox. Herderite	av/h	poor	subcon.
Heulandite	av	perfect	uneven
Kyanite	h/vh	perfect	uneven
Laumontite	av	perfect	uneven
Lazurite	av	imperfect	uneven
Lepidocrocite	h	perfect	uneven
Limonite	h	none	uneven
Magnesite	h	perfect rhom.	con. - un.
Malachite	h	perfect	subcon. - un.
Manganite	h	perfect	uneven
Mesolite	av	perfect	uneven
Mimetite	vh	none	subcon. - un.
Monazite	h/vh	distinct	con. - un.
Natrolite	av	perfect	uneven
Nickeline	vh	none	uneven
Nosean	av	indistinct	un. - con.
Pectolite	av	perfect	uneven
Pentlandite	h	none	con.
Perovskite	h	imperfect	subcon. - un.
Phillipsite	av	distinct	uneven
Pyrochlore	h	distinct	subcon. - un.
Pyromorphite	vh	v. poor prism	un. - subcon.
Pyrrhotite	h	none	subcon. - un.
Rhodochrosite	h	perfect rhom.	uneven
Riebeckite	h	perfect	uneven
Scheelite	vh	distinct	subcon. - un.
Scolecite	av	perfect	uneven
Scorodite	h	imperfect	subcon.
Siderite	h	perfect rhom.	uneven
Smithsonite	h	perfect rhom.	subcon. - un.
Sphalerite	h	perfect	con.
Stilbite	av	perfect	uneven
Tennantite	h	none	un. - subcon.
Tetrahedrite	h/vh	none	un. - subcon.
Thomsonite	av	perfect	un. - subcon.
Titanite	h	distinct	con.
Wavellite	av	perfect	subcon. - un.
Willemite	h	basal	uneven
Wolframite	vh	perfect	uneven
Wollastonite	av/h	perfect	splintery
Xenotime	h/vh	per. prismatic	uneven
Zincite	vh	perfect	con.
HARDNESS <6			
Actinolite	h	good	un. - subcon.
Aegirine	h	good	uneven
Akermanite	av	distinct	un. - con.
Amblygonite	h	perfect	uneven
Anatase	h	perfect basal	subcon.
Anthophyllite	av/h	perfect	uneven
Arfvedsonite	h	perfect	uneven
Arsenopyrite	vh	indistinct	uneven
Augite	h	good	un. - con.
Brookite	h	poor	subcon. - un.
Cancrinite	av	perfect	uneven
Chloanthite	vh	distinct	uneven
Enstatite	h	good	uneven
Gehlenite	h	distinct	un. - con.
Glaucophane	h	perfect	un. - con.
Grunerite	h	good	uneven
Hauyne	av	indistinct	un. - con.
Hedenbergite	h	good	un. - con.
Hematite	vh	none	un. - subcon.
Hornblende	h	perfect	uneven
Humite	h	poor	uneven
Hypersthene	h	good	uneven
Ilmenite	h	none	con. - un.
Ilvaite	h	distinct	uneven

MINERAL	SG	CLEAVAGE	FRACTURE
Lazulite	h	indis. - pris.	un.- splintery
Leucite	av	very poor	con.
Milarite	av	none	con. - un.
Nepheline	av	indistinct	con.
Neptunite	h	perfect	con.
Richterite	av/h	perfect	uneven
Romanechite	vh	not det.	uneven
Samarskite	vh	indistinct	con.
Scapolite	av	distinct	un. - con.
Skutterudite	vh	distinct	uneven
Smaltite	vh	distinct	uneven
Sodalite	av	poor	un. - con.
Tremolite	av/h	good	un. - subcon.
Turquoise	av	good	con.
HARDNESS <7			
Albite	av	distinct	uneven
Andesine	av	perfect	un. - con.
Anorthite	av	perfect	con. - un.
Anorthoclase	av	perfect	uneven
Axinite	h	good	un. - con.
Bytownite	av	perfect	un. - con.
Cassiterite	vh	poor	subcon. - un.
Chloritoid	h	perfect	uneven
Chondrodite	h	poor	uneven
Clinozoisite	h	perfect	uneven
Columbite	vh	distinct	subcon. - un.
Diaspore	h	perfect	con.
Diopside	h	good	uneven
Epidote	h	perfect	uneven
Franklinite	vh	none	un. - subcon.
Gadolinite	h	none	con.
Jadeite	h	good	splintery
Labradorite	av	perfect	un. - con.
Magnetite	vh	none	subcon. - un.
Marcasite	h	distinct	uneven
Microcline	av	perfect	uneven
Oligoclase	av	perfect	un. - con.
Opal	av	none	con.
Orthoclase	av	perfect	un. - con.
Petalite	av	perfect	subcon.
Prehnite	av	distinct	uneven
Pyrite	h	indistinct	con. - un.
Pyrolusite	vh	perfect	uneven
Quartz	av	none	con.
Rhodonite	h	perfect	con. - un.
Rutile	h	distinct	con. - un.
Sanidine	av	perfect	con. - un.
Stibiconite	h/vh	not det.	uneven
Tourmaline	h	very ind.	un. - con.
Vesuvianite	h	indistinct	un. - con.
Zoisite	h	perfect	un. - con.
HARDNESS >7			
Andalusite	h	dis. prismatic	un. - subcon.
Beryl	av	indistinct	un. - con.
Chalcedony	av	none	con.
Chrysoberyl	h	dis. prismatic	con. - un.
Cordierite	av	distinct	con.
Corundum	h	none	con. - un.
Diamond	h	per. oct.	con.
Dumortierite	h	good	uneven
Euclase	h	perfect	con.
Garnet	h	none	un. - con.
Olivine	h	imperfect	con.
Phenakite	av	distinct	con.
Ruby	h	none	con. - un.
Sillimanite	h	perfect	uneven
Spinel	h	none	con. - un.
Spodumene	h	perfect	uneven
Staurolite	h	distinct	un. - subcon.
Topaz	h	perfect	subcon. - un.
Zircon	h	imperfect	un. - con.

HOW ROCKS ARE FORMED

ROCK FORMS in cycles. Molten magma inside the earth's crust slowly rises towards the surface. This may form into large masses, called plutons (**1**); smaller intrusions, called dikes (**2**); or lava flows and volcanoes. On cooling, igneous rocks such as granite are formed. Rocks are brought to the surface by earth

ROCK CYCLE
The rock-making cycle, shown below, spans millions of years.

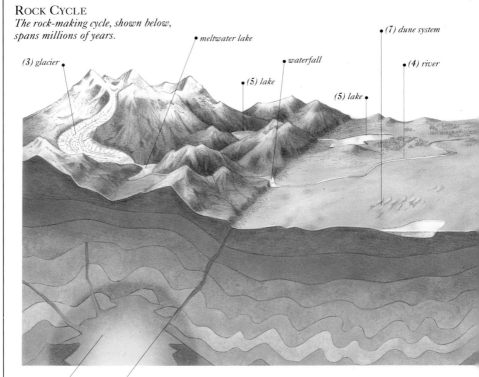

• *(7) dune system*

• *meltwater lake*

(3) glacier •

• *waterfall*

• *(4) river*

• *(5) lake*

(5) lake •

(1) plutons •   *(2) dikes* •

• *granite*

schist •

IGNEOUS
Molten magma forces its way through other rocks. On cooling, it can form granite dikes (left).

METAMORPHIC
Heat and pressure in mountain-building change sedimentary and igneous rocks to metamorphic rocks.

movements, and they are exposed by erosion and weathering. Further erosion by ice, water, wind, and weathering breaks down the rocks into mineral particles, which are transported by glaciers (**3**), rivers (**4**), and wind. The particles are deposited as sedimentary layers in lakes (**5**), deltas (**6**), dunes (**7**), and on the sea-bed to form sedimentary rocks such as clay or shale (**8**). Much sediment is deposited on the continental shelf (**9**), and some is carried to the greater depths of the ocean floor by dense currents channeled by ocean canyons (**10**). When sedimentary and igneous rocks are subjected to intense heat and pressure during large-scale mountain-building, they become metamorphic rocks, such as schist and gneiss. Further increases in temperature and pressure may cause the rock to become molten, and the rock cycle is completed.

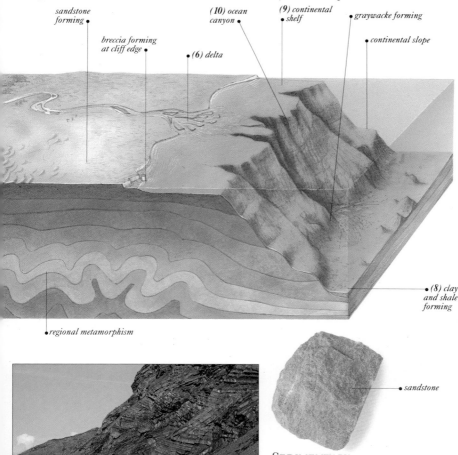

sandstone forming

breccia forming at cliff edge

(10) ocean canyon

(6) delta

(9) continental shelf

graywacke forming

continental slope

(8) clay and shale forming

regional metamorphism

sandstone

SEDIMENTARY
Sandstones consist of particles of quartz worn from pre-existing rocks, which have then been deposited on sea or river beds. After burial and compression, sandstones may be folded, as seen on the sea cliff (left).

IGNEOUS ROCK CHARACTERISTICS

IGNEOUS ROCKS crystallize from molten magma or lava. The starting composition of the magma, the manner in which it travels towards the earth's surface, and the rate at which it cools all help to determine its composition and resultant characteristics. These characteristics include grain size, crystal shape, mineral content, and overall color.

coarse-grained gabbro, a plutonic-igneous rock with large crystals •

ORIGIN

Origin indicates whether the rock is intrusive (magma crystallized beneath the earth's surface) or extrusive (lava crystallized at the earth's surface).

INTRUSIVE BASIC DIKE
A dolerite dike is an igneous rock which has intruded sedimentary shale.

• *augite, a ferro-magnesium*

OCCURRENCE

This describes the form of the molten mass when it cooled. A pluton, for instance, is a very large, deep intrusion that can measure many miles across; a dike is a narrow, discordant sheet of rock; a sill is a concordant sheet.

MINERAL CONTENT

Feldspars (right), micas, quartz, and ferro-magnesians (above) make up the bulk of igneous rocks. How minerals affect the rock's chemistry is described under the term "composition."

labradorite, a feldspar •

GRAIN SIZE

This indicates whether a rock is plutonic (coarse-grained) or extrusive (fine-grained). Coarse-grained igneous rocks such as gabbro have crystals over ⅟₁₆ in (5 mm) in diameter; medium-grained rocks such as dolerite have crystals ⅟₆₄–⅟₁₆ in (0.5–5 mm) in size; and fine-grained rocks, such as basalt, have crystals that are less than ⅟₆₄ in (0.5 mm) in size.

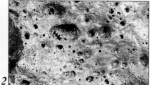

SEEING THE GRAINS

Individual grains of gabbro (1) can be seen with the naked eye, but you need a hand lens to see the separate grains in dolerite (2). Basalt (3) is fine-grained, requiring the use of a microscope.

CRYSTAL SHAPE

Slow cooling gives the minerals time to develop well-formed (euhedral) crystals. Fast cooling allows time only for poorly-formed (anhedral) crystals to grow.

TEXTURE

Texture refers to the way the grains or crystals are arranged and their size relative to one another.

EUHEDRAL CRYSTALS

Highly magnified section of dolerite (left) with well-formed crystals.

COLOR

Color is generally an accurate indicator of chemistry, reflecting a mineral's content. Light color indicates an acid rock, with over 65 percent silica. Basic rocks are dark colored, with low silica, and a high proportion of dark, dense ferro-magnesian minerals such as augite.

COMPOSITION

Igneous rocks are arranged into groups according to chemical composition: acid rocks, with over 65 percent total silica content (including over 10 percent modal quartz); intermediate rocks, with 55–65 percent silica content; basic rocks, with 45–55 percent total silica content (less than 10 percent modal quartz). Ultrabasic rocks have less than 45 percent total silica content.

LIGHT COLOR
Rhyolite has over 65 percent silica and over 10 percent modal quartz.

MEDIUM COLOR
Andesite, an intermediate rock with 55–65 percent total silica content.

DARK COLOR
Basalt, a basic rock with 45–55 percent silica content.

TYPES OF METAMORPHISM

METAMORPHIC ROCKS are rocks that have been changed considerably from their original igneous, sedimentary, or earlier metamorphic structure and composition. The rocks are formed by the application of heat and pressure (greatest near mountain-building) to a pre-existing rock.

REGIONAL METAMORPHISM

When rock in a mountain-building region is transformed by both heat and pressure it becomes regionally metamorphosed rock. The metamorphosed area can cover thousands of square miles. The sequence below demonstrates how the nature of a rock changes as the heat and pressure intensify.

METAMORPHIC LANDSCAPE
Gneiss, a rock altered by a high degree of regional metamorphism, forms a rugged landscape.

SHALE

1. NO PRESSURE
Fossiliferous shale, a fine-grained sedimentary rock, rich in clay minerals and quartz, with fossil brachiopod shells, unaffected by metamorphism.

2. LOW PRESSURE
When fossiliferous shale is subjected to low pressure, the fossils may be distorted or destroyed. The resulting rock is slate.

SLATE

SCHIST

4. HIGH PRESSURE
At the highest pressures and temperatures, and where active fluids may be circulating through the rocks, gneiss, a coarse-grained rock, is formed. Any rock can be altered by these conditions.

3. MODERATE PRESSURE
Slate, as well as many other rocks, forms medium-grained schist when subjected to moderate increases in temperature and pressure.

GNEISS

CONTACT METAMORPHISM

Rocks in the metamorphic aureole, the area surrounding an igneous intrusion or near a lava flow, may be altered by direct heat alone. These rocks are called contact metamorphic rocks. The heat may change the minerals in the original rock so that the resulting metamorphic rock is more crystalline, and features such as fossils may disappear. The extent of the metamorphic aureole is determined by the magma's or lava's temperature and the size of the intrusion.

SANDSTONE

• *grains loosely held together*

MAGMA INTRUSION

A mass of dark-colored dolerite (at the base of the cliff), has intruded and heated layers of originally black shale, metamorphosing them to a lighter rock (hornfels).

HEAT ALONE

When heated, sandstone (above) – a porous, sedimentary rock – becomes metaquartzite (right) – a crystalline, non-porous rock, composed of an interlocking mosaic of quartz crystals.

• *interlocking quartz crystals*

METAQUARTZITE

DYNAMIC METAMORPHISM

When large-scale movements take place in the earth's crust, especially along fault lines, dynamic metamorphism occurs. Huge masses of rock are forced over other rocks. Where these rock masses come into contact with each other, a crushed and powdered metamorphic rock called mylonite forms.

MYLONITE

MOVEMENT OF ROCK MASSES

A low-angled thrust fault, halfway up the cliff.

• *highly altered and distorted by forces of thrust movement*

METAMORPHIC ROCK CHARACTERISTICS

METAMORPHIC ROCKS exhibit certain typical features. The minerals of which they are made usually occur as crystals. Crystal orientation is determined by whether the rock formed as a result of both heat and pressure, or heat alone. Their size reflects the degree of heat and pressure to which they were subjected. Thus, examination of the crystals in a metamorphic rock can help to establish its origin and its identity.

foliated gneiss shows bands of dark biotite mica

STRUCTURE
This indicates the way minerals are oriented in a rock. Contact metamorphic rocks have a crystalline structure: the minerals are usually randomly arranged. Regional metamorphic rocks, however, are foliated: the pressure forces certain minerals to become aligned.

FOLIATED

CRYSTALLINE

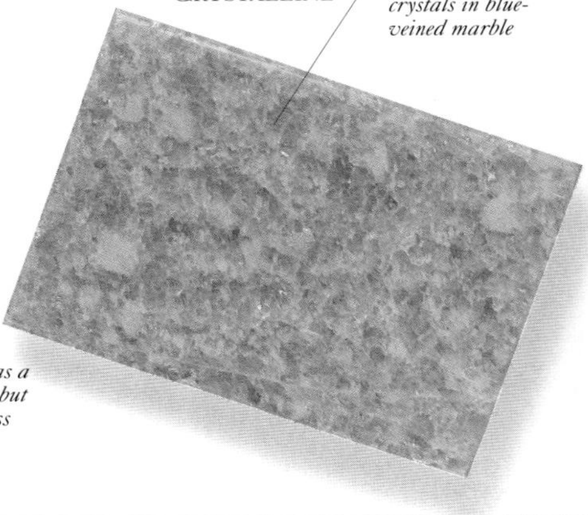

mass of randomly organized, fused crystals in blue-veined marble

kyanite schist has a foliated structure, but alignment here is less evident than in gneiss

GRAIN SIZE

Grain size indicates the temperature
and pressure conditions to which
the rock was subjected: generally,
the higher the pressure and
temperature, the coarser the
grain size. Thus slate, which
forms under low pressure, is
fine-grained. Schist, formed by
moderate temperature and pressure,
is medium-grained, and gneiss,
formed at high temperatures
and pressures, is coarse-grained.

COARSE-GRAINED

schist

gneiss

black slate

MEDIUM-GRAINED

PRESSURE AND TEMPERATURE

Medium- to high-grade metamorphism
occurs at a minimum temperature of
approximately 480° F (250° C) – temperatures in some metamorphic rocks can be
much lower – and a maximum temperature
of 1,472° F (800° C); above this, the rock
melts to become magma or lava. Intensity of
pressure ranges from 2,000 to 10,000 kilobars.

FINE-GRAINED

MINERAL CONTENT

The presence of certain minerals in
metamorphic rocks can help the
identification process. Garnet and kyanite
occur in gneiss and schists, while crystals of
pyrite grow on the cleavage
surfaces of slate. Minerals
such as brucite can occur
in marble.

GNEISS

*Under a microscope,
gneiss reveals quartz
and mica (left).*

quartz   *mica*

MILKY QUARTZ
*found in meta-
quartzite and gneiss*

*found in gneiss
and schist*

**ORTHOCLASE
FELDSPAR**
*found in gneiss
and schist*

MUSCOVITE MICA

SEDIMENTARY ROCK CHARACTERISTICS

A S SEDIMENTARY ROCKS form in layers, or strata, they can be distinguished from igneous and metamorphic rocks in the field. A hand specimen usually breaks along layered surfaces. Another key feature that sets them apart is their fossil content – fossils are never found in crystalline igneous rocks, and only rarely in metamorphic rocks. The origins of the particles that make up sedimentary rocks determine their appearance, and give clues to their identity.

ORIGIN
Sedimentary rocks form at, or very near, the earth's surface, where rock particles transported by wind, water, and ice are deposited on dry land, on the beds of rivers and lakes, and in marine environments: beaches, deltas, and the sea.

• *quartz conglomerate*

LAYERS OF SEDIMENT
The pebbles and sand collecting on this beach may eventually form sedimentary rocks.

FOSSIL CONTENT
Fossils occur mainly in sedimentary rocks. They are the remains of animals and plants preserved in layers of sediment. The types of fossil that are found in a rock give an indication of the rock's origin: a marine fossil, for instance, suggests that the rock formed from sediments deposited in the sea. Rocks that are especially rich in fossils include limestone.

• *brachiopod fossils in limestone*

GRAIN SIZE

Although the classification of grain size in sedimentary rocks can be complex, the terms coarse-, medium-, and fine-grained are usually used. Grains may range in size from boulders to minute particles of clay. Coarse-grained rocks composed of fragments easily seen with the naked eye include conglomerate, breccia, and some sandstones. Medium-grained rocks, the grains of which can be seen with a hand lens, include other sandstones. Fine-grained rock, includes shale, clay, and mudstone.

COARSE-GRAINED

• quartz conglomerate

shale •

MEDIUM-GRAINED

FINE-GRAINED

• sandstone

MAGNIFIED GRAINS
Highly magnified rock specimens reveal the shape of the grains in

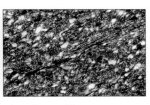

the sediment. These can vary from rounded (above left) to angular (above right).

GRAIN SHAPE
The way the grains that make up sedimentary rocks are transported influences their shape. Wind erosion creates round sand particles, but angular pebbles. Water-based erosion gives rise to angular, sand-sized particles, but smooth, round pebbles.

CLASSIFICATION
This explains the source of the rock's grains. Detrital rocks contain particles from pre-existing rocks; the term biogenic indicates that the rock is made of shells or other fossil fragments; and the term chemical indicates that the minerals were produced by chemical precipitation.

CHEMICAL

CHEMICAL

• rock gypsum

• oolitic limestone

• breccia

DETRITAL

DETRITAL

• pink orthoquartzite

ROCK IDENTIFICATION KEY

THIS KEY IS DESIGNED to help identify your rock specimens. In Stage 1, decide whether the rock is igneous, metamorphic, or sedimentary. In Stage 2, determine the grain size – follow the key to find the correct category: an eye represents coarse-grained; a hand lens represents medium-grained; and a microscope suggests fine-grained. In Stage 3 (see pages 42–45), you have to take into consideration other rock properties (color, structure, and mineral content) to direct you finally to a specific rock entry in this book.

STAGE 1

IGNEOUS?

If you have an igneous rock, it will show a crystalline structure; that is, it will be composed of an interlocking mosaic of mineral crystals. These crystals may be randomly set into the rock or they may show some form of alignment. They lack structures like bedding planes (sedimentary rocks) and foliation (metamorphic rocks). Some lavas may be full of small gas-bubble hollows. No fossils will be evident.

• *randomly oriented crystals*

• *interlocking crystals cannot be easily broken from the rock*

METAMORPHIC?

If you have a metamorphic rock, it will be one of two major types. A regionally metamorphosed rock will have a characteristic structure, or foliation. This foliation is often wavy, not flat like the bedding planes of a sedimentary rock. Contact metamorphism produces a more random arrangement.

• *foliated gneiss with wavy bands*

SEDIMENTARY?

If your sample is a sedimentary rock, layers may be evident in it. Grains may be poorly held together, and you may be able to rub them off with your fingers. Quartz is a dominant mineral in many sediments, and calcite is present in limestones. The presence of fossils also helps to distinguish sedimentary rocks from igneous or metamorphic specimens.

• *grains of quartz, weakly cemented together*

STAGE 2

Once you have established the formation of the rock, the next step is to categorize it by grain size. This refers to the size of the grains in the body of rock, not to the odd large crystal that may be set into it.

VISIBLE TO
NAKED EYE

HAND LENS
NEEDED

MICROSCOPE
NEEDED

IGNEOUS

Coarse-grained

Medium-grained

Fine-grained

METAMORPHIC

Coarse-grained

Medium-grained

Fine-grained

SEDIMENTARY

Coarse-grained

Medium-grained

Fine-grained

STAGE 3

You have decided whether the rock is igneous, sedimentary, or metamorphic, and you have identified its grain size. If you have an igneous rock, look at its color, next. Acid rocks, rich in low density, pale silicates, are light colored. Basic and ultrabasic rocks, rich in heavy ferro-magnesian minerals, are dark. The

IGNEOUS	COARSE-GRAINED		MEDIUM-GRAINED
		LIGHT COLOR *Pink granite* **180**, *White granite* **180**, *Porphyritic granite* **181**, *Graphic granite* **181**, *Adamellite* **182**, *Pegmatite* **185**, *White granodiorite* **187**, *Syenite* **188**, *Anorthosite* **191**.	
		MEDIUM COLOR *Hornblende granite* **181**, *Granodiorite* **187**, *Diorite* **187**, *Syenite* **188**, *Nepheline syenite* **188**, *Agglomerate* **204**.	
		DARK COLOR *Gabbro* **189**, *Larvikite* **189**, *Olivine gabbro* **190**, *Bojite* **191**, *Serpentinite* **194**, *Pyroxenite* **194**, *Kimberlite* **195**, *Peridotite* **195**.	

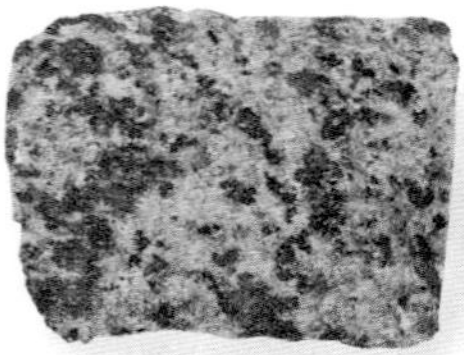

METAMORPHIC	COARSE-GRAINED		MEDIUM-GRAINED
		FOLIATED *Gneiss* **213**, *Folded gneiss* **213**, *Augen gneiss* **214**, *Granular gneiss* **214**, *Migmatite* **214**, *Amphibolite* **215**, *Eclogite* **215**.	
		UNFOLIATED *Granulite* **215**, *Marble* **216–217**, *Skarn* **220**.	

intermediate rocks, as the description implies, lie between the above two categories in mineral content and therefore, color. If you have a metamorphic rock, examine whether it is foliated (some min- erals align) or unfoliated (crystalline, with no apparent structure). Decide which of these categories your specimen falls into, and then refer to the pages indicated in bold for further identification information.

FINE-GRAINED		
LIGHT COLOR *Microgranite* **183**, *Quartz porphyry* **184**, *Granophyre* **186**, *Leuco gabbro* **190**.		**LIGHT COLOR** *Rhyolite* **196**, *Ignimbrite* **206**, *Volcanic bomb* **206**.
MEDIUM COLOR *Lamprophyre* **199**, *Rhomb porphyry* **201**.		**MEDIUM COLOR** *Dacite* **197**, *Lamprophyre* **199**, *Andesite* **199**, *Trachyte* **201**, *Pumice* **205**, *Tuff* **205**, *Ignimbrite* **206**.
DARK COLOR *Dolerite* **192**, *Norite* **192**, *Troctolite* **193**.		**DARK COLOR** *Xenolith* **184**, *Dunite* **193**, *Obsidian* **197**, *Pitchstone* **198**, *Basalt* **202**, *Spilite* **203**, *Tuff* **204**, *Volcanic bomb* **206**, *Ropy lava* **207**.

FINE-GRAINED		
FOLIATED *Phyllite* **210**, *Folded schist* **211**, *Garnet schist* **211**, *Muscovite schist* **211**, *Biotite schist* **212**, *Kyanite schist* **212**.		**FOLIATED** *Green slate* **208**, *Black slate* **208**, *Slate with pyrite* **209**, *Slate with distorted fossils* **209**, *Phyllite* **210**.
UNFOLIATED *Marbles* **216–217**, *Hornfels* **218–219**, *Spotted slate* **219**, *Metaquartzite* **220**, *Skarn* **220**.		**UNFOLIATED** *Marble* **216**, *Spotted slate* **219**, *Skarn* **220**, *Halleflinta* **221**, *Mylonite* **221**.

STAGE 3 *continued*

If you have a sedimentary rock, look at its mineral composition. Is it made up mainly of rock fragments, in effect miniature rocks? Or is it composed mainly of quartz? Quartz is easily recognizable, because it is usually gray in color and very hard. You

SEDIMENTARY	COARSE-GRAINED	MEDIUM-GRAINED

MAINLY ROCK FRAGMENTS
Polygenetic conglomerate **222**, *Breccia* **223**.

MAINLY QUARTZ FRAGMENTS
No rocks in this category.

CALCIUM CARBONATE DOMINANT
Limestone breccia **223**, *Pisolitic limestone* **236**, *Crinoidal limestone* **238**.

OTHER MINERALS
No rocks in this category.

may have a limestone, rich in calcium carbonate and identifiable by its pale color and its effervescing reaction with dilute hydrochloric acid. Or your sedimentary rock specimen may be composed mainly of minerals other than calcium carbonate and quartz. Decide which of these four categories your specimen falls into and then refer to the pages indicated for further identification information.

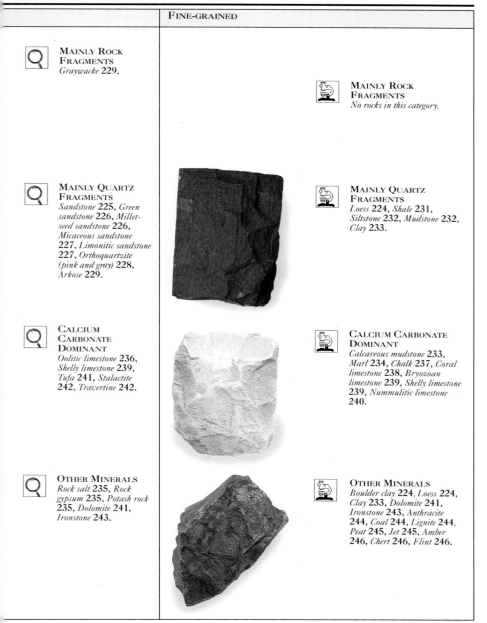

FINE-GRAINED

MAINLY ROCK FRAGMENTS
Graywacke **229.**

MAINLY ROCK FRAGMENTS
No rocks in this category.

MAINLY QUARTZ FRAGMENTS
Sandstone **225,** *Green sandstone* **226,** *Millet-seed sandstone* **226,** *Micaceous sandstone* **227,** *Limonitic sandstone* **227,** *Orthoquartzite (pink and gray)* **228,** *Arkose* **229.**

MAINLY QUARTZ FRAGMENTS
Loess **224,** *Shale* **231,** *Siltstone* **232,** *Mudstone* **232,** *Clay* **233.**

CALCIUM CARBONATE DOMINANT
Oolitic limestone **236,** *Shelly limestone* **239,** *Tufa* **241,** *Stalactite* **242,** *Travertine* **242.**

CALCIUM CARBONATE DOMINANT
Calcareous mudstone **233,** *Marl* **234,** *Chalk* **237,** *Coral limestone* **238,** *Bryozoan limestone* **239,** *Shelly limestone* **239,** *Nummulitic limestone* **240.**

OTHER MINERALS
Rock salt **235,** *Rock gypsum* **235,** *Potash rock* **235,** *Dolomite* **241,** *Ironstone* **243.**

OTHER MINERALS
Boulder clay **224,** *Loess* **224,** *Clay* **233,** *Dolomite* **241,** *Ironstone* **243,** *Anthracite* **244,** *Coal* **244,** *Lignite* **244,** *Peat* **245,** *Jet* **245,** *Amber* **246,** *Chert* **246,** *Flint* **246.**

MINERALS

NATIVE ELEMENTS

NATIVE ELEMENTS are free, uncombined elements which are classified into three groups: Metals such as gold, silver, and copper; semimetals such as arsenic and antimony; and non-metals, including carbon and sulfur. Metallic elements are very dense, soft, malleable, ductile, and opaque. Massive dendritic, wire-like habits are common. Distinct crystals are rare. Unlike metals, semimetals are poor conductors of electricity and they usually occur in nodular masses. Non-metallic elements are transparent to translucent, do not conduct electricity, and tend to form distinct crystals.

Group Native Elements	Composition Au		Hardness 2½–3

GOLD

Crystals form as cubes or octahedra, but distinct examples are rare. The usual habits are as grains, flakes, nuggets, and dendritic masses. The bright, rich yellow color is resistant to tarnishing. Gold is often rich in silver, when it is paler in color. The streak is golden-yellow. Gold is opaque, and its luster is metallic.

• **FORMATION** Forms mainly in hydrothermal veins, often associated with quartz and sulfides. It also occurs in placer deposits of unconsolidated sand, and in sandstone and conglomerate. It is possible to find alluvial gold in grains or nuggets, in stream beds. Panning for gold by sifting the sediment is an age-old method of looking for this rare and valuable mineral. Gold can be confused with pyrite and chalcopyrite at first, but only a few tests are needed to identify it.

• **TESTS** Insoluble in all single acids; soluble in aqua regia.

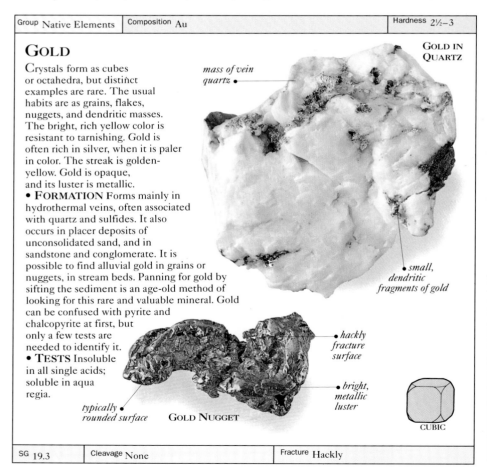

GOLD IN QUARTZ

mass of vein quartz

small, dendritic fragments of gold

hackly fracture surface

bright, metallic luster

typically rounded surface GOLD NUGGET

CUBIC

SG 19.3	Cleavage None		Fracture Hackly

Group Native Elements	Composition Ag		Hardness 2½–3

SILVER

Crystals are rare. They form as cubes and octahedra, sometimes in parallel bands. The usual habits are wires, scales, dendrites, and massive. Silver is silver-white in color, though it tarnishes on exposure to the atmosphere. It produces a silvery white streak. Silver is opaque, and the luster is metallic.
• **FORMATION** Forms in hydrothermal veins, and in the oxidized regions of ore deposits, with gold, and other silver minerals, and metallic sulfides. Silver forms 20 to 25 percent of the gold and silver alloy, called electrum.
• **TESTS** Silver is soluble in nitric acid, and is fusible. It tarnishes if exposed to the fumes of hydrogen sulfide. It is the best conductor of electricity and heat.

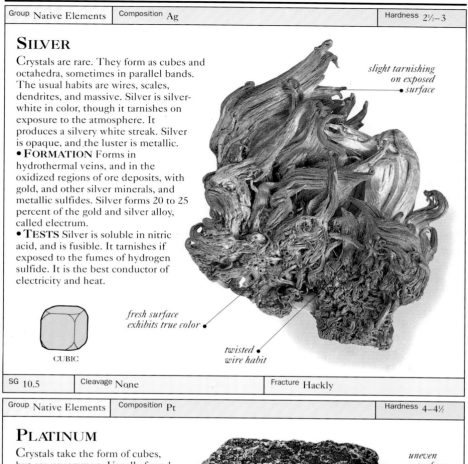

slight tarnishing on exposed • surface

fresh surface exhibits true color •

CUBIC

twisted • wire habit

SG 10.5	Cleavage None	Fracture Hackly

Group Native Elements	Composition Pt		Hardness 4–4½

PLATINUM

Crystals take the form of cubes, but are uncommon. Usually found as grains, nuggets, and scales, platinum is silvery gray to white in color. The streak is white to silvery gray. Platinum is opaque, and has a metallic luster. This luster is not altered by tarnishing if the mineral is exposed to the atmosphere.
• **FORMATION** Originally formed in basic and ultrabasic igneous rocks, and rarely in contact aureoles, platinum also occurs in placer sediments because of its very high specific gravity.
• **TESTS** When there are iron impurities present, platinum can be weakly magnetic. It is insoluble in all acids, except aqua regia.

uneven • surface

CUBIC

rounded nugget

SG 21.4	Cleavage None	Fracture Hackly

Group Native elements	Composition Cu		Hardness 2½–3

COPPER

It is rare for copper to form crystals; when it does, they take the form of cubes, octahedra, or dodecahedra. The usual habits are dendritic and massive. Copper can also form in wires. Color is a key identification feature, and is copper-red or pale rose-red on fresh surfaces. It tarnishes to copper-brown. The streak is copper-red. Copper is an opaque mineral. Its luster is metallic.
• **FORMATION** Copper forms in basic volcanic rocks, and in the reducing environments of sulfide deposits.
• **TESTS** It is soluble in nitric acid.

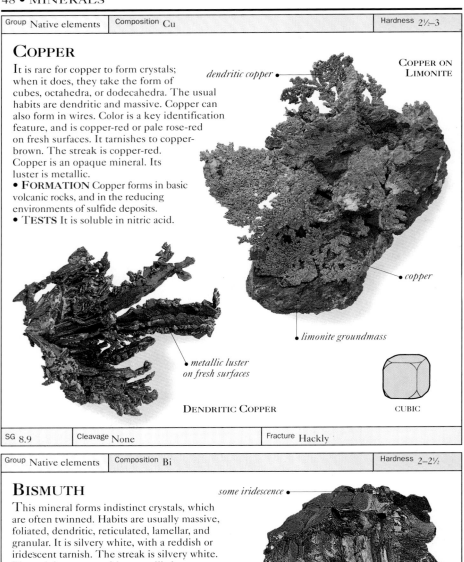

dendritic copper •

COPPER ON LIMONITE

• *copper*

• *limonite groundmass*

• *metallic luster on fresh surfaces*

DENDRITIC COPPER

CUBIC

SG 8.9	Cleavage None		Fracture Hackly

Group Native elements	Composition Bi		Hardness 2–2½

BISMUTH

This mineral forms indistinct crystals, which are often twinned. Habits are usually massive, foliated, dendritic, reticulated, lamellar, and granular. It is silvery white, with a reddish or iridescent tarnish. The streak is silvery white. Bismuth is opaque, with a metallic luster.
• **FORMATION** Forms in hydro-thermal veins, and pegmatites.
• **TESTS** Fuses at low temperature, and dissolves easily in nitric acid.

some iridescence •

lamellar habit •

metallic luster •

TRIGONAL / HEXAGONAL

SG 9.7–9.8	Cleavage Perfect basal		Fracture Uneven

Group Native elements	Composition As		Hardness 3½

ARSENIC

On rare occasions, arsenic forms rhombohedral crystals. It commonly occurs as granular, botryoidal, or stalactitic masses. It is pale gray, and tarnishes to dark gray. The streak is pale gray. Arsenic is an opaque mineral, and it has a metallic luster.
• **FORMATION** Forms mainly in hydrothermal veins.
• **TESTS** Heated, arsenic gives off fumes smelling of garlic.

metallic luster

TRIGONAL / HEXAGONAL

botryoidal habit

SG 5.7	Cleavage Perfect basal	Fracture Uneven

Group Native elements	Composition Sb		Hardness 3–3½

ANTIMONY

Crystals, though rare, are pseudo-cubic, or tabular, and often twinned. Usual habits are massive, lamellar, granular, or acicular. It is pale silvery gray, with a gray streak. It is opaque, and the luster is brilliant metallic.
• **FORMATION** Forms in hydrothermal veins with arsenic and silver, as well as galena, sphalerite, pyrite, and stibnite.
• **TESTS** Burns white fumes in the air; turns flame greenish blue.

massive habit

crystal apparent

TRIGONAL / HEXAGONAL

SG 6.6–6.7	Cleavage Perfect basal	Fracture Uneven

Group Native elements	Composition S		Hardness 1½–2½

SULFUR

The crystal forms of this mineral are tabular, and bipyramidal. Sulfur also occurs in massive, encrusting, powdery, and stalactitic habits. It is bright lemon-yellow to yellowish brown, and the streak is white. Sulfur is transparent to translucent, and has a resinous to greasy luster.
• **FORMATION** Forms around volcanic craters and hot springs.
• **TESTS** Fuses at low temperature, giving off sulfur dioxide.

tabular crystal

resinous luster

bipyramidal crystal

ORTHORHOMBIC

SG 2.0–2.1	Cleavage Imperfect basal	Fracture Uneven to conchoidal

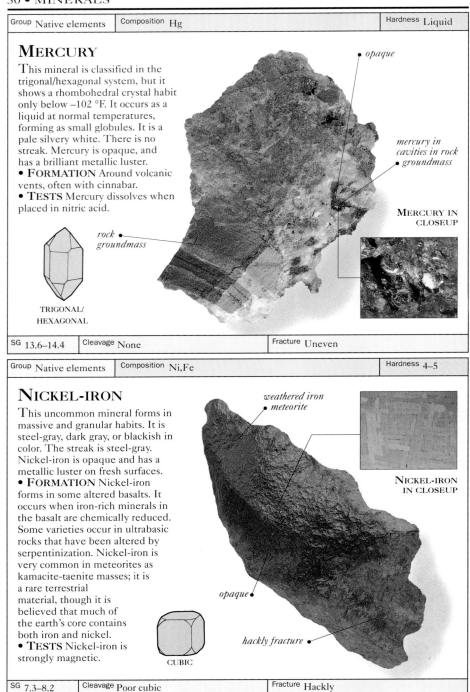

Group Native elements	Composition Hg		Hardness Liquid

MERCURY

This mineral is classified in the trigonal/hexagonal system, but it shows a rhombohedral crystal habit only below −102 °F. It occurs as a liquid at normal temperatures, forming as small globules. It is a pale silvery white. There is no streak. Mercury is opaque, and has a brilliant metallic luster.
• **FORMATION** Around volcanic vents, often with cinnabar.
• **TESTS** Mercury dissolves when placed in nitric acid.

opaque

mercury in cavities in rock groundmass

MERCURY IN CLOSEUP

rock groundmass

TRIGONAL/ HEXAGONAL

SG 13.6–14.4	Cleavage None	Fracture Uneven

Group Native elements	Composition Ni,Fe	Hardness 4–5

NICKEL-IRON

This uncommon mineral forms in massive and granular habits. It is steel-gray, dark gray, or blackish in color. The streak is steel-gray. Nickel-iron is opaque and has a metallic luster on fresh surfaces.
• **FORMATION** Nickel-iron forms in some altered basalts. It occurs when iron-rich minerals in the basalt are chemically reduced. Some varieties occur in ultrabasic rocks that have been altered by serpentinization. Nickel-iron is very common in meteorites as kamacite-taenite masses; it is a rare terrestrial material, though it is believed that much of the earth's core contains both iron and nickel.
• **TESTS** Nickel-iron is strongly magnetic.

weathered iron meteorite

NICKEL-IRON IN CLOSEUP

opaque

hackly fracture

CUBIC

SG 7.3–8.2	Cleavage Poor cubic	Fracture Hackly

Group Native elements	Composition C		Hardness 10

DIAMOND

The crystals form as octahedra, cubes, dodecahedra, and tetrahedra, often with curved faces. Diamond also occurs in rounded masses with a radiating structure (bort), and as micro-crystalline masses (carbonado). It may be colorless, white, gray, orange, yellow, brown, pink, red, blue, green, or black. The streak is white. Diamond is transparent to opaque, and has an adamantine to greasy luster. It is used chiefly as an industrial abrasive and is also a highly valued and sought-after gem.
• **FORMATION** Found in ultrabasic rocks (kimberlites), forming pipelike intrusions.
• **TESTS** The hardest of all the known minerals – it can only be scratched by another diamond.

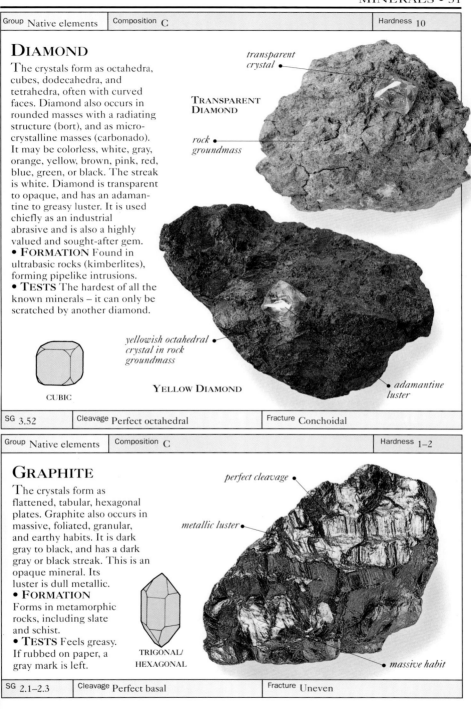

transparent crystal

TRANSPARENT DIAMOND

rock groundmass

yellowish octahedral crystal in rock groundmass

YELLOW DIAMOND

adamantine luster

CUBIC

SG 3.52	Cleavage Perfect octahedral	Fracture Conchoidal

Group Native elements	Composition C		Hardness 1–2

GRAPHITE

The crystals form as flattened, tabular, hexagonal plates. Graphite also occurs in massive, foliated, granular, and earthy habits. It is dark gray to black, and has a dark gray or black streak. This is an opaque mineral. Its luster is dull metallic.
• **FORMATION** Forms in metamorphic rocks, including slate and schist.
• **TESTS** Feels greasy. If rubbed on paper, a gray mark is left.

perfect cleavage

metallic luster

TRIGONAL/
HEXAGONAL

massive habit

SG 2.1–2.3	Cleavage Perfect basal	Fracture Uneven

SULFIDES AND SULFOSALTS

SULFIDES ARE chemical compounds in which sulfur has combined with metallic and semi-metallic elements. When tellurium substitutes for sulfur, the resultant compound is a telluride; if arsenic substitutes, arsenide is formed. The properties of sulfides, tellurides, and arsenides are somewhat variable.

———— • ————

Many sulfides have metallic lusters, and are soft and dense (such as galena and molybdenite). Some are nonmetallic (orpiment, realgar), or relatively hard (marcasite, cobaltite). Well-formed, highly symmetrical crystals are the rule.

———— • ————

Sulfides are very important ores of lead, zinc, iron, and copper. They form in hydrothermal veins below the water table as they are easily oxidized to sulfates. Sulfosalts are compounds in which metallic elements combine with sulfur plus a semimetallic element (such as antimony and arsenic). Their properties are similar to sulfides.

Group Sulfides	Composition PbS		Hardness 2½

GALENA

This very common ore mineral forms cubes, octahedra, or cubo-octahedral crystals, and also occurs in massive, granular, and fibrous habits. Both the color and streak are lead-gray. Galena is opaque, with a metallic luster.
• **FORMATION** Galena forms in hydrothermal veins, when hot fluids find their way to higher levels in the earth's crust. It can occur with several other minerals, including fluorite, quartz, calcite, sphalerite and pyrite.
• **TESTS** This mineral is soluble in hydrochloric acid, producing the "rotten egg" smell of hydrogen sulfide.

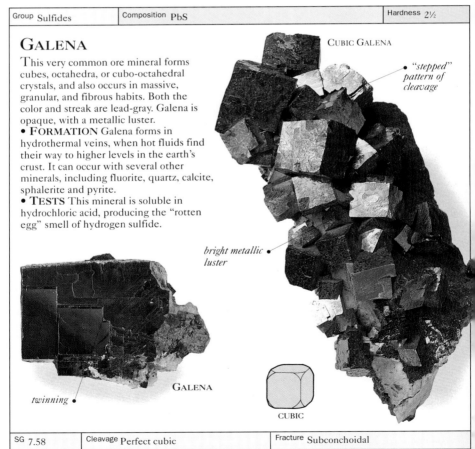

CUBIC GALENA

"stepped" pattern of cleavage

bright metallic luster

twinning •

GALENA

CUBIC

SG 7.58	Cleavage Perfect cubic		Fracture Subconchoidal

Group Sulfides	Composition HgS	Hardness 2–2½

CINNABAR

This mineral forms as thick
tabular, rhombohedral, and
prismatic crystals, which are
commonly twinned. It also
occurs in massive, encrusting,
or granular habits. The color is
typically brownish red or
scarlet. The streak is scarlet.
Cinnabar is transparent to
opaque, and has an adamantine,
submetallic, or dull luster.
• **FORMATION** Forms with
realgar and pyrite around volcanic
vents and hot springs. Other associated minerals include native
mercury, marcasite, opal, quartz,
stibnite, and calcite. It may also
occur in mineral veins, and in
sedimentary rocks associated
with recent volcanic activity.
• **TESTS** Does not alter when
exposed to the atmosphere.

adamantine luster

mass of small crystals

TRIGONAL/
HEXAGONAL

SG 8.0–8.2	Cleavage Perfect prismatic	Fracture Conchoidal to uneven

Group Sulfides	Composition CdS	Hardness 3–3½

GREENOCKITE

This mineral occurs as tabular, pyramidal,
and prismatic crystals, but more often as
earthy coatings on other minerals. It is
yellow, orange-yellow, orange, or red in
color, and the streak is orange-yellow
to brick-red. It is a transparent to
translucent mineral. It has a
resinous or adamantine luster.
• **FORMATION** Greenockite
occurs as a replacement and
alteration product of sphalerite,
when the sphalerite is cadmium-
rich. Although it is not a
common mineral, green-
ockite sometimes forms
as minute crystals with
other minerals, including
prehnite, and zeolites.
• **TESTS** Greenockite
is soluble in hydrochloric
acid, producing hydrogen
sulfide, which gives off
a "rotten egg" smell.

resinous luster

coating of greenockite on rock surface

conchoidal fracture

TRIGONAL/
HEXAGONAL

SG 4.7–4.8	Cleavage Distinct	Fracture Conchoidal

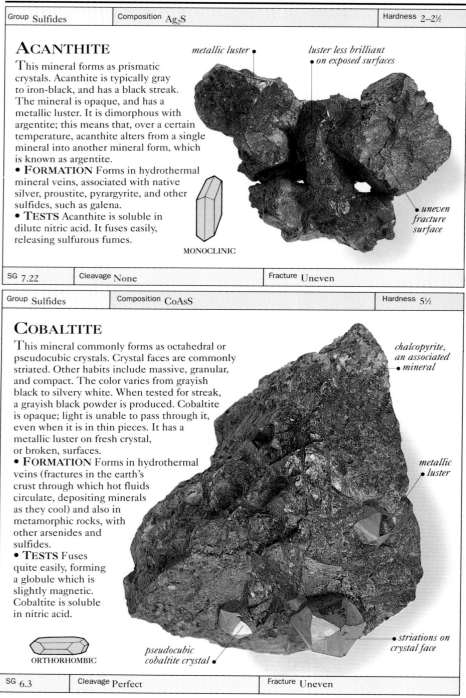

Group Sulfides	Composition Ag₂S		Hardness 2–2½

ACANTHITE

metallic luster •

• *luster less brilliant on exposed surfaces*

This mineral forms as prismatic crystals. Acanthite is typically gray to iron-black, and has a black streak. The mineral is opaque, and has a metallic luster. It is dimorphous with argentite; this means that, over a certain temperature, acanthite alters from a single mineral into another mineral form, which is known as argentite.
• **FORMATION** Forms in hydrothermal mineral veins, associated with native silver, proustite, pyrargyrite, and other sulfides, such as galena.
• **TESTS** Acanthite is soluble in dilute nitric acid. It fuses easily, releasing sulfurous fumes.

• *uneven fracture surface*

MONOCLINIC

SG 7.22	Cleavage None	Fracture Uneven

Group Sulfides	Composition CoAsS		Hardness 5½

COBALTITE

This mineral commonly forms as octahedral or pseudocubic crystals. Crystal faces are commonly striated. Other habits include massive, granular, and compact. The color varies from grayish black to silvery white. When tested for streak, a grayish black powder is produced. Cobaltite is opaque; light is unable to pass through it, even when it is in thin pieces. It has a metallic luster on fresh crystal, or broken, surfaces.
• **FORMATION** Forms in hydrothermal veins (fractures in the earth's crust through which hot fluids circulate, depositing minerals as they cool) and also in metamorphic rocks, with other arsenides and sulfides.
• **TESTS** Fuses quite easily, forming a globule which is slightly magnetic. Cobaltite is soluble in nitric acid.

chalcopyrite, an associated • *mineral*

metallic • *luster*

ORTHORHOMBIC

pseudocubic cobaltite crystal •

• *striations on crystal face*

SG 6.3	Cleavage Perfect	Fracture Uneven

Group Sulfides	Composition ZnS		Hardness 3½–4

SPHALERITE

This mineral, known also as "blende" or "black jack," forms tetrahedral and dodecahedral crystals; it often exhibits curved crystal faces. Other habits include massive, granular, concretionary, and botryoidal. The color ranges from black, brown, yellow, and red, to green, gray, and white. It can also be colorless. The streak is pale brown to colorless. Sphalerite varies from translucent to transparent. It has a resinous to adamantine luster.

• **FORMATION** Common in hydro-thermal veins, it occurs with minerals such as dolomite, quartz, pyrite, galena, fluorite, barite, and calcite.

• **TESTS** The addition of dilute hydrochloric acid to sphalerite produces a smell reminiscent of hydrogen sulfide ("rotten eggs"). If pure, it is infusible, but as the iron content of sphalerite rises, the mineral specimen melts with increasing ease.

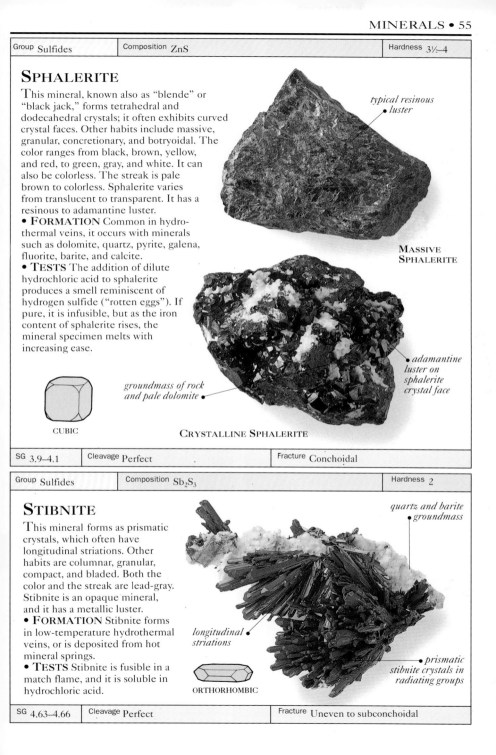

typical resinous luster

MASSIVE SPHALERITE

groundmass of rock and pale dolomite

adamantine luster on sphalerite crystal face

CUBIC

CRYSTALLINE SPHALERITE

SG 3.9–4.1	Cleavage Perfect		Fracture Conchoidal

Group Sulfides	Composition Sb₂S₃		Hardness 2

STIBNITE

This mineral forms as prismatic crystals, which often have longitudinal striations. Other habits are columnar, granular, compact, and bladed. Both the color and the streak are lead-gray. Stibnite is an opaque mineral, and it has a metallic luster.

• **FORMATION** Stibnite forms in low-temperature hydrothermal veins, or is deposited from hot mineral springs.

• **TESTS** Stibnite is fusible in a match flame, and it is soluble in hydrochloric acid.

quartz and barite groundmass

longitudinal striations

prismatic stibnite crystals in radiating groups

ORTHORHOMBIC

SG 4.63–4.66	Cleavage Perfect		Fracture Uneven to subconchoidal

Group Sulfides	Composition Cu_5FeS_4	Hardness 3

BORNITE

The crystals formed by bornite are cubic, octahedral, or dodecahedral, and they often have curved or rough faces. More usually, it forms in compact, granular, or massive habits. Bornite can be coppery red, coppery brown, or bronze, tarnishing to iridescent blue, purple, and red – leading to its common name "peacock ore." The streak is grayish black. Bornite is opaque, with a metallic luster.
• **FORMATION** Forms in hydrothermal veins, with minerals such as quartz, chalcopyrite, and galena. It also forms in some igneous rocks. The oxidation zone of copper veins can contain bornite.
• **TESTS** Bornite is soluble in nitric acid.

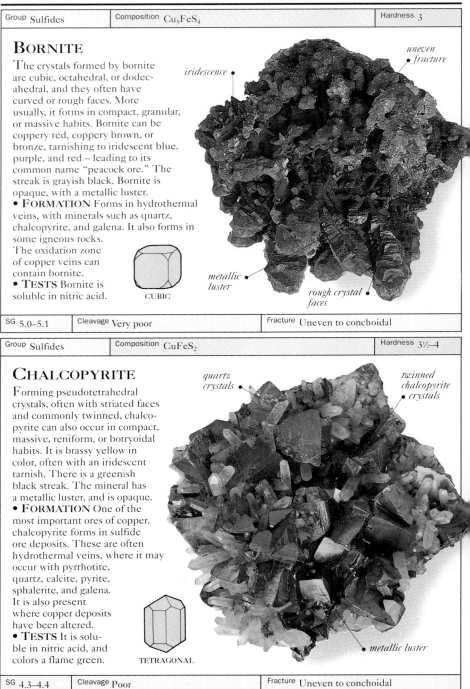

iridescence

uneven fracture

metallic luster

CUBIC

rough crystal faces

SG 5.0–5.1	Cleavage Very poor	Fracture Uneven to conchoidal

Group Sulfides	Composition $CuFeS_2$	Hardness 3½–4

CHALCOPYRITE

Forming pseudotetrahedral crystals, often with striated faces and commonly twinned, chalcopyrite can also occur in compact, massive, reniform, or botryoidal habits. It is brassy yellow in color, often with an iridescent tarnish. There is a greenish black streak. The mineral has a metallic luster, and is opaque.
• **FORMATION** One of the most important ores of copper, chalcopyrite forms in sulfide ore deposits. These are often hydrothermal veins, where it may occur with pyrrhotite, quartz, calcite, pyrite, sphalerite, and galena. It is also present where copper deposits have been altered.
• **TESTS** It is soluble in nitric acid, and colors a flame green.

quartz crystals

twinned chalcopyrite crystals

metallic luster

TETRAGONAL

SG 4.3–4.4	Cleavage Poor	Fracture Uneven to conchoidal

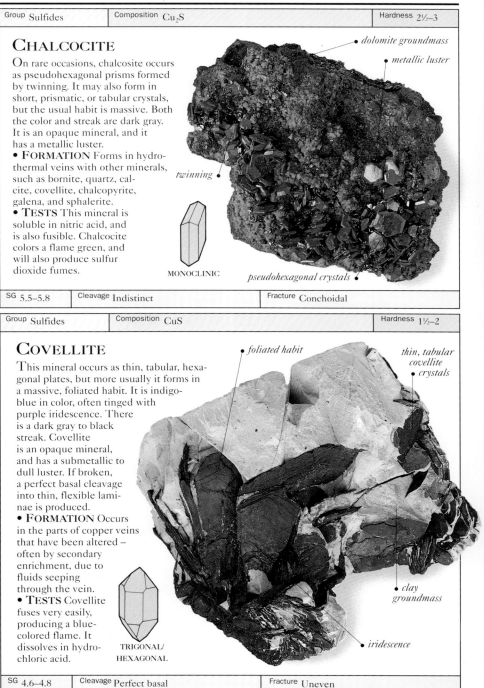

Group Sulfides	Composition Cu_2S	Hardness $2\frac{1}{2}$–3

CHALCOCITE

On rare occasions, chalcosite occurs as pseudohexagonal prisms formed by twinning. It may also form in short, prismatic, or tabular crystals, but the usual habit is massive. Both the color and streak are dark gray. It is an opaque mineral, and it has a metallic luster.
• **FORMATION** Forms in hydrothermal veins with other minerals, such as bornite, quartz, calcite, covellite, chalcopyrite, galena, and sphalerite.
• **TESTS** This mineral is soluble in nitric acid, and is also fusible. Chalcocite colors a flame green, and will also produce sulfur dioxide fumes.

dolomite groundmass

metallic luster

twinning

MONOCLINIC

pseudohexagonal crystals

SG 5.5–5.8	Cleavage Indistinct	Fracture Conchoidal

Group Sulfides	Composition CuS	Hardness $1\frac{1}{2}$–2

COVELLITE

This mineral occurs as thin, tabular, hexagonal plates, but more usually it forms in a massive, foliated habit. It is indigo-blue in color, often tinged with purple iridescence. There is a dark gray to black streak. Covellite is an opaque mineral, and has a submetallic to dull luster. If broken, a perfect basal cleavage into thin, flexible laminae is produced.
• **FORMATION** Occurs in the parts of copper veins that have been altered – often by secondary enrichment, due to fluids seeping through the vein.
• **TESTS** Covellite fuses very easily, producing a blue-colored flame. It dissolves in hydrochloric acid.

foliated habit

thin, tabular covellite crystals

clay groundmass

TRIGONAL/
HEXAGONAL

iridescence

SG 4.6–4.8	Cleavage Perfect basal	Fracture Uneven

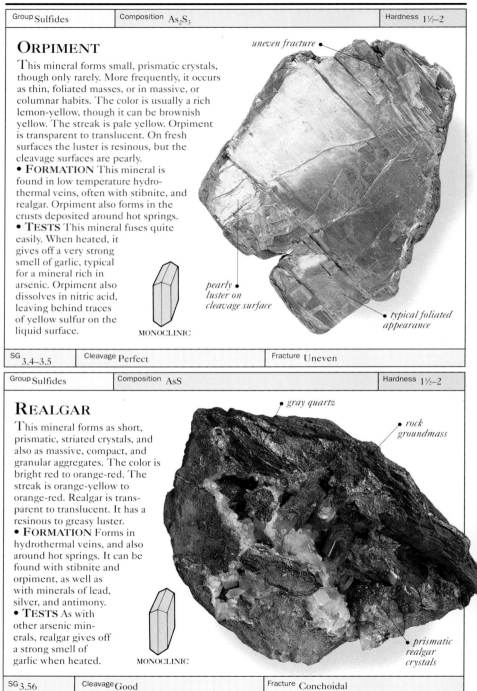

Group Sulfides	Composition As_2S_3	Hardness $1\frac{1}{2}$–2

ORPIMENT

uneven fracture

This mineral forms small, prismatic crystals, though only rarely. More frequently, it occurs as thin, foliated masses, or in massive, or columnar habits. The color is usually a rich lemon-yellow, though it can be brownish yellow. The streak is pale yellow. Orpiment is transparent to translucent. On fresh surfaces the luster is resinous, but the cleavage surfaces are pearly.

• **FORMATION** This mineral is found in low temperature hydrothermal veins, often with stibnite, and realgar. Orpiment also forms in the crusts deposited around hot springs.

• **TESTS** This mineral fuses quite easily. When heated, it gives off a very strong smell of garlic, typical for a mineral rich in arsenic. Orpiment also dissolves in nitric acid, leaving behind traces of yellow sulfur on the liquid surface.

pearly luster on cleavage surface

MONOCLINIC

typical foliated appearance

SG 3.4–3.5	Cleavage Perfect	Fracture Uneven

Group Sulfides	Composition AsS	Hardness $1\frac{1}{2}$–2

REALGAR

gray quartz

rock groundmass

This mineral forms as short, prismatic, striated crystals, and also as massive, compact, and granular aggregates. The color is bright red to orange-red. The streak is orange-yellow to orange-red. Realgar is transparent to translucent. It has a resinous to greasy luster.

• **FORMATION** Forms in hydrothermal veins, and also around hot springs. It can be found with stibnite and orpiment, as well as with minerals of lead, silver, and antimony.

• **TESTS** As with other arsenic minerals, realgar gives off a strong smell of garlic when heated.

MONOCLINIC

prismatic realgar crystals

SG 3.56	Cleavage Good	Fracture Conchoidal

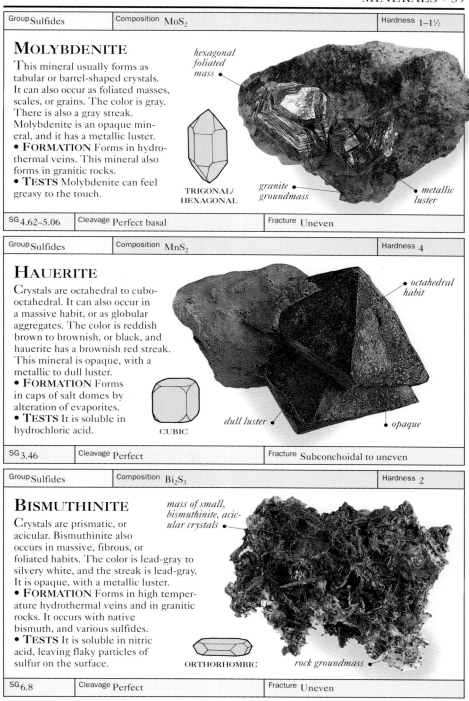

Group Sulfides	Composition MoS_2	Hardness $1-1\frac{1}{2}$

MOLYBDENITE

This mineral usually forms as tabular or barrel-shaped crystals. It can also occur as foliated masses, scales, or grains. The color is gray. There is also a gray streak. Molybdenite is an opaque mineral, and it has a metallic luster.
• **FORMATION** Forms in hydrothermal veins. This mineral also forms in granitic rocks.
• **TESTS** Molybdenite can feel greasy to the touch.

hexagonal foliated mass

TRIGONAL/ HEXAGONAL

granite groundmass

metallic luster

SG 4.62–5.06	Cleavage Perfect basal	Fracture Uneven

Group Sulfides	Composition MnS_2	Hardness 4

HAUERITE

Crystals are octahedral to cubo-octahedral. It can also occur in a massive habit, or as globular aggregates. The color is reddish brown to brownish, or black, and hauerite has a brownish red streak. This mineral is opaque, with a metallic to dull luster.
• **FORMATION** Forms in caps of salt domes by alteration of evaporites.
• **TESTS** It is soluble in hydrochloric acid.

octahedral habit

CUBIC

dull luster

opaque

SG 3.46	Cleavage Perfect	Fracture Subconchoidal to uneven

Group Sulfides	Composition Bi_2S_3	Hardness 2

BISMUTHINITE

Crystals are prismatic, or acicular. Bismuthinite also occurs in massive, fibrous, or foliated habits. The color is lead-gray to silvery white, and the streak is lead-gray. It is opaque, with a metallic luster.
• **FORMATION** Forms in high temperature hydrothermal veins and in granitic rocks. It occurs with native bismuth, and various sulfides.
• **TESTS** It is soluble in nitric acid, leaving flaky particles of sulfur on the surface.

mass of small, bismuthinite, acicular crystals

ORTHORHOMBIC

rock groundmass

SG 6.8	Cleavage Perfect	Fracture Uneven

Group Sulfides	Composition FeS_2	Hardness 6–6½

PYRITE

This mineral forms as cubic, pyritohedral, or octahedral crystals; twinning is common. The crystal faces are often striated. Pyrite can be massive, granular, reniform, stalactitic, botryoidal, and nodular. The pale yellow color gives rise to its nickname, "fool's gold." The streak is greenish black. It is opaque, with a metallic luster.
• **FORMATION** A common accessory mineral in igneous, sedimentary, and metamorphic rocks. Fine crystals occur with sphalerite, and other sulfides in hydrothermal veins.
• **TESTS** Gives off sparks when struck with a hard metal object.

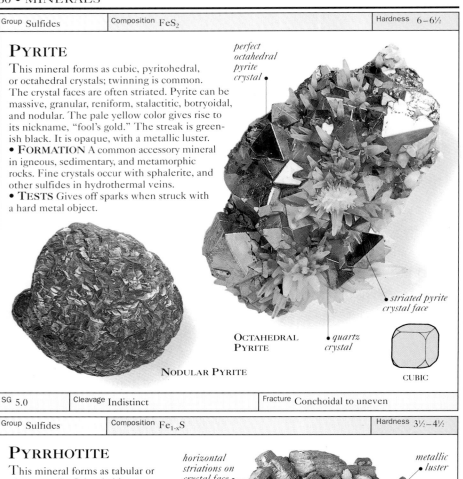

perfect octahedral pyrite crystal

striated pyrite crystal face

OCTAHEDRAL PYRITE

quartz crystal

NODULAR PYRITE

CUBIC

SG 5.0	Cleavage Indistinct	Fracture Conchoidal to uneven

Group Sulfides	Composition $Fe_{1-x}S$	Hardness 3½–4½

PYRRHOTITE

This mineral forms as tabular or platy crystals. Other habits are massive and granular. The color varies from bronze-yellow to a coppery bronze-red; the mineral tarnishes to brown, often with iridescence. The streak is dark gray to black. Pyrrhotite is an opaque mineral and has a metallic luster.
• **FORMATION** Commonly forms in magmatic igneous deposits, especially those of basic and ultrabasic composition. It occurs with pyrite, galena, sphalerite, and other sulfides.
• **TESTS** Pyrrhotite is magnetic.

horizontal striations on crystal face

mass of twinned crystals

metallic luster

MONOCLINIC

tabular, six-sided crystal

SG 4.53–4.77	Cleavage None	Fracture Subconchoidal to uneven

Group Sulfides	Composition FeAsS	Hardness $5\frac{1}{2}-6$

ARSENOPYRITE

This mineral forms as prismatic crystals, often twinned. It also exhibits massive, columnar, and granular habits. Typically silvery white, arsenopyrite tarnishes to pink, brown, and copper shades, with iridescence. The streak is black to gray. It is opaque, and has a metallic luster.
• **FORMATION** Forms in hydrothermal veins, in metamorphic rocks, and in basic igneous rocks.
• **TESTS** When a specimen is heated, or if it is struck with a hard object, arsenopyrite produces a smell reminiscent of garlic.

MONOCLINIC

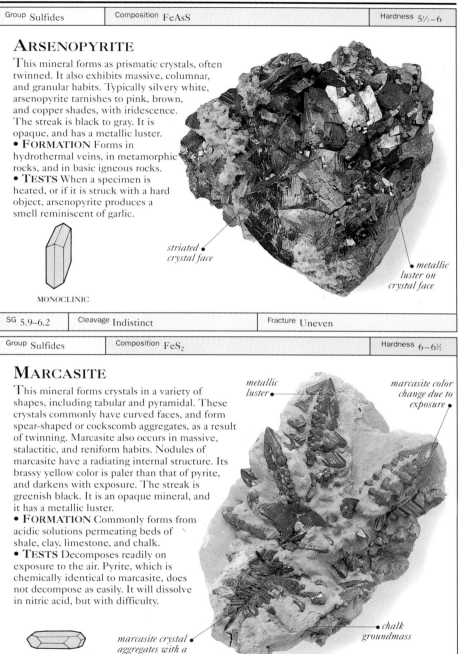

striated
crystal face

metallic
luster on
crystal face

SG 5.9–6.2	Cleavage Indistinct	Fracture Uneven

Group Sulfides	Composition FeS_2	Hardness $6-6\frac{1}{2}$

MARCASITE

This mineral forms crystals in a variety of shapes, including tabular and pyramidal. These crystals commonly have curved faces, and form spear-shaped or cockscomb aggregates, as a result of twinning. Marcasite also occurs in massive, stalactitic, and reniform habits. Nodules of marcasite have a radiating internal structure. Its brassy yellow color is paler than that of pyrite, and darkens with exposure. The streak is greenish black. It is an opaque mineral, and it has a metallic luster.
• **FORMATION** Commonly forms from acidic solutions permeating beds of shale, clay, limestone, and chalk.
• **TESTS** Decomposes readily on exposure to the air. Pyrite, which is chemically identical to marcasite, does not decompose as easily. It will dissolve in nitric acid, but with difficulty.

metallic
luster

marcasite color
change due to
exposure

chalk
groundmass

marcasite crystal
aggregates with a
spear-shaped habit

ORTHORHOMBIC

SG 4.92	Cleavage Distinct	Fracture Uneven

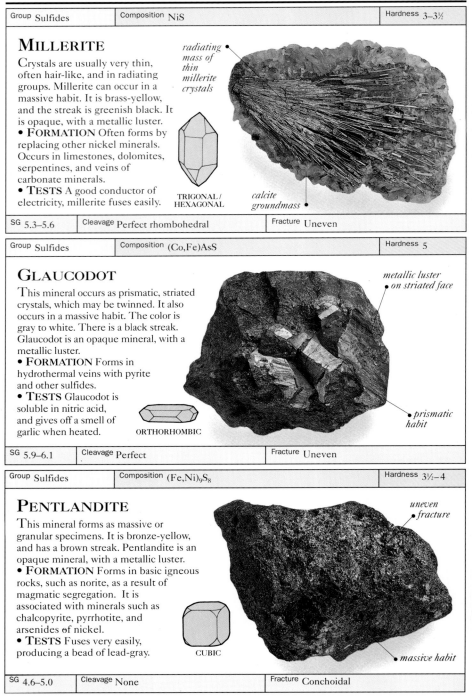

Group Sulfides	Composition NiS	Hardness 3–3½

MILLERITE

Crystals are usually very thin, often hair-like, and in radiating groups. Millerite can occur in a massive habit. It is brass-yellow, and the streak is greenish black. It is opaque, with a metallic luster.
• **FORMATION** Often forms by replacing other nickel minerals. Occurs in limestones, dolomites, serpentines, and veins of carbonate minerals.
• **TESTS** A good conductor of electricity, millerite fuses easily.

radiating mass of thin millerite crystals

TRIGONAL / HEXAGONAL

calcite groundmass

SG 5.3–5.6	Cleavage Perfect rhombohedral	Fracture Uneven

Group Sulfides	Composition (Co,Fe)AsS	Hardness 5

GLAUCODOT

This mineral occurs as prismatic, striated crystals, which may be twinned. It also occurs in a massive habit. The color is gray to white. There is a black streak. Glaucodot is an opaque mineral, with a metallic luster.
• **FORMATION** Forms in hydrothermal veins with pyrite and other sulfides.
• **TESTS** Glaucodot is soluble in nitric acid, and gives off a smell of garlic when heated.

metallic luster on striated face

prismatic habit

ORTHORHOMBIC

SG 5.9–6.1	Cleavage Perfect	Fracture Uneven

Group Sulfides	Composition (Fe,Ni)$_9$S$_8$	Hardness 3½–4

PENTLANDITE

This mineral forms as massive or granular specimens. It is bronze-yellow, and has a brown streak. Pentlandite is an opaque mineral, with a metallic luster.
• **FORMATION** Forms in basic igneous rocks, such as norite, as a result of magmatic segregation. It is associated with minerals such as chalcopyrite, pyrrhotite, and arsenides of nickel.
• **TESTS** Fuses very easily, producing a bead of lead-gray.

uneven fracture

CUBIC

massive habit

SG 4.6–5.0	Cleavage None	Fracture Conchoidal

Group Tellurides	Composition AuAgTe₄	Hardness 1½−2

SYLVANITE

This mineral forms short, prismatic crystals, which are commonly twinned. Sylvanite also occurs as bladed, columnar, and granular masses. The color is silvery white, gray, or yellow. The streak is silvery white to steel-gray. Sylvanite is opaque, and it has a metallic luster.
• FORMATION Forms in hydrothermal veins with fluorite, other tellurides, sulfides, carbonates, gold, tellurium, and quartz. Very fine crystals, up to ⅜ inch (1 cm) long, have been found with native gold.
• TESTS It is soluble in nitric acid, leaving a yellow-gold residue. When heated in concentrated sulfuric acid, the solution becomes reddish in color.

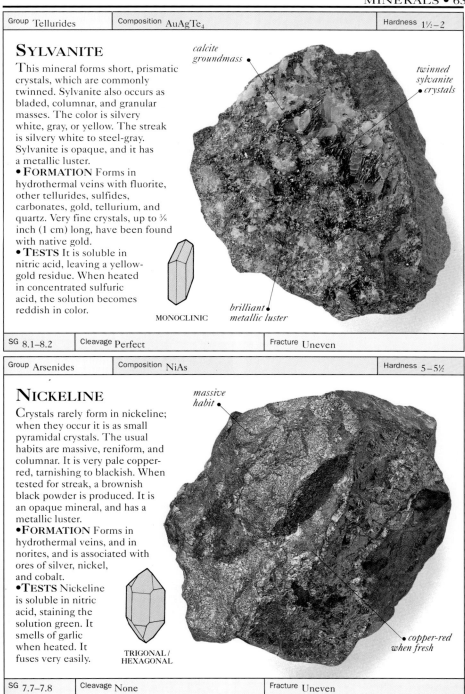

calcite groundmass

twinned sylvanite crystals

MONOCLINIC

brilliant metallic luster

SG 8.1−8.2	Cleavage Perfect	Fracture Uneven

Group Arsenides	Composition NiAs	Hardness 5−5½

NICKELINE

Crystals rarely form in nickeline; when they occur it is as small pyramidal crystals. The usual habits are massive, reniform, and columnar. It is very pale copper-red, tarnishing to blackish. When tested for streak, a brownish black powder is produced. It is an opaque mineral, and has a metallic luster.
•FORMATION Forms in hydrothermal veins, and in norites, and is associated with ores of silver, nickel, and cobalt.
•TESTS Nickeline is soluble in nitric acid, staining the solution green. It smells of garlic when heated. It fuses very easily.

massive habit

TRIGONAL / HEXAGONAL

copper-red when fresh

SG 7.7−7.8	Cleavage None	Fracture Uneven

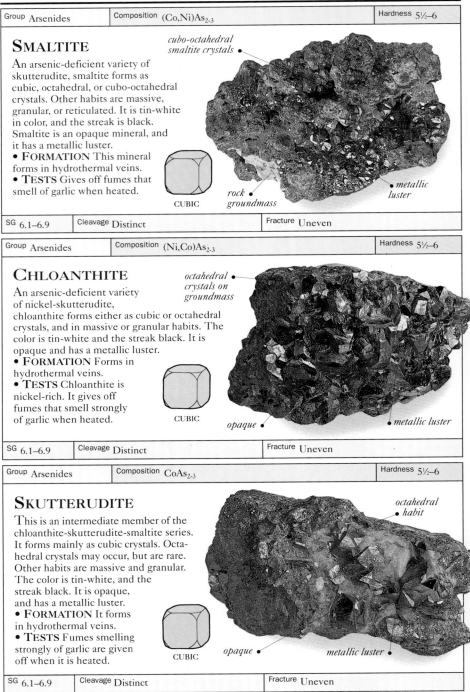

Group Arsenides	Composition $(Co,Ni)As_{2-3}$		Hardness $5\frac{1}{2}$–6

SMALTITE

cubo-octahedral
smaltite crystals •

An arsenic-deficient variety of
skutterudite, smaltite forms as
cubic, octahedral, or cubo-octahedral
crystals. Other habits are massive,
granular, or reticulated. It is tin-white
in color, and the streak is black.
Smaltite is an opaque mineral, and
it has a metallic luster.
• **FORMATION** This mineral
forms in hydrothermal veins.
• **TESTS** Gives off fumes that
smell of garlic when heated.

CUBIC

rock •
groundmass

• metallic
luster

SG 6.1–6.9	Cleavage Distinct	Fracture Uneven

Group Arsenides	Composition $(Ni,Co)As_{2-3}$		Hardness $5\frac{1}{2}$–6

CHLOANTHITE

octahedral •
crystals on
groundmass

An arsenic-deficient variety
of nickel-skutterudite,
chloanthite forms either as cubic or octahedral
crystals, and in massive or granular habits. The
color is tin-white and the streak black. It is
opaque and has a metallic luster.
• **FORMATION** Forms in
hydrothermal veins.
• **TESTS** Chloanthite is
nickel-rich. It gives off
fumes that smell strongly
of garlic when heated.

CUBIC

opaque •

• metallic luster

SG 6.1–6.9	Cleavage Distinct	Fracture Uneven

Group Arsenides	Composition $CoAs_{2-3}$		Hardness $5\frac{1}{2}$–6

SKUTTERUDITE

octahedral
• habit

This is an intermediate member of the
chloanthite-skutterudite-smaltite series.
It forms mainly as cubic crystals. Octahedral crystals may occur, but are rare.
Other habits are massive and granular.
The color is tin-white, and the
streak black. It is opaque,
and has a metallic luster.
• **FORMATION** It forms
in hydrothermal veins.
• **TESTS** Fumes smelling
strongly of garlic are given
off when it is heated.

CUBIC

opaque •

metallic luster •

SG 6.1–6.9	Cleavage Distinct	Fracture Uneven

Group Sulfosalts	Composition Cu_3AsS_4		Hardness 3

ENARGITE

Crystals are prismatic or tabular, and often twinned. The crystal faces show vertical striations. Enargite may also form in massive or granular habits. The color and streak are dark gray to black. It is opaque, with a metallic luster.
• **FORMATION** Found in hydrothermal veins, or replacement deposits. These mineral veins are formed when hot fluids circulating in the earth's crust move upwards, where the elements held in them are precipitated. Enargite is associated with many minerals, such as quartz, and sulfides, including galena, bornite, sphalerite, pyrite, and chalcopyrite. It also occurs in the cap rocks of salt domes, with minerals such as anhydrite.
• **TESTS** When heated, it smells of garlic. It is soluble in nitric acid and melts in a match flame.

twinned crystals with striations

uneven fracture

ORTHORHOMBIC

metallic luster

SG 4.4–4.5	Cleavage Perfect	Fracture Uneven

Group Sulfosalts	Composition $Pb_4FeSb_6S_{14}$		Hardness 2½

JAMESONITE

This mineral forms as acicular to fibrous crystals, and in massive and plumose habits. The color and streak are both dark gray. Jamesonite is an opaque mineral, and has a metallic luster.
• **FORMATION** Forms in hydrothermal veins, where hot, chemically rich fluids have permeated joints and fault lines, depositing minerals in the process of cooling. Jamesonite is associated with other sulfosalts, with sulfides, carbonates, and also with the common mineral quartz.
• **TESTS** Jamesonite is soluble in hydrochloric acid.

rock groundmass

metallic luster

mass of fibrous, twisted jamesonite crystals

MONOCLINIC

SG 5.63	Cleavage Good basal	Fracture Uneven to conchoidal

Group Sulfosalts	Composition Ag_5SbS_4	Hardness $2–2\frac{1}{2}$

STEPHANITE

This mineral forms as short, prismatic, or tabular crystals, which are sometimes twinned. The habit can also be massive. Stephanite is typically iron-black in color, with a black streak. It is an opaque mineral, and the luster is metallic.
• **FORMATION** Forms in veins, with native silver, and with sulfides and other sulfosalts, such as acanthite, tetrahedrite, polybasite, proustite, and argentite.
• **TESTS** Stephanite is soluble in nitric acid, and produces arsenic and sulfur oxide when this test is carried out. This mineral fuses very easily.

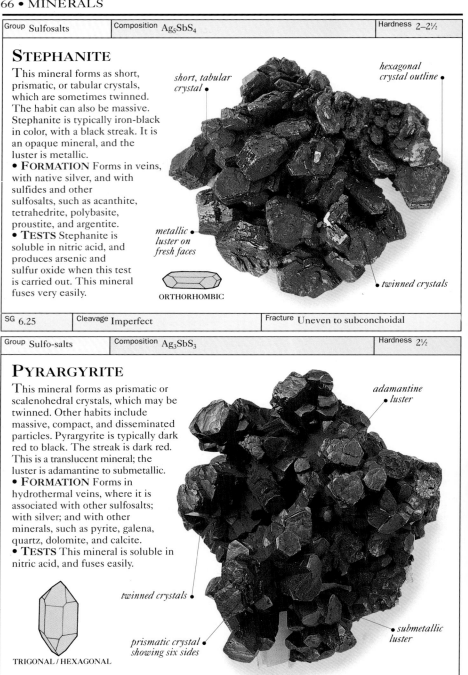

short, tabular crystal

hexagonal crystal outline

metallic luster on fresh faces

ORTHORHOMBIC

twinned crystals

SG 6.25	Cleavage Imperfect	Fracture Uneven to subconchoidal

Group Sulfo-salts	Composition Ag_3SbS_3	Hardness $2\frac{1}{2}$

PYRARGYRITE

This mineral forms as prismatic or scalenohedral crystals, which may be twinned. Other habits include massive, compact, and disseminated particles. Pyrargyrite is typically dark red to black. The streak is dark red. This is a translucent mineral; the luster is adamantine to submetallic.
• **FORMATION** Forms in hydrothermal veins, where it is associated with other sulfosalts; with silver; and with other minerals, such as pyrite, galena, quartz, dolomite, and calcite.
• **TESTS** This mineral is soluble in nitric acid, and fuses easily.

adamantine luster

twinned crystals

prismatic crystal showing six sides

TRIGONAL / HEXAGONAL

submetallic luster

SG 5.8–5.9	Cleavage Distinct rhombohedral	Fracture Conchoidal to uneven

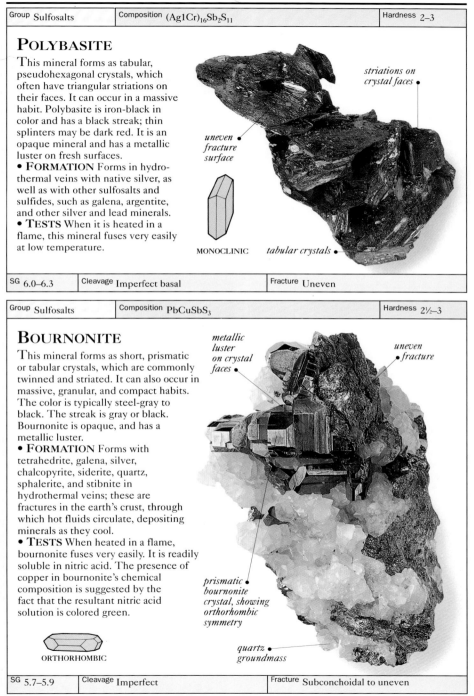

Group Sulfosalts	Composition $(Ag1Cr)_{16}Sb_2S_{11}$	Hardness 2–3

POLYBASITE

This mineral forms as tabular, pseudohexagonal crystals, which often have triangular striations on their faces. It can occur in a massive habit. Polybasite is iron-black in color and has a black streak; thin splinters may be dark red. It is an opaque mineral and has a metallic luster on fresh surfaces.
• **FORMATION** Forms in hydrothermal veins with native silver, as well as with other sulfosalts and sulfides, such as galena, argentite, and other silver and lead minerals.
• **TESTS** When it is heated in a flame, this mineral fuses very easily at low temperature.

striations on crystal faces

uneven fracture surface

MONOCLINIC *tabular crystals*

SG 6.0–6.3	Cleavage Imperfect basal	Fracture Uneven

Group Sulfosalts	Composition $PbCuSbS_3$	Hardness 2½–3

BOURNONITE

This mineral forms as short, prismatic or tabular crystals, which are commonly twinned and striated. It can also occur in massive, granular, and compact habits. The color is typically steel-gray to black. The streak is gray or black. Bournonite is opaque, and has a metallic luster.
• **FORMATION** Forms with tetrahedrite, galena, silver, chalcopyrite, siderite, quartz, sphalerite, and stibnite in hydrothermal veins; these are fractures in the earth's crust, through which hot fluids circulate, depositing minerals as they cool.
• **TESTS** When heated in a flame, bournonite fuses very easily. It is readily soluble in nitric acid. The presence of copper in bournonite's chemical composition is suggested by the fact that the resultant nitric acid solution is colored green.

metallic luster on crystal faces

uneven fracture

prismatic bournonite crystal, showing orthorhombic symmetry

ORTHORHOMBIC

quartz groundmass

SG 5.7–5.9	Cleavage Imperfect	Fracture Subconchoidal to uneven

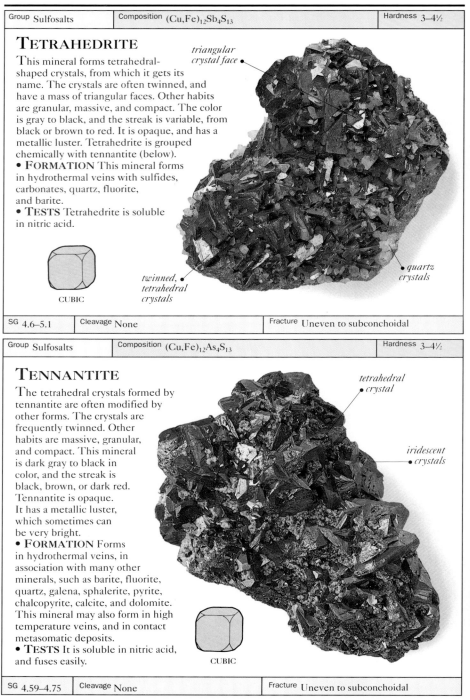

Group Sulfosalts	Composition $(Cu,Fe)_{12}Sb_4S_{13}$	Hardness $3-4\frac{1}{2}$

TETRAHEDRITE

This mineral forms tetrahedral-shaped crystals, from which it gets its name. The crystals are often twinned, and have a mass of triangular faces. Other habits are granular, massive, and compact. The color is gray to black, and the streak is variable, from black or brown to red. It is opaque, and has a metallic luster. Tetrahedrite is grouped chemically with tennantite (below).
• **FORMATION** This mineral forms in hydrothermal veins with sulfides, carbonates, quartz, fluorite, and barite.
• **TESTS** Tetrahedrite is soluble in nitric acid.

triangular crystal face

quartz crystals

CUBIC

twinned, tetrahedral crystals

SG 4.6–5.1	Cleavage None	Fracture Uneven to subconchoidal

Group Sulfosalts	Composition $(Cu,Fe)_{12}As_4S_{13}$	Hardness $3-4\frac{1}{2}$

TENNANTITE

The tetrahedral crystals formed by tennantite are often modified by other forms. The crystals are frequently twinned. Other habits are massive, granular, and compact. This mineral is dark gray to black in color, and the streak is black, brown, or dark red. Tennantite is opaque. It has a metallic luster, which sometimes can be very bright.
• **FORMATION** Forms in hydrothermal veins, in association with many other minerals, such as barite, fluorite, quartz, galena, sphalerite, pyrite, chalcopyrite, calcite, and dolomite. This mineral may also form in high temperature veins, and in contact metasomatic deposits.
• **TESTS** It is soluble in nitric acid, and fuses easily.

tetrahedral crystal

iridescent crystals

CUBIC

SG 4.59–4.75	Cleavage None	Fracture Uneven to subconchoidal

Group Sulfosalts	Composition $Pb_5Sb_4S_{11}$		Hardness $2\frac{1}{2}$–3

BOULANGERITE

This mineral forms long, prismatic crystals, which may be acicular. Other habits are massive, fibrous, or plumose. The color is lead-gray to bluish gray, and the streak is brownish. Boulangerite is opaque and has a dull or metallic luster.
• **FORMATION** Forms in hydrothermal veins, together with galena, pyrite, and sphalerite; with sulfosalts, including tetrahedrite, tennantite, and proustite; and with other minerals, such as quartz, and various carbonates.
• **TESTS** When it is heated in a flame, boulangerite fuses very easily. It does not react with cold, dilute acids, but is soluble in hot, strong acids.

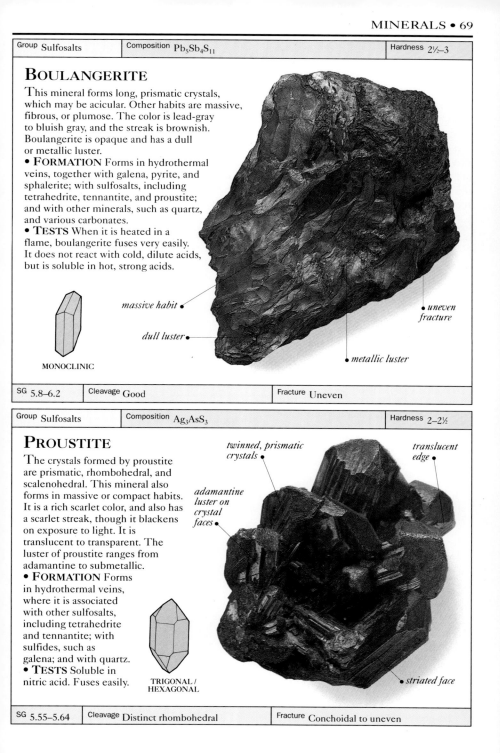

massive habit •

• uneven fracture

dull luster •

MONOCLINIC

• metallic luster

SG 5.8–6.2	Cleavage Good	Fracture Uneven

Group Sulfosalts	Composition Ag_3AsS_3		Hardness 2–2½

PROUSTITE

The crystals formed by proustite are prismatic, rhombohedral, and scalenohedral. This mineral also forms in massive or compact habits. It is a rich scarlet color, and also has a scarlet streak, though it blackens on exposure to light. It is translucent to transparent. The luster of proustite ranges from adamantine to submetallic.
• **FORMATION** Forms in hydrothermal veins, where it is associated with other sulfosalts, including tetrahedrite and tennantite; with sulfides, such as galena; and with quartz.
• **TESTS** Soluble in nitric acid. Fuses easily.

twinned, prismatic crystals •

translucent edge •

adamantine luster on crystal faces •

TRIGONAL / HEXAGONAL

• striated face

SG 5.55–5.64	Cleavage Distinct rhombohedral	Fracture Conchoidal to uneven

HALIDES

HALIDES ARE compounds in which metallic elements combine with halogens (the elements chlorine, bromine, fluorine, and iodine). Halides are common in a number of geological environments. Some, such as halite, are found in evaporite sequences. These are alternating layers of sedimentary rock, which contain evaporites, such as gypsum, halite, and potash rock in a strict sequence, interbedded with rocks such as marl and limestone.

———— • ————

Other halides, like fluorite, occur in hydrothermal veins. The halides are usually very soft minerals, and many have cubic crystal symmetry. Their specific gravity tends to be low.

Group Halides	Composition NaCl	Hardness 2

HALITE

The crystals formed by halite are cube-shaped and frequently have concave faces. They are called hopper crystals. Very rarely, halite occurs as octahedral crystals. Other habits include massive, granular, and compact. In a compact habit, the mineral is known as rock salt. It can be white, colorless, orange, yellow, reddish, blue, purple, and black. The streak, however, is consistently white. Halite is transparent to translucent, and has a vitreous luster.
• **FORMATION** This is an evaporite mineral, formed by precipitation, as the water in a salt lake or a lagoon dries out. Halite is associated with other evaporite minerals, such as sylvite, gypsum, dolomite, and anhydrite.
• **TESTS** There are several very easy tests that can be applied to halite. It has a salty taste. It is also readily soluble in cold water; if some of the resulting solution is left to dry out, small hopper crystals will form by precipitation. Halite feels greasy when handled. It colors a flame yellow. Minute impurities may produce green, orange, or reddish fluorescence.

HOPPER CRYSTALS

• *twinned, cube-shaped crystals*

cubic cleavage faces with vitreous • luster

ORANGE HALITE

uneven fracture •

• *transparency visible around margins*

CUBIC

SG 2.1–2.2	Cleavage Perfect cubic	Fracture Uneven to conchoidal

Group Halides	Composition KCl	Hardness 2

SYLVITE

The crystals usually form as cubes and, rarely, as octahedra. Sylvite can also occur in crusts, and in massive or granular habits. It can be colorless, whitish, gray, pink, bluish, yellow, purple, or red. The streak is white. This is a transparent mineral, which has a vitreous luster.
• **FORMATION** Forms as an evaporite mineral, by precipitation from salt solutions. It is associated with minerals such as halite, gypsum, polyhalite, carnallite, and anhydrite.
• **TESTS** Like halite, sylvite is soluble in cold water. It has a bitter taste.

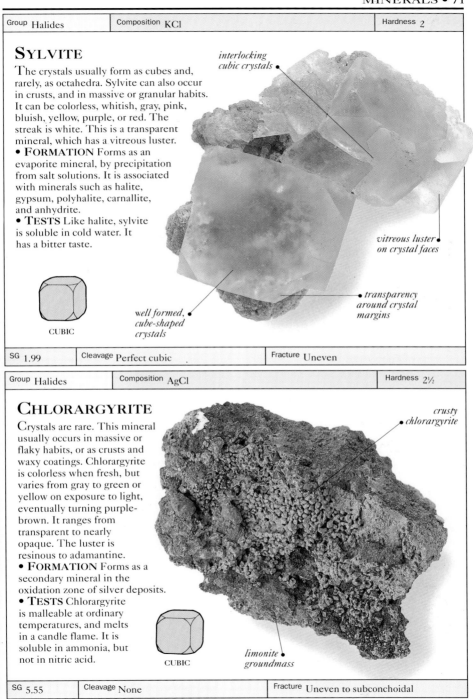

interlocking cubic crystals

vitreous luster on crystal faces

transparency around crystal margins

well formed, cube-shaped crystals

CUBIC

SG 1.99	Cleavage Perfect cubic	Fracture Uneven

Group Halides	Composition AgCl	Hardness 2½

CHLORARGYRITE

Crystals are rare. This mineral usually occurs in massive or flaky habits, or as crusts and waxy coatings. Chlorargyrite is colorless when fresh, but varies from gray to green or yellow on exposure to light, eventually turning purple-brown. It ranges from transparent to nearly opaque. The luster is resinous to adamantine.
• **FORMATION** Forms as a secondary mineral in the oxidation zone of silver deposits.
• **TESTS** Chlorargyrite is malleable at ordinary temperatures, and melts in a candle flame. It is soluble in ammonia, but not in nitric acid.

crusty chlorargyrite

limonite groundmass

CUBIC

SG 5.55	Cleavage None	Fracture Uneven to subconchoidal

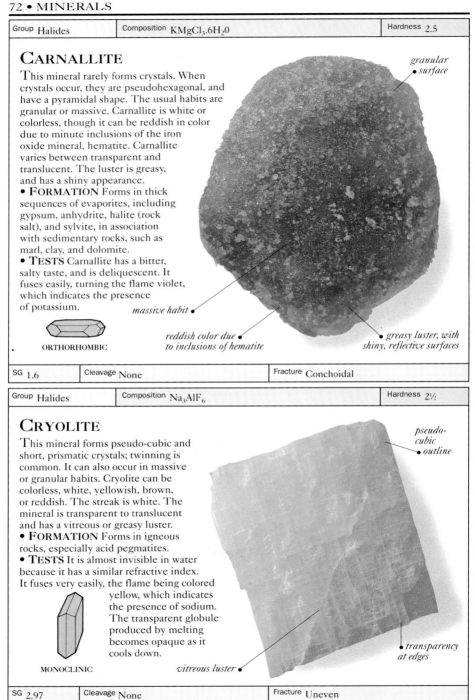

Group Halides	Composition $KMgCl_3.6H_2O$	Hardness 2.5

CARNALLITE

This mineral rarely forms crystals. When crystals occur, they are pseudohexagonal, and have a pyramidal shape. The usual habits are granular or massive. Carnallite is white or colorless, though it can be reddish in color due to minute inclusions of the iron oxide mineral, hematite. Carnallite varies between transparent and translucent. The luster is greasy, and has a shiny appearance.
• **FORMATION** Forms in thick sequences of evaporites, including gypsum, anhydrite, halite (rock salt), and sylvite, in association with sedimentary rocks, such as marl, clay, and dolomite.
• **TESTS** Carnallite has a bitter, salty taste, and is deliquescent. It fuses easily, turning the flame violet, which indicates the presence of potassium.

granular surface

massive habit

ORTHORHOMBIC

reddish color due to inclusions of hematite

greasy luster, with shiny, reflective surfaces

SG 1.6	Cleavage None	Fracture Conchoidal

Group Halides	Composition Na_3AlF_6	Hardness 2½

CRYOLITE

This mineral forms pseudo-cubic and short, prismatic crystals; twinning is common. It can also occur in massive or granular habits. Cryolite can be colorless, white, yellowish, brown, or reddish. The streak is white. The mineral is transparent to translucent and has a vitreous or greasy luster.
• **FORMATION** Forms in igneous rocks, especially acid pegmatites.
• **TESTS** It is almost invisible in water because it has a similar refractive index. It fuses very easily, the flame being colored yellow, which indicates the presence of sodium. The transparent globule produced by melting becomes opaque as it cools down.

pseudo-cubic outline

MONOCLINIC

vitreous luster

transparency at edges

SG 2.97	Cleavage None	Fracture Uneven

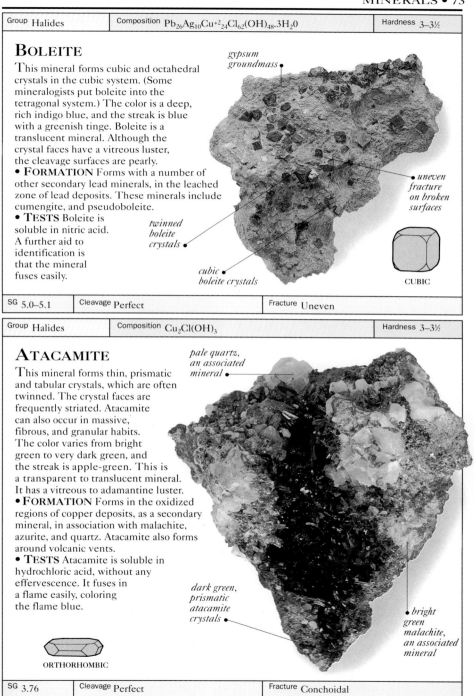

Group Halides	Composition $Pb_{26}Ag_{10}Cu^{+2}_{24}Cl_{62}(OH)_{48} \cdot 3H_2O$	Hardness $3–3\frac{1}{2}$

BOLEITE

This mineral forms cubic and octahedral crystals in the cubic system. (Some mineralogists put boleite into the tetragonal system.) The color is a deep, rich indigo blue, and the streak is blue with a greenish tinge. Boleite is a translucent mineral. Although the crystal faces have a vitreous luster, the cleavage surfaces are pearly.
• **FORMATION** Forms with a number of other secondary lead minerals, in the leached zone of lead deposits. These minerals include cumengite, and pseudoboleite.
• **TESTS** Boleite is soluble in nitric acid. A further aid to identification is that the mineral fuses easily.

gypsum groundmass

uneven fracture on broken surfaces

twinned boleite crystals

cubic boleite crystals

CUBIC

SG 5.0–5.1	Cleavage Perfect	Fracture Uneven

Group Halides	Composition $Cu_2Cl(OH)_3$	Hardness $3–3\frac{1}{2}$

ATACAMITE

This mineral forms thin, prismatic and tabular crystals, which are often twinned. The crystal faces are frequently striated. Atacamite can also occur in massive, fibrous, and granular habits. The color varies from bright green to very dark green, and the streak is apple-green. This is a transparent to translucent mineral. It has a vitreous to adamantine luster.
• **FORMATION** Forms in the oxidized regions of copper deposits, as a secondary mineral, in association with malachite, azurite, and quartz. Atacamite also forms around volcanic vents.
• **TESTS** Atacamite is soluble in hydrochloric acid, without any effervescence. It fuses in a flame easily, coloring the flame blue.

pale quartz, an associated mineral

dark green, prismatic atacamite crystals

bright green malachite, an associated mineral

ORTHORHOMBIC

SG 3.76	Cleavage Perfect	Fracture Conchoidal

Group Halides	Composition CaF_2	Hardness 4

FLUORITE

The crystals formed by this mineral are cubes and octahedra, and are often twinned. Fluorite may also be in massive, granular, and compact habits. It occurs in a great variety of colors, ranging from purple, green, colorless, white, and yellow, to pink, red, blue, and black. The streak is white. Fluorite is a transparent to translucent mineral and has a vitreous luster. If broken, its perfect octahedral cleavage produces triangular shapes on the corners of the cubic crystals.

• **FORMATION** Forms in hydrothermal veins, and around hot springs. Fluorite is a fairly common mineral, and is associated with quartz, calcite, dolomite, galena, pyrite, chalcopyrite, sphalerite, barite, and various other hydrothermal-vein minerals.

• **TESTS** As its name suggests, it can be strongly fluorescent in ultraviolet light.

PURPLE FLUORITE

• *octahedral crystal, showing translucency*

GREEN FLUORITE

transparent •

• *twinned cubes*

YELLOW FLUORITE

• *twinning*

vitreous luster •

• *striations on crystal faces*

octahedral crystal •

alternating light and dark bands •

BLUE JOHN

• *vitreous luster*

PINK FLUORITE

CUBIC

SG 3.1–3.3	Cleavage Perfect octahedral	Fracture Conchoidal

Group Halides	Composition $Pb_2Cu^{+2}Cl_2(OH)_4$	Hardness $2\frac{1}{2}$

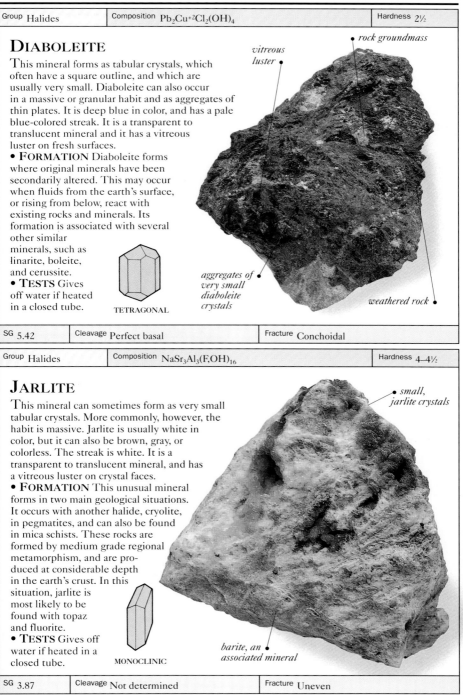

rock groundmass

DIABOLEITE

This mineral forms as tabular crystals, which often have a square outline, and which are usually very small. Diaboleite can also occur in a massive or granular habit and as aggregates of thin plates. It is deep blue in color, and has a pale blue-colored streak. It is a transparent to translucent mineral and it has a vitreous luster on fresh surfaces.

vitreous luster

- **FORMATION** Diaboleite forms where original minerals have been secondarily altered. This may occur when fluids from the earth's surface, or rising from below, react with existing rocks and minerals. Its formation is associated with several other similar minerals, such as linarite, boleite, and cerussite.
- **TESTS** Gives off water if heated in a closed tube.

TETRAGONAL

aggregates of very small diaboleite crystals

weathered rock

SG 5.42	Cleavage Perfect basal	Fracture Conchoidal

Group Halides	Composition $NaSr_3Al_3(F,OH)_{16}$	Hardness $4-4\frac{1}{2}$

JARLITE

This mineral can sometimes form as very small tabular crystals. More commonly, however, the habit is massive. Jarlite is usually white in color, but it can also be brown, gray, or colorless. The streak is white. It is a transparent to translucent mineral, and has a vitreous luster on crystal faces.

small, jarlite crystals

- **FORMATION** This unusual mineral forms in two main geological situations. It occurs with another halide, cryolite, in pegmatites, and can also be found in mica schists. These rocks are formed by medium grade regional metamorphism, and are produced at considerable depth in the earth's crust. In this situation, jarlite is most likely to be found with topaz and fluorite.
- **TESTS** Gives off water if heated in a closed tube.

MONOCLINIC

barite, an associated mineral

SG 3.87	Cleavage Not determined	Fracture Uneven

OXIDES AND HYDROXIDES

OXIDES are composed of elements combined with oxygen. A particularly common example is the iron oxide hematite, which is iron combined with oxygen (O). Oxides form a variable group, occurring in many geological environments and in most rock types. Some, such as hematite, magnetite (another iron oxide), cassiterite (tin oxide), and chromite (chromium oxide), are important ores of metals. Others, like corundum (aluminum oxide), have gemstone varieties such as ruby and sapphire. The properties of the oxides are varied. The gem varieties, and metallic ores, are very hard and of high specific gravity. They also vary considerably in color, from the rich red of ruby, the blue of sapphire, and the red, green, and blue of spinel (magnesium, aluminum oxide), to the black of magnetite.

———— • ————

Hydroxides form when a metallic element combines with water and hydroxyl (OH). A common example is brucite (magnesium hydroxide). Hydroxides, formed through a chemical reaction between an oxide and water, are usually of low hardness: brucite, for example, has a hardness of 2½; gibbsite (aluminum hydroxide) is 2½–3½.

Group Oxides	Composition $MgAl_2O_4$		Hardness 7½–8

SPINEL

This mineral forms as octahedral and sometimes cubic or dodecahedral crystals. Other habits are massive, granular, and compact. The color ranges from red, to green, blue, brown, and black. The streak is white. Spinel is transparent to opaque, and has a vitreous luster.
• **FORMATION** Forms in a variety of metamorphic rocks, including serpentinites, gneiss, and marble, as well as in igneous rocks of basic chemistry.
• **TESTS** A characteristic of this mineral is that it is infusible. Picotite is the chromium-rich variety, and pleonaste is the dark, iron-rich variety of spinel.

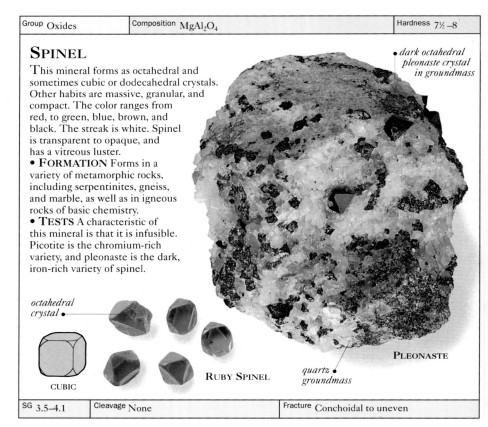

dark octahedral pleonaste crystal in groundmass

octahedral crystal •

CUBIC

RUBY SPINEL

quartz groundmass •

PLEONASTE

SG 3.5–4.1	Cleavage None	Fracture Conchoidal to uneven

Group Oxides	Composition $(Zn, Mn^{+2})O$	Hardness $4–4\frac{1}{2}$

ZINCITE

Pyramidal, hemimorphic crystals are formed by this mineral, but only rarely. Usually, zincite occurs in massive, granular, and foliated habits. The color is dark red to orange-yellow. The streak is orange-yellow. Zincite is translucent to transparent, and it has a subadamantine luster.
• **FORMATION** Forms in contact metamorphic rocks, and is associated with minerals such as calcite, willemite, franklinite, and tephrite. Zincite is an important zinc mineral, prized by collectors and mineralogists for its rarity.
• **TESTS** Zincite is soluble in hydrochloric acid, but shows no effervescence. It is fluorescent and infusible when placed in a flame.

subadamantine luster

mass of foliated zincite crystals

calcite groundmass

TRIGONAL / HEXAGONAL

SG 5.68	Cleavage Perfect	Fracture Conchoidal

Group Oxides	Composition $(Zn,Mn^{+2},Fe^{+2})(Fe^{+3},Mn^{+3})_2O_4$	Hardness $5\frac{1}{2}–6\frac{1}{2}$

FRANKLINITE

This mineral is in the spinel group. It occurs as octahedral crystals, frequently with rounded edges, and in granular or massive habits. The color is black, with a reddish brown to black streak. Franklinite is opaque, and it has a metallic luster.
• **FORMATION** Forms in zinc deposits in metamorphosed limestones and dolomites. It is associated with a number of other minerals, including calcite, willemite, zincite, rhodonite, and garnet.
• **TESTS** This mineral is weakly magnetic. When heated in a flame, it becomes strongly magnetic, and is infusible. It is soluble in hydrochloric acid, with no effervescence.

octahedral franklinite crystal

CUBIC

uneven fracture

calcite groundmass

SG 5.07–5.22	Cleavage None	Fracture Uneven to subconchoidal

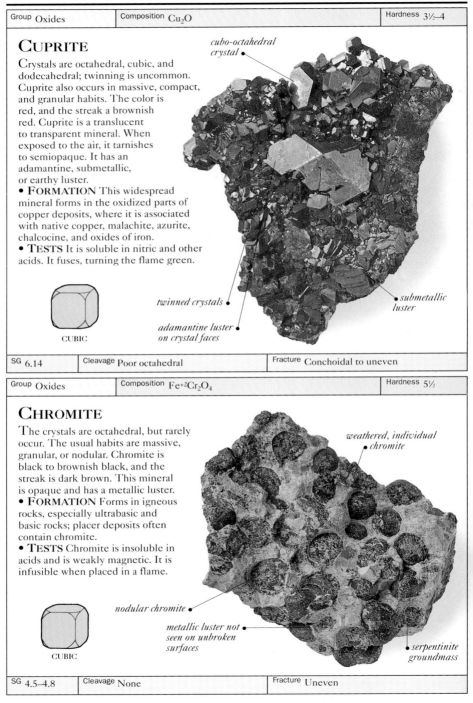

Group Oxides	Composition Cu_2O	Hardness $3\frac{1}{2}$–4

CUPRITE

Crystals are octahedral, cubic, and dodecahedral; twinning is uncommon. Cuprite also occurs in massive, compact, and granular habits. The color is red, and the streak a brownish red. Cuprite is a translucent to transparent mineral. When exposed to the air, it tarnishes to semiopaque. It has an adamantine, submetallic, or earthy luster.

• **FORMATION** This widespread mineral forms in the oxidized parts of copper deposits, where it is associated with native copper, malachite, azurite, chalcocine, and oxides of iron.

• **TESTS** It is soluble in nitric and other acids. It fuses, turning the flame green.

cubo-octahedral crystal

twinned crystals

adamantine luster on crystal faces

CUBIC

submetallic luster

SG 6.14	Cleavage Poor octahedral	Fracture Conchoidal to uneven

Group Oxides	Composition $Fe^{+2}Cr_2O_4$	Hardness $5\frac{1}{2}$

CHROMITE

The crystals are octahedral, but rarely occur. The usual habits are massive, granular, or nodular. Chromite is black to brownish black, and the streak is dark brown. This mineral is opaque and has a metallic luster.

• **FORMATION** Forms in igneous rocks, especially ultrabasic and basic rocks; placer deposits often contain chromite.

• **TESTS** Chromite is insoluble in acids and is weakly magnetic. It is infusible when placed in a flame.

weathered, individual chromite

nodular chromite

metallic luster not seen on unbroken surfaces

CUBIC

serpentinite groundmass

SG 4.5–4.8	Cleavage None	Fracture Uneven

Group Oxides	Composition $Fe^{+2}Fe^{+3}_2O_4$	Hardness $5\frac{1}{2}$–$6\frac{1}{2}$

MAGNETITE

This common oxide mineral forms octahedral and dodecahedral crystals and also occurs in massive and granular habits. The color is black, and so is the streak. Magnetite is an opaque mineral. The luster may be either metallic or dull.
• **FORMATION** Magnetite forms in igneous rocks, and also in veins and replacement deposits.
• **TESTS** As the name suggests, this mineral is highly magnetic, attracting iron filings. It will also deflect a compass needle.

granular habit of small particles

OCTAHEDRAL CRYSTAL

CUBIC

triangular crystal face

GRANULAR MAGNETITE

SG 5.2	Cleavage None	Fracture Subconchoidal to uneven

Group Oxides	Composition $Fe^{+2}TiO_3$	Hardness 5–6

ILMENITE

This mineral usually forms thick, tabular crystals; sometimes it forms rhombohedral crystals. Twinning is common. Other habits are lamellar, massive, compact, and granular. It is black or brownish black, with a black to brownish red streak. It is opaque. Ilmenite has a luster ranging from metallic to dull.
• **FORMATION** Forms in many igneous rocks as an accessory mineral, including pegmatites, and in mineral veins. It is also found as a placer in black sands.
• **TESTS** Soluble in concentrated hydrochloric acid if powdered first. Weakly magnetic when cold.

twinned ilmenite crystals

TRIGONAL / HEXAGONAL

lamellar ilmenite

oligoclase feldspar groundmass

SG 4.72	Cleavage None	Fracture Conchoidal to uneven

Group Oxides	Composition $\propto - Fe_2O_3$	Hardness 5–6

HEMATITE

The crystals of this mineral are tabular or rhombohedral, and occasionally prismatic or pyramidal. Tabular crystals may form as rosettes, when they are called iron roses. Other habits are massive, compact, columnar, fibrous, reniform, botryoidal, stalactitic, foliated, and granular. When hematite forms in a reniform habit, it is known as kidney ore. Its color ranges from brownish, bright red, blood-red, and brownish red, to steel-gray, and iron-black. The streak is brownish-red. It is an opaque mineral, with a metallic to dull luster.
• **FORMATION** Occurs as a hydrothermal and replacement mineral. It also forms in igneous rocks as an accessory mineral.
• **TESTS** This mineral may become magnetic when heated.

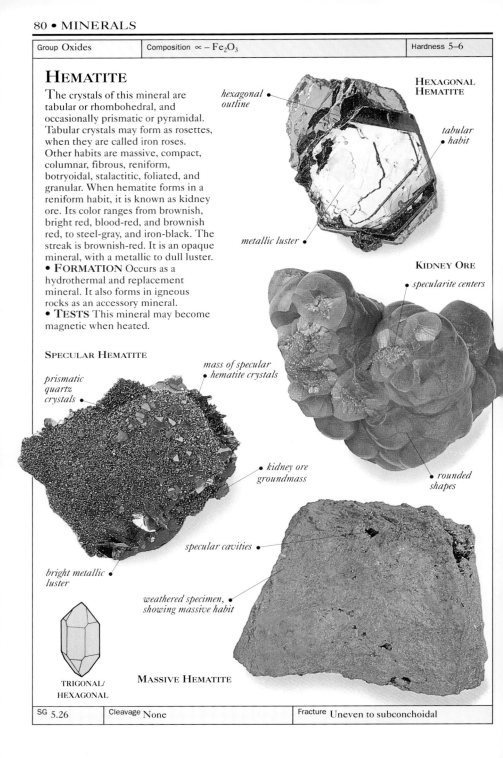

HEXAGONAL HEMATITE

hexagonal outline

tabular habit

metallic luster

KIDNEY ORE

specularite centers

SPECULAR HEMATITE

prismatic quartz crystals

mass of specular hematite crystals

kidney ore groundmass

rounded shapes

specular cavities

bright metallic luster

weathered specimen, showing massive habit

TRIGONAL/ HEXAGONAL

MASSIVE HEMATITE

SG 5.26	Cleavage None	Fracture Uneven to subconchoidal

Group Oxides	Composition BeAl$_2$O$_4$		Hardness 8½

CHRYSOBERYL

The chrysoberyl crystals are tabular or prismatic, and commonly twinned. Other habits are granular and massive. The color varies from green or yellow to brownish or gray. The gem variety, alexandrite, is green in daylight but is red in tungsten light. Chrysoberyl is a transparent to translucent mineral, and it has a vitreous luster.
• **FORMATION** Forms in many rocks, including pegmatites, schists, gneisses, and marbles. Chrysoberyl also occurs in placer sands, which are alluvial deposits. Its occurrence here is largely due to its great hardness and resistance to weathering and erosion.
• **TESTS** It is an insoluble mineral.

vitreous luster

striations on crystal faces

crystals are transparent to translucent

ORTHORHOMBIC

tabular crystal

twinned crystals

SG 3.7–3.8	Cleavage Distinct prismatic	Fracture Conchoidal to uneven

Group Oxides	Composition SnO$_2$		Hardness 6–7

CASSITERITE

This mineral may form as short or slender prismatic, or bipyramidal, crystals. Other habits are massive, granular, botryoidal, and reniform. The typical color is brown to black, but it may also be yellowish or colorless. The streak is white, gray, or brownish. Cassiterite is transparent to nearly opaque. The luster is adamantine on crystal faces, and greasy when fractured.
• **FORMATION** Forms in high temperature hydrothermal veins, where associated minerals include quartz, chalcopyrite, and tourmaline. It also forms in some contact metamorphic rocks.
• **TESTS** This mineral is insoluble in acids. Cassiterite is also infusible.

adamantine luster on crystal faces

twinned crystals

opaque

TETRAGONAL

short, prismatic crystals

SG 7.0	Cleavage Poor	Fracture Subconchoidal to uneven

Group Oxides	Composition Al_2O_3	Hardness 9

CORUNDUM

This mineral forms steep bipyramidal, prismatic, tabular, or rhombohedral crystals. It also occurs in massive and granular habits. Corundum can be many colors but always has a white streak. It is transparent to translucent with a vitreous to adamantine luster.
• **FORMATION** Forms in silica-poor igneous rocks, and metamorphic rocks rich in aluminum.
• **TESTS** It is insoluble.

TRIGONAL/
HEXAGONAL

pyramidal crystal

translucent

SG 4.0–4.1	Cleavage None	Fracture Conchoidal to uneven

Group Oxides	Composition Al_2O_3	Hardness 9

RUBY

vitreous luster

A variety of corundum, ruby forms as bipyramidal, prismatic, tabular, or rhombohedral crystals. It is red in color, and has a white-colored streak. Ruby is translucent to transparent, with a vitreous or adamantine luster.
• **FORMATION** Forms in igneous and metamorphic rocks. Because of its hardness and density, ruby also occurs in river gravels.
• **TESTS** Insoluble in acids.

TRIGONAL/
HEXAGONAL

ruby crystals in groundmass

ruby crystal

SG 4.0–4.1	Cleavage None	Fracture Conchoidal to uneven

Group Oxides	Composition Al_2O_3	Hardness 9

SAPPHIRE

sapphire crystals in rock groundmass

The blue-colored variety of corundum, sapphire forms as bipyramidal, prismatic, tabular, or rhombohedral crystals. Other habits are massive and granular. It may also be green, yellow, purple, or colorless. It is transparent to translucent, with a vitreous or adamantine luster.
• **FORMATION** Sapphire forms in certain igneous and metamorphic rocks. It also occurs in sedimentary alluvial deposits.
• **TESTS** Insoluble in acids.

TRIGONAL/
HEXAGONAL

bipyramidal crystal

SG 4.0–4.1	Cleavage None	Fracture Conchoidal to uneven

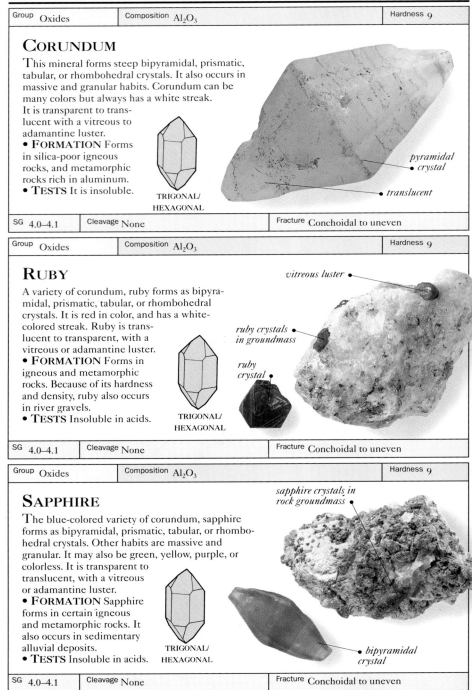

Group Oxides	Composition $Mn^{+4}O_2$		Hardness $2-6\frac{1}{2}$

PYROLUSITE

Crystals are prismatic, but very rare. The usual habits are massive, compact, columnar, or fibrous. Dendritic coatings are common. It is black to dark gray in color, and has a black or bluish black streak. Pyrolusite is an opaque mineral and it has a metallic to dull or earthy luster.

• **FORMATION** Forms as a precipitate in lakes and bogs and also in nodules on deep ocean beds. Pyrolusite is a secondary mineral in manganese veins.

• **TESTS** Soluble in hydrochloric acid. It will leave sooty marks if touched.

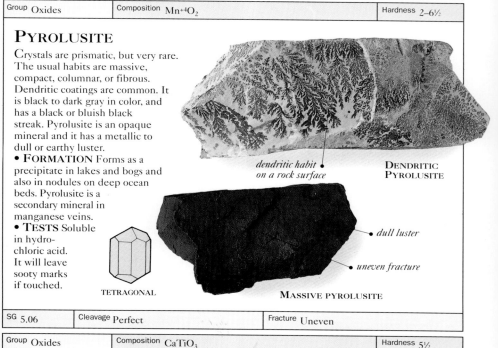

dendritic habit on a rock surface

DENDRITIC PYROLUSITE

dull luster

uneven fracture

TETRAGONAL

MASSIVE PYROLUSITE

SG 5.06	Cleavage Perfect		Fracture Uneven

Group Oxides	Composition $CaTiO_3$		Hardness $5\frac{1}{2}$

PEROVSKITE

This mineral forms pseudo-cubic crystals, with striations parallel to the edges. It also occurs as reniform masses. The color is yellow, amber, dark brown, or black, and there is a colorless to pale gray streak. Perovskite is a transparent to opaque mineral, and it has a metallic to adamantine luster.

• **FORMATION** Forms in certain basic and ultrabasic igneous rocks, schists rich in talc and chlorite, and in some marbles. Perovskite is also an accessory mineral in some rocks. An accessory mineral is not an important rock-former, and its presence does not influence the bulk chemistry or classification of the rock.

• **TESTS** It is soluble only in hot sulfuric acid. Perovskite is infusible.

pseudo-cubic crystal

striated crystal

ORTHORHOMBIC

SG 4.01	Cleavage Imperfect		Fracture Subconchoidal to uneven

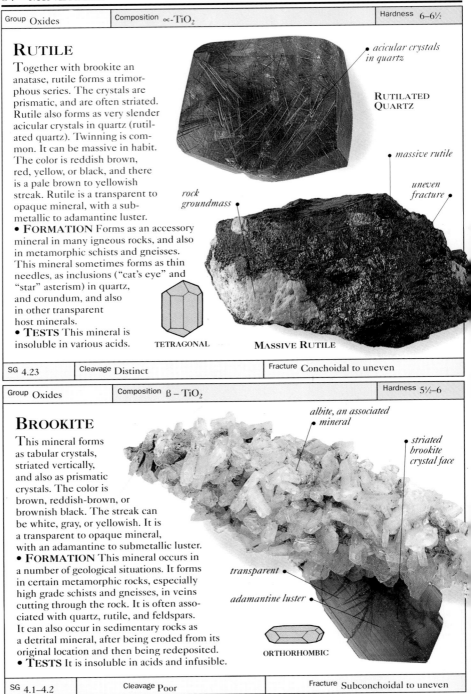

Group Oxides	Composition ∝-TiO₂	Hardness 6–6½

RUTILE

Together with brookite an anatase, rutile forms a trimorphous series. The crystals are prismatic, and are often striated. Rutile also forms as very slender acicular crystals in quartz (rutilated quartz). Twinning is common. It can be massive in habit. The color is reddish brown, red, yellow, or black, and there is a pale brown to yellowish streak. Rutile is a transparent to opaque mineral, with a submetallic to adamantine luster.

• **FORMATION** Forms as an accessory mineral in many igneous rocks, and also in metamorphic schists and gneisses. This mineral sometimes forms as thin needles, as inclusions ("cat's eye" and "star" asterism) in quartz, and corundum, and also in other transparent host minerals.

• **TESTS** This mineral is insoluble in various acids.

acicular crystals in quartz

RUTILATED QUARTZ

massive rutile

uneven fracture

rock groundmass

TETRAGONAL

MASSIVE RUTILE

SG 4.23	Cleavage Distinct	Fracture Conchoidal to uneven

Group Oxides	Composition ß – TiO₂	Hardness 5½–6

BROOKITE

This mineral forms as tabular crystals, striated vertically, and also as prismatic crystals. The color is brown, reddish-brown, or brownish black. The streak can be white, gray, or yellowish. It is a transparent to opaque mineral, with an adamantine to submetallic luster.

• **FORMATION** This mineral occurs in a number of geological situations. It forms in certain metamorphic rocks, especially high grade schists and gneisses, in veins cutting through the rock. It is often associated with quartz, rutile, and feldspars. It can also occur in sedimentary rocks as a detrital mineral, after being eroded from its original location and then being redeposited.

• **TESTS** It is insoluble in acids and infusible.

albite, an associated mineral

striated brookite crystal face

transparent

adamantine luster

ORTHORHOMBIC

SG 4.1–4.2	Cleavage Poor	Fracture Subconchoidal to uneven

Group Oxides	Composition $Y - TiO_2$	Hardness 5½–6

ANATASE

The pyramidal crystals formed by anatase are often striated. The crystals may also be tabular, and these are often highly modified. The color may be brown, deep blue, or black, and the streak may be colorless, white, or pale yellow. Anatase is a transparent to nearly opaque mineral, and it has an adamantine to submetallic luster.

• **FORMATION** This particular type of titanium dioxide forms in certain metamorphic rocks, especially schist and gneiss. It can also occur in some igneous rocks, such as diorite and granite, where it is an accessory mineral. Anatase is also found in placer deposits, after it has been removed from its original location and then redeposited alluvially.

• **TESTS** This mineral is insoluble in all acids.

ORTHORHOMBIC

small, bipyramidal anatase crystal

albite, an associated mineral

opaque crystal

SG 3.82–3.97	Cleavage Perfect basal	Fracture Subconchcoidal

Group Oxides	Composition UO_2	Hardness 5–6

URANINITE

Occurs as cubic, cubo-octahedral, octahedral, or dodecahedral crystals. More often, it forms in massive (when it is known as pitchblende), botryoidal, or granular habits. The color and streak can be black to brownish black, or grayish black. Uraninite is an opaque mineral and it has a submetallic, greasy, dull, or pitchlike luster.

• **FORMATION** It forms in hydrothermal veins. It also occurs in stratified sedimentary rocks, such as sandstone and conglomerate, and in some igneous rocks, including pegmatites and granites.

• **TESTS** Uraninite is highly radioactive. It is infusible, and insoluble in hydrochloric acid. It does dissolve slowly, however, in nitric acid.

CUBIC

botryoidal habit

opaque

submetallic to dull luster

SG 6.5–10.0	Cleavage Indistinct	Fracture Conchoidal to uneven

Group Oxides	Composition SiO_2	Hardness 7

QUARTZ

One of the most common minerals, quartz forms hexagonal prisms, terminated by rhombohedra, or pyramidal shapes. Quartz faces are often striated and the crystals twinned and distorted. It also occurs in massive, granular, concretionary, stalactitic, and cryptocrystalline habits. The coloring is amazingly variable, and quartz may be white, gray, red, purple, pink, yellow, green, brown, and black, as well as being colorless. It is also the source of a wide variety of semiprecious gemstones – many of which are shown here. The streak is colorless to white. Quartz is a transparent to translucent mineral, and it has a vitreous luster on fresh surfaces.

• **FORMATION** This mineral occurs commonly in igneous, metamorphic, and sedimentary rocks, and can be frequently found in mineral veins with metal ores.

• **TESTS** Quartz is insoluble, unless placed in hydrofluoric acid.

TRIGONAL/
HEXAGONAL

milky quartz groundmass

SMOKY QUARTZ

vitreous luster

translucent

ROSE QUARTZ

uneven fracture

vitreous luster

mass of pyramidal crystals

AMETHYST

SG 2.65	Cleavage None	Fracture Conchoidal to uneven

prismatic crystal

MILKY QUARTZ

transparent specimens

ROCK CRYSTAL

vitreous luster

prismatic crystal habit

hexagonal crystal

CITRINE

conchoidal fracture

vitreous luster on crystal face

uneven fracture at base of crystal

Group Oxides	Composition SiO_2	Hardness 7

CHALCEDONY

A microcrystalline variety of quartz, chalcedony usually occurs as mammillary or botryoidal masses. The color is highly variable, and may be white, blue, red, green, brown, or black. Varieties of chalcedony include jasper, an opaque form; agate, a form with concentric banding of different colors; moss agate, with dark dendritic patterns; chrysoprase, a green variety; and onyx, in which the banding is parallel. Carnelian is red to reddish brown, and sard is light to dark brown. There is a white streak. Chalcedony is a transparent to translucent or opaque mineral, and it has a vitreous to waxy luster.

• **FORMATION** This mineral forms in cavities in rocks of different types, especially lavas. A lot of chalcedony develops at relatively low temperatures, as a precipitate from silica-rich solutions. It can also be formed as a dehydration product of opal.

• **TESTS** Its higher specific gravity can help to distinguish chalcedony from opal.

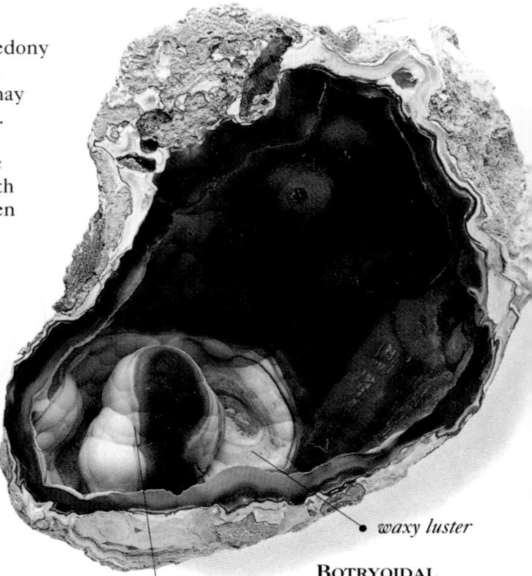

waxy luster

BOTRYOIDAL CHALCEDONY

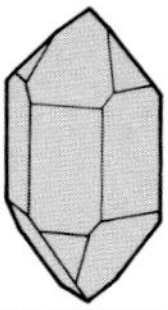

botryoidal habit

TRIGONAL/
HEXAGONAL

different colored bands

cut specimens

waxy luster

concentric bands

uneven fracture

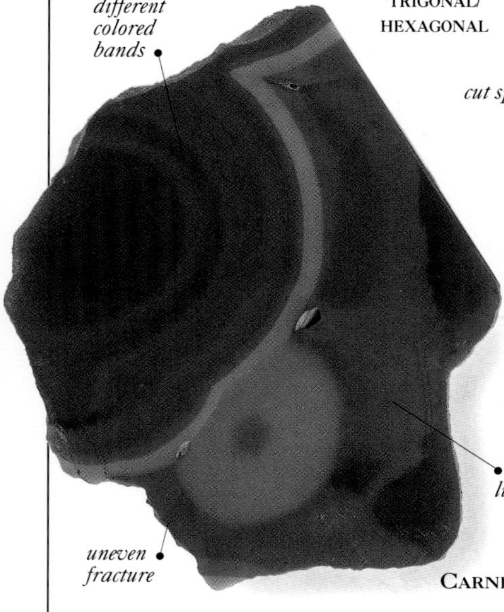

CARNELIAN

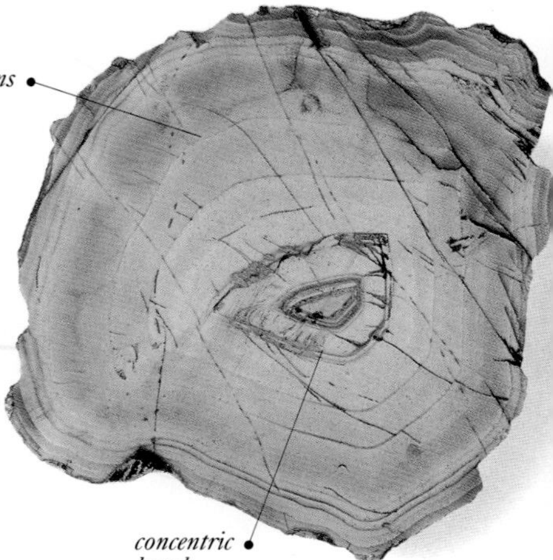

FORTIFICATION AGATE

SG 2.65	Cleavage None	Fracture Conchoidal

waxy luster

mammillary habit

JASPER

CHRYSOPRASE

bands of different colors

uneven fracture

vitreous luster

ONYX

parallel bands

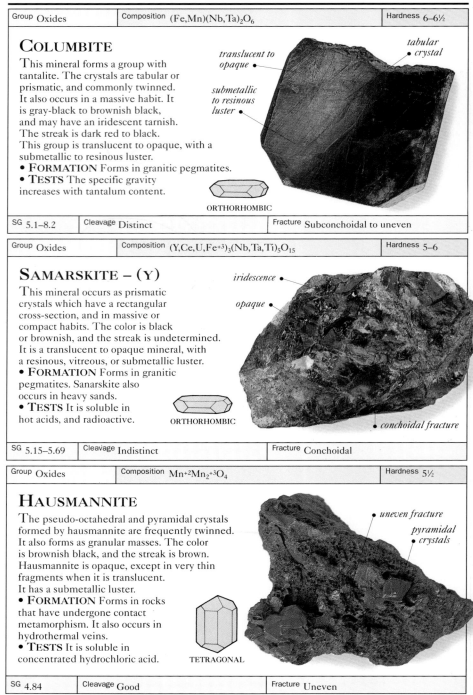

Group Oxides	Composition $(Fe,Mn)(Nb,Ta)_2O_6$	Hardness 6–6½

COLUMBITE

This mineral forms a group with
tantalite. The crystals are tabular or
prismatic, and commonly twinned.
It also occurs in a massive habit. It
is gray-black to brownish black,
and may have an iridescent tarnish.
The streak is dark red to black.
This group is translucent to opaque, with a
submetallic to resinous luster.
• **FORMATION** Forms in granitic pegmatites.
• **TESTS** The specific gravity
increases with tantalum content.

translucent to opaque •

submetallic to resinous luster •

tabular • crystal

ORTHORHOMBIC

SG 5.1–8.2	Cleavage Distinct	Fracture Subconchoidal to uneven

Group Oxides	Composition $(Y,Ce,U,Fe^{+3})_3(Nb,Ta,Ti)_5O_{15}$	Hardness 5–6

SAMARSKITE – (Y)

This mineral occurs as prismatic
crystals which have a rectangular
cross-section, and in massive or
compact habits. The color is black
or brownish, and the streak is undetermined.
It is a translucent to opaque mineral, with
a resinous, vitreous, or submetallic luster.
• **FORMATION** Forms in granitic
pegmatites. Sanarskite also
occurs in heavy sands.
• **TESTS** It is soluble in
hot acids, and radioactive.

iridescence •

opaque •

• conchoidal fracture

ORTHORHOMBIC

SG 5.15–5.69	Cleavage Indistinct	Fracture Conchoidal

Group Oxides	Composition $Mn^{+2}Mn_2^{+3}O_4$	Hardness 5½

HAUSMANNITE

The pseudo-octahedral and pyramidal crystals
formed by hausmannite are frequently twinned.
It also forms as granular masses. The color
is brownish black, and the streak is brown.
Hausmannite is opaque, except in very thin
fragments when it is translucent.
It has a submetallic luster.
• **FORMATION** Forms in rocks
that have undergone contact
metamorphism. It also occurs in
hydrothermal veins.
• **TESTS** It is soluble in
concentrated hydrochloric acid.

• uneven fracture

pyramidal • crystals

TETRAGONAL

SG 4.84	Cleavage Good	Fracture Uneven

Group Oxides	Composition Oxides and hydroxides		Hardness Soft

"WAD"

Not strictly a mineral, wad is a mixture of several oxide and hydroxide minerals, especially of manganese. It usually contains pyrolusite and psilomelane. It has an amorphous appearance, and may be reniform, arborescent, encrusting, or massive in habit. Wad is often a dull black color, though it may be lead-gray, bluish, or brownish black. The streak is dark brown or blackish. It is an opaque mineral, with a dull or earthy luster.
• **FORMATION** Occurs in sedimentary environments with manganese minerals.
• **TESTS** When heated in a closed test tube, water is given off.

massive habit

rock groundmass

dull luster

SG 2.8–4.4	Cleavage None		Fracture Uneven

Group Hydroxides	Composition $(Ba,H_2O)Mn^{+4},Mn^{+3})_5O_{10}$		Hardness 5–6

ROMANECHITE

MASSIVE ROMANECHITE

In the past, psilomelane was regarded as a distinct mineral species. However, recent studies have found that psilomelane is actually the amorphous species, romanechite. It forms in massive, botryoidal, reniform, stalactitic, and earthy habits. It is black to dark gray, and the streak is black, or brownish black, and shining. It is an opaque mineral, with a submetallic luster.
• **FORMATION** Forms by the alteration of other minerals, especially manganese-rich silicates and carbonates. Romanechite is a common mineral and forms in concretions and where limestones have been replaced by other materials.
• **TESTS** It is soluble in hydrochloric acid, giving off chlorine gas. It gives off water if heated in a closed test tube.

massive habit

BOTRYOIDAL ROMANECHITE

botryoidal habit

MONOCLINIC

opaque

submetallic luster

SG 6.4	Cleavage Not determined		Fracture Uneven

Group Oxides	Composition $(Na,Ca)_2 Nb_2O_6(OH,F) - (Ca,Na)_2Ta_2O_6(O1,OH,F)$	Hardness 5–5½

PYROCHLORE-MICROLITE

This series of minerals forms as octahedral crystals, which are sometimes twinned. Other habits are as grains and irregular masses. Its color is brown, reddish brown, or black. The streak is yellowish to brown. The Pyrochlore-Microlite series is translucent to opaque and has a vitreous to resinous luster.

• **FORMATION** Forms in pegmatites and carbonatites. Pyrochlore-Microlite is also found as an accessory mineral in nepheline syenites.

• **TESTS** This series of minerals is infusible. It is soluble in hydrochloric acid, but only with great difficulty. A number of elements, such as thorium and uranium, can replace calcium and sodium in the chemical structure, when the mineral becomes radioactive.

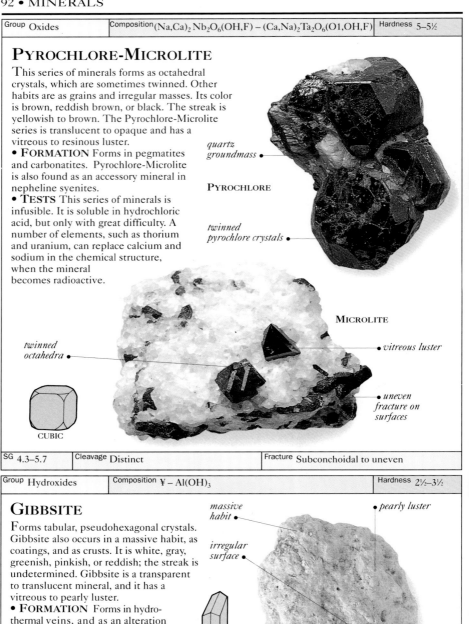

quartz groundmass •

PYROCHLORE

twinned pyrochlore crystals •

MICROLITE

twinned octahedra •

• *vitreous luster*

• *uneven fracture on surfaces*

CUBIC

SG 4.3–5.7	Cleavage Distinct	Fracture Subconchoidal to uneven

Group Hydroxides	Composition ¥ – $Al(OH)_3$	Hardness 2½–3½

GIBBSITE

Forms tabular, pseudohexagonal crystals. Gibbsite also occurs in a massive habit, as coatings, and as crusts. It is white, gray, greenish, pinkish, or reddish; the streak is undetermined. Gibbsite is a transparent to translucent mineral, and it has a vitreous to pearly luster.

• **FORMATION** Forms in hydrothermal veins, and as an alteration product of aluminum minerals.

• **TESTS** Gibbsite smells of wet clay when you breathe over it.

massive habit •

• *pearly luster*

irregular surface •

MONOCLINIC

SG 2.4	Cleavage Perfect	Fracture Uneven

Group Oxides	Composition SiO_2,nH_2O	Hardness $5\frac{1}{2}-6\frac{1}{2}$

OPAL

The structure of opal is amorphous. It forms in a great variety of habits, including massive, botryoidal, reniform, stalactitic, globular, and concretionary. Precious opal is milky white, or black, with a brilliant interplay of colors, commonly red, blue, and yellow. The colors often change as a result of the warming of water in the mineral. Precious opals warmed in the hand will be particularly brilliant. Fire opal is orange or reddish, and may or may not have an interplay of colors. Common opal is gray, black, or green, and has no interplay of colors. The streak is white. Opal is transparent to opaque. Its luster can be vitreous to resinous, waxy or pearly, though vitreous is the most common.

- **FORMATION** Forms at low temperatures from silica-rich water, especially around hot springs, but it can occur in almost any geological environment.
- **TESTS** Opal often fluoresces in ultraviolet light and is insoluble in acids. When heated, it decomposes and may turn into quartz as the water molecules are removed. When opal is exposed to air for any length of time, the mineral structure becomes fragile because of the loss of water and infilling with fractures.

iron nodule

nodule broken to reveal opal

PRECIOUS OPAL

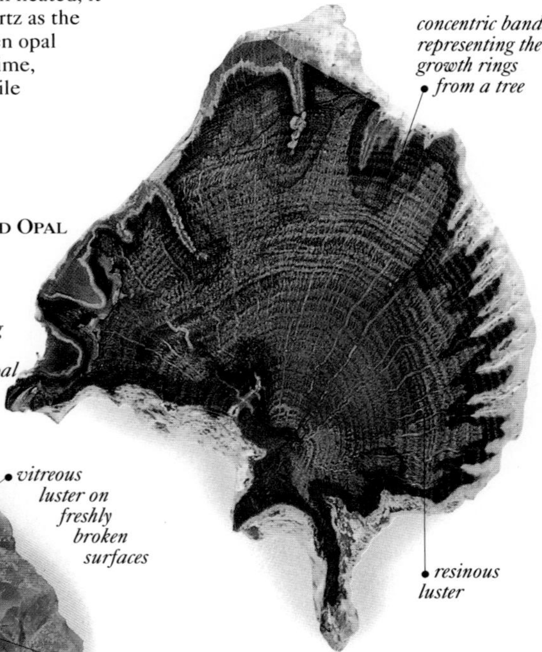

concentric bands, representing the growth rings from a tree

WOOD OPAL

resinous luster

red coloring typical of fire opal

vitreous luster on freshly broken surfaces

FIRE OPAL

conchoidal fracture well displayed

SG 1.9–2.3	Cleavage Uneven	Fracture Conchoidal

Group Hydroxides	Composition $Mg(OH)_2$	Hardness $2\frac{1}{2}$

BRUCITE

CRYSTALLINE BRUCITE

This mineral forms as broad, tabular crystals. It can be massive, foliated, fibrous (nemalite), and granular in habit. It is white, pale green, gray, bluish, and, when it contains manganese, yellow to brown in color. There is a white streak. Brucite is transparent. It has a waxy, vitreous, or pearly luster (the fibrous varieties are silky). Flexible, inelastic laminae are produced from the perfect cleavage when this mineral is carefully broken.

• **FORMATION** Forms in metamorphosed limestones, and in schists, and serpentinites.

• **TESTS** Brucite is soluble in hydrochloric acid, with no effervescence. It is also infusible.

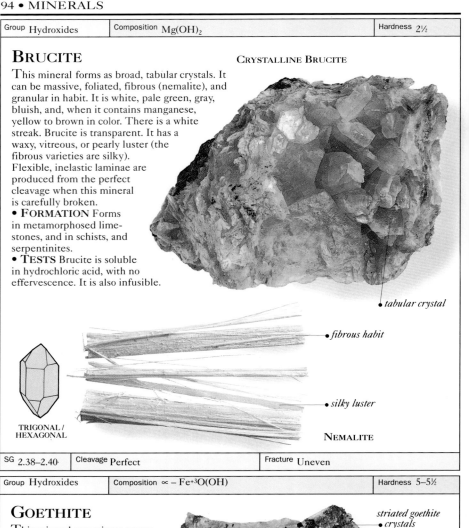

• tabular crystal

• fibrous habit

• silky luster

TRIGONAL /
HEXAGONAL

NEMALITE

SG 2.38–2.40	Cleavage Perfect	Fracture Uneven

Group Hydroxides	Composition $\propto - Fe^{+3}O(OH)$	Hardness 5–5½

GOETHITE

striated goethite
• crystals

This mineral sometimes occurs as vertically striated, prismatic crystals, but more frequently as massive, botryoidal, stalactitic, and earthy specimens. The color is blackish brown, or reddish to yellowish brown. The streak is orange to brownish. Goethite is opaque. The luster is adamantine on crystal faces, and otherwise dull.

groundmass
• of quartz

• **FORMATION** Goethite forms by the oxidation of iron-rich deposits.

• **TESTS** Turns magnetic when heated.

ORTHORHOMBIC

SG 3.3–4.3	Cleavage Perfect	Fracture Uneven

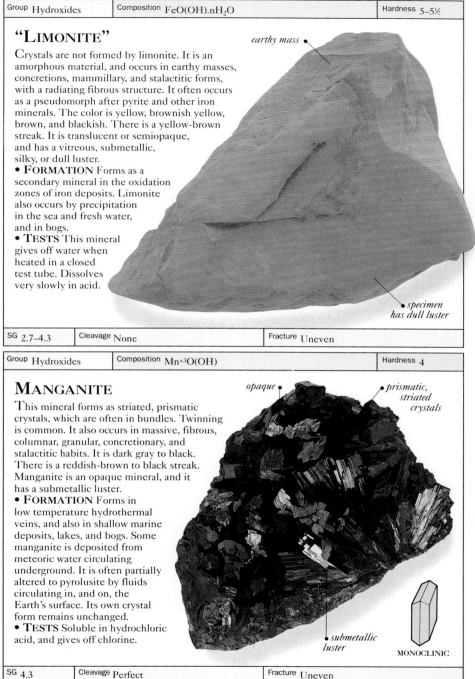

Group Hydroxides	Composition $FeO(OH).nH_2O$		Hardness 5–5½

"LIMONITE"

earthy mass •

Crystals are not formed by limonite. It is an amorphous material, and occurs in earthy masses, concretions, mammillary, and stalactitic forms, with a radiating fibrous structure. It often occurs as a pseudomorph after pyrite and other iron minerals. The color is yellow, brownish yellow, brown, and blackish. There is a yellow-brown streak. It is translucent or semiopaque, and has a vitreous, submetallic, silky, or dull luster.
• **FORMATION** Forms as a secondary mineral in the oxidation zones of iron deposits. Limonite also occurs by precipitation in the sea and fresh water, and in bogs.
• **TESTS** This mineral gives off water when heated in a closed test tube. Dissolves very slowly in acid.

• specimen has dull luster

SG 2.7–4.3	Cleavage None	Fracture Uneven

Group Hydroxides	Composition $Mn^{+3}O(OH)$		Hardness 4

MANGANITE

opaque •   • prismatic, striated crystals

This mineral forms as striated, prismatic crystals, which are often in bundles. Twinning is common. It also occurs in massive, fibrous, columnar, granular, concretionary, and stalactitic habits. It is dark gray to black. There is a reddish-brown to black streak. Manganite is an opaque mineral, and it has a submetallic luster.
• **FORMATION** Forms in low temperature hydrothermal veins, and also in shallow marine deposits, lakes, and bogs. Some manganite is deposited from meteoric water circulating underground. It is often partially altered to pyrolusite by fluids circulating in, and on, the Earth's surface. Its own crystal form remains unchanged.
• **TESTS** Soluble in hydrochloric acid, and gives off chlorine.

• submetallic luster

MONOCLINIC

SG 4.3	Cleavage Perfect	Fracture Uneven

Group Hydroxides	Composition FeO(OH) and $Al_2O_3 2H_2O$	Hardness 1–3

"BAUXITE"

A mixture of several minerals, bauxite's composition includes hydrated aluminium oxides, such as gibbsite, boehmite, diaspore, and iron oxides. Strictly speaking, bauxite should be classified as a rock, but it is sometimes grouped with minerals. The varied composition means that the properties are also variable. The habit is generally massive, concretionary, oolitic, or pisolitic. The color varies from white to yellowish or red and reddish brown. The streak is normally white. Bauxite has a dull or earthy luster, and is opaque.
• **FORMATION** Forms by the weathering and decay of rocks that contain aluminum silicates. This is most likely to occur under tropical conditions, when heavy rains leach the silicates from the rock, leaving behind the aluminum minerals.
• **TESTS** Bauxite smells of wet clay if breathed on. It is infusible and virtually insoluble.

pisolitic habit

rounded fragments in groundmass

SG 2.3–2.7	Cleavage None	Fracture Uneven

Group Hydroxides	Composition AlO(OH)	Hardness 6½–7

DIASPORE

This mineral forms as platy, acicular, or tabular crystals, as well as in massive, foliated, scaly, or stalactitic habits. It is frequently disseminated and granular. The color may be white, colorless, grayish, yellowish, greenish, brown, purple, or pink. There is a white streak. Diaspore is a transparent to translucent mineral. The luster is vitreous, but pearly on cleavages.
• **FORMATION** Forms in altered igneous rocks and in marbles. It occurs with many minerals, including magnetite, spinel, dolomite, chlorite, and corundum. Diaspore is also found in clay deposits, when it occurs with bauxite and aluminum-rich clay minerals.
• **TESTS** It is insoluble and infusible.

vitreous luster

emery groundmass

platy habit

translucent to transparent

ORTHORHOMBIC

SG 3.3–3.5	Cleavage Perfect	Fracture Conchoidal

Group Hydroxides	Composition ¥ – Fe^{+3}O(OH)	Hardness 5

LEPIDOCROCITE

This mineral may form as flattened, platy crystals, but it
more commonly occurs in
massive or fibrous habits. The
color is deep red to reddish brown, and the streak
is orange. Lepidocrocite is a transparent mineral,
and it has a submetallic luster.
• **FORMATION** Forms with minerals such as
goethite as a secondary mineral.
• **TESTS** It is strongly magnetic
when heated. It dissolves slowly in
hydrochloric acid but much more
quickly in nitric acid.

submetallic luster

goethite, an associated mineral

platy lepidocrocite crystals

ORTHORHOMBIC

SG 3.9	Cleavage Perfect	Fracture Uneven

Group Oxides	Composition WO$_3$.H$_2$O	Hardness 1–2½

TUNGSTITE

Crystals are microscopic and platy but
rarely occur. Tungstite more commonly
forms in massive, earthy, or powdery
habits. The color may be yellow or
yellowish green, and the streak is
yellow. It is a transparent to translucent
mineral, with an earthy or resinous luster.
• **FORMATION** This mineral forms in
environments where primary tungsten
minerals have been altered.
• **TESTS** Tungstite is soluble in
alkaline solutions, but it is
insoluble in acids.

resinous luster

quartz groundmass

earthy tungstite

ORTHORHOMBIC

SG 5.5	Cleavage Perfect	Fracture Uneven

Group Hydroxides	Composition Sb^{+3}Sb$_2$$^{+5}O_6$(OH)	Hardness 4½–5

STIBICONITE

This mineral may be prismatic after the
shape of the mineral it replaced. The
usual habits are massive, compact, or
botryoidal, though stibiconite also forms
in crusts. The color is white to pale
yellowish; it may also be orange, brown,
gray, or black, due to impurities. The
streak is yellow white. It is transparent to
translucent, with a pearly to earthy luster.
• **FORMATION** Forms by the
alteration of stibnite.
• **TESTS** Gives off water when heated
in a closed test tube.

pseudomorphic after stibnite

earthy luster

uneven fracture

CUBIC

SG 3.3–5.5	Cleavage Not determined	Fracture Uneven

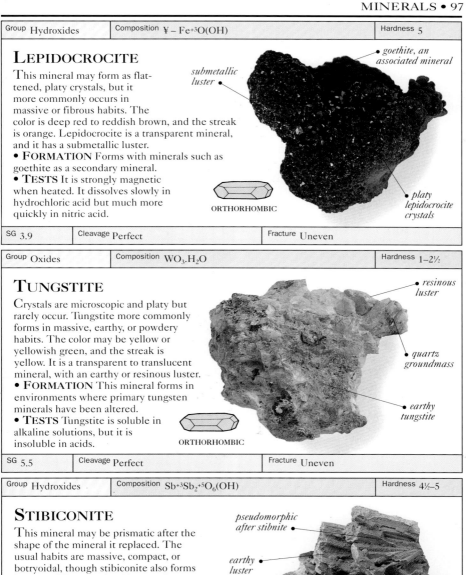

CARBONATES, NITRATES, AND BORATES

CARBONATES ARE compounds in which one or more metallic or semimetallic elements combine with the $(CO_3)^{-2}$ carbonate radical. Calcite, the commonest carbonate, forms when calcium combines with the carbonate radical. When barium substitutes for calcium, witherite is formed; when manganese substitutes, rhodochrosite is formed. Carbonates usually form well-developed rhombohedral crystals.

They tend to dissolve readily in hydrochloric acid, and can be colorless or vividly colored.

———— • ————

Nitrates are compounds in which one or more metallic elements combine with the nitrate $(NO_2)^{-1}$ radical (e.g. nitratine). Borates, also included in this section, are formed when metallic elements combine with the borate $(BO_3)^{-3}$ radical (e.g. ulexite, colemanite).

Group Carbonates	Composition $CaCO_3$	Hardness $3\frac{1}{2}-4$

ARAGONITE

The prismatic and elongated crystals formed by aragonite are often twinned. If intergrown, such twins may produce pseudo-hexagonal forms. The habit can also be columnar, stalactitic, fibrous, radiating, and coral-like, when it is called flos ferri, meaning "flower of iron." Aragonite is white, colorless, gray, yellowish, green, blue, violet, reddish, or brown. There is a white streak. It is transparent to translucent, and has a vitreous luster.

• **FORMATION** Widespread, forming in metamorphic and sedimentary rocks, in caves in limestone areas, in mineral veins, and around hot springs.
• **TESTS** It is soluble in cold, diluted hydrochloric acid, with effervescence, and is often fluorescent under ultraviolet light.

coral-like habit

resinous luster

FLOS FERRI ARAGONITE

PSEUDO-HEXAGONAL ARAGONITE

rock groundmass

vitreous luster

pseudo-hexagonal twinned crystals

ORTHORHOMBIC

SG 2.94–2.95	Cleavage Distinct pinacoidal	Fracture Subconchoidal

Group Carbonates	Composition $CaCO_3$		Hardness 3

CALCITE

Crystals are rhombohedral and scalenohedral, with combinations producing "nail-head" and "dog-tooth" forms. Iceland spar rhombs show double refraction. Twinning is common. Calcite can also form in massive, granular, fibrous, and stalactitic habits. It is white, colorless, gray, red, brown, green, and black. The streak is white to grayish. Calcite is transparent to translucent, with a vitreous to pearly or dull luster.
• **FORMATION** Forms in many rocks. Calcite makes up the bulk of limestones and marbles.
• **TESTS** It effervesces with cold, diluted hydrochloric acid.

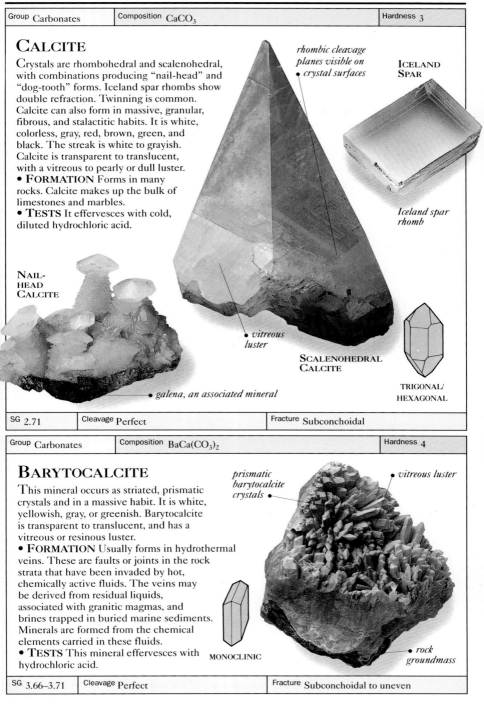

rhombic cleavage planes visible on • *crystal surfaces*

ICELAND SPAR

Iceland spar rhomb

NAIL-HEAD CALCITE

• *vitreous luster*

SCALENOHEDRAL CALCITE

galena, an associated mineral

TRIGONAL/ HEXAGONAL

SG 2.71	Cleavage Perfect		Fracture Subconchoidal

Group Carbonates	Composition $BaCa(CO_3)_2$		Hardness 4

BARYTOCALCITE

This mineral occurs as striated, prismatic crystals and in a massive habit. It is white, yellowish, gray, or greenish. Barytocalcite is transparent to translucent, and has a vitreous or resinous luster.
• **FORMATION** Usually forms in hydrothermal veins. These are faults or joints in the rock strata that have been invaded by hot, chemically active fluids. The veins may be derived from residual liquids, associated with granitic magmas, and brines trapped in buried marine sediments. Minerals are formed from the chemical elements carried in these fluids.
• **TESTS** This mineral effervesces with hydrochloric acid.

prismatic barytocalcite crystals •

• *vitreous luster*

MONOCLINIC

• *rock groundmass*

SG 3.66–3.71	Cleavage Perfect		Fracture Subconchoidal to uneven

Group Carbonates	Composition $MnCO_3$	Hardness $3\frac{1}{2}-4$

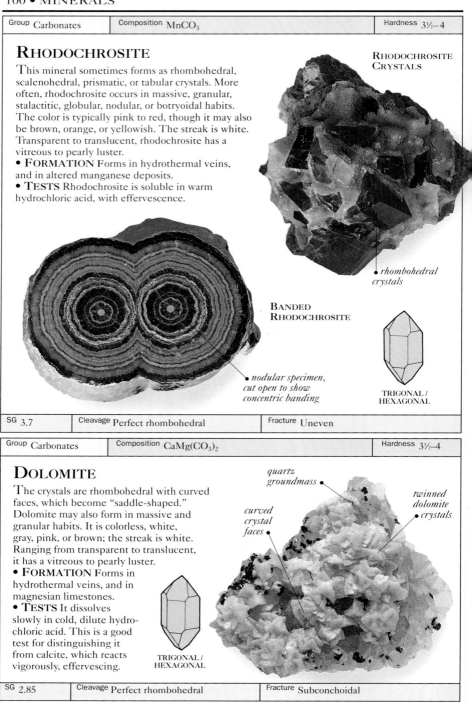

RHODOCHROSITE

This mineral sometimes forms as rhombohedral, scalenohedral, prismatic, or tabular crystals. More often, rhodochrosite occurs in massive, granular, stalactitic, globular, nodular, or botryoidal habits. The color is typically pink to red, though it may also be brown, orange, or yellowish. The streak is white. Transparent to translucent, rhodochrosite has a vitreous to pearly luster.
• **FORMATION** Forms in hydrothermal veins, and in altered manganese deposits.
• **TESTS** Rhodochrosite is soluble in warm hydrochloric acid, with effervescence.

RHODOCHROSITE CRYSTALS

• rhombohedral crystals

BANDED RHODOCHROSITE

• nodular specimen, cut open to show concentric banding

TRIGONAL / HEXAGONAL

SG 3.7	Cleavage Perfect rhombohedral	Fracture Uneven

Group Carbonates	Composition $CaMg(CO_3)_2$	Hardness $3\frac{1}{2}-4$

DOLOMITE

The crystals are rhombohedral with curved faces, which become "saddle-shaped." Dolomite may also form in massive and granular habits. It is colorless, white, gray, pink, or brown; the streak is white. Ranging from transparent to translucent, it has a vitreous to pearly luster.
• **FORMATION** Forms in hydrothermal veins, and in magnesian limestones.
• **TESTS** It dissolves slowly in cold, dilute hydrochloric acid. This is a good test for distinguishing it from calcite, which reacts vigorously, effervescing.

quartz groundmass •

curved crystal faces •

twinned dolomite • crystals

TRIGONAL / HEXAGONAL

SG 2.85	Cleavage Perfect rhombohedral	Fracture Subconchoidal

Group Carbonates	Composition $Ca(Fe^{+2},Mg,Mn)(CO_3)_2$	Hardness $3\frac{1}{2}-4$

ANKERITE

This mineral, which is part of a group with dolomite, forms rhombohedral crystals. Other habits in which it occurs are massive and granular. Ankerite is white, gray, yellowish brown, or brown in color, and the streak is white. This is a translucent mineral, with a vitreous to pearly luster.
• **FORMATION** Ankerite forms in mineral veins, sometimes with gold and sulfides.
• **TESTS** Ankerite is soluble when placed in hydrochloric acid.

twinned, rhombohedral crystals

pearly luster

TRIGONAL / HEXAGONAL

SG 2.97	Cleavage Perfect rhombohedral	Fracture Subconchoidal

Group Carbonates	Composition $ZnCO_3$	Hardness $4-4\frac{1}{2}$

SMITHSONITE

This mineral forms rhombohedral crystals, often with curved faces; sometimes it forms scalenohedral crystals. Smithsonite may also occur in massive, botryoidal, reniform, granular, and stalactitic habits. It can be white, gray, yellow, green, blue, pink, purple, or brown. The streak is white. It is a translucent mineral, and it has a vitreous or pearly luster.
• **FORMATION** Forms in parts of oxidized copper-zinc deposits. It is associated with malachite, azurite, pyromorphite, cerussite, and hemimorphite.
• **TESTS** It is soluble in hydrochloric acid.

small rounded masses indicate botryoidal habit

BLUE SMITHSONITE

rock groundmass

pearly luster

TRIGONAL / HEXAGONAL

botryoidal smithsonite

WHITE SMITHSONITE

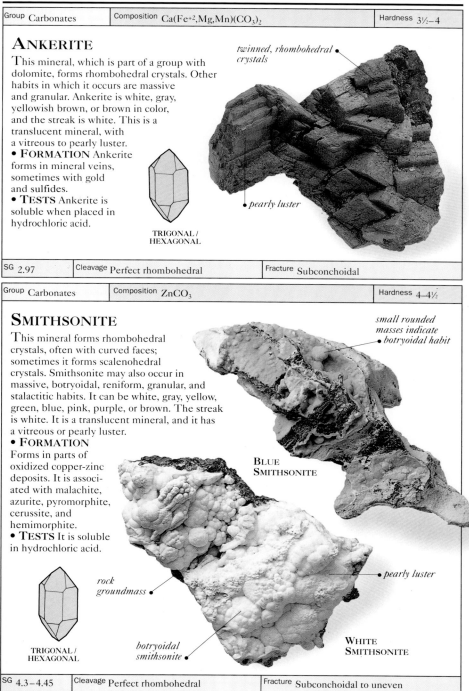

SG $4.3-4.45$	Cleavage Perfect rhombohedral	Fracture Subconchoidal to uneven

Group Carbonates	Composition $Fe^{+2}CO_3$	Hardness 4

SIDERITE

This mineral forms as rhombohedral, tabular, prismatic, and scalenohedral crystals, often with curved faces, and sometimes twinned. It also occurs in massive, granular, compact, botryoidal, and oolitic habits. Siderite is pale yellowish, gray, brown, greenish, reddish, or almost black in colour. The streak is white. It is a translucent mineral, and it has a vitreous, pearly, or silky luster.
• **FORMATION** Forms in hydrothermal veins, as well as in sedimentary strata.
• **TESTS** Siderite becomes magnetic when heated, and it dissolves slowly in cold hydrochloric acid. When the acid is heated, the solution effervesces.

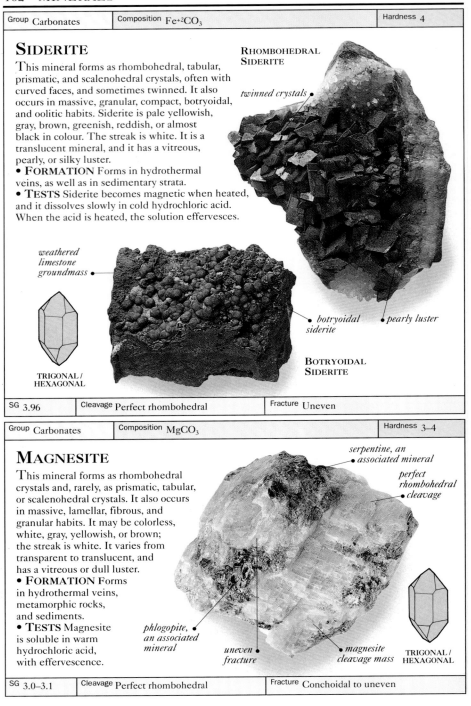

RHOMBOHEDRAL
SIDERITE

twinned crystals

weathered limestone groundmass

botryoidal siderite

pearly luster

BOTRYOIDAL
SIDERITE

TRIGONAL /
HEXAGONAL

SG 3.96	Cleavage Perfect rhombohedral	Fracture Uneven

Group Carbonates	Composition $MgCO_3$	Hardness 3–4

MAGNESITE

This mineral forms as rhombohedral crystals and, rarely, as prismatic, tabular, or scalenohedral crystals. It also occurs in massive, lamellar, fibrous, and granular habits. It may be colorless, white, gray, yellowish, or brown; the streak is white. It varies from transparent to translucent, and has a vitreous or dull luster.
• **FORMATION** Forms in hydrothermal veins, metamorphic rocks, and sediments.
• **TESTS** Magnesite is soluble in warm hydrochloric acid, with effervescence.

serpentine, an associated mineral

perfect rhombohedral cleavage

phlogopite, an associated mineral

uneven fracture

magnesite cleavage mass

TRIGONAL /
HEXAGONAL

SG 3.0–3.1	Cleavage Perfect rhombohedral	Fracture Conchoidal to uneven

Group Carbonates	Composition $BaCO_3$	Hardness 3–3½

WITHERITE

The crystals form as twinned prismatic, often pseudohexagonal, dipyramids. Witherite also occurs in massive, granular, fibrous, and columnar habits. It may be colorless, white, gray, yellow, green, or brown, with a white streak. Transparent to translucent, it has a vitreous to resinous luster.
• FORMATION Forms in hydrothermal veins, with quartz, calcite, and barite.
• TESTS Witherite is soluble in dilute hydrochloric acid, with effervescence. Barium in the structure raises specific gravity. Powdered witherite colors a flame apple-green.

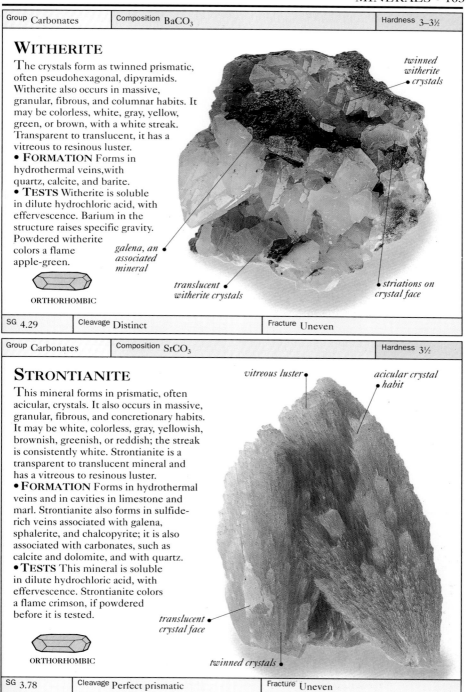

twinned witherite crystals

galena, an associated mineral

translucent witherite crystals

striations on crystal face

ORTHORHOMBIC

SG 4.29	Cleavage Distinct	Fracture Uneven

Group Carbonates	Composition $SrCO_3$	Hardness 3½

STRONTIANITE

This mineral forms in prismatic, often acicular, crystals. It also occurs in massive, granular, fibrous, and concretionary habits. It may be white, colorless, gray, yellowish, brownish, greenish, or reddish; the streak is consistently white. Strontianite is a transparent to translucent mineral and has a vitreous to resinous luster.
• FORMATION Forms in hydrothermal veins and in cavities in limestone and marl. Strontianite also forms in sulfide-rich veins associated with galena, sphalerite, and chalcopyrite; it is also associated with carbonates, such as calcite and dolomite, and with quartz.
• TESTS This mineral is soluble in dilute hydrochloric acid, with effervescence. Strontianite colors a flame crimson, if powdered before it is tested.

vitreous luster

acicular crystal habit

translucent crystal face

twinned crystals

ORTHORHOMBIC

SG 3.78	Cleavage Perfect prismatic	Fracture Uneven

Group Carbonates	Composition $PbCO_3$	Hardness 3–3½

CERUSSITE

Crystals are often tabular, but can be acicular. Clusters of twinned crystals are common. Cerussite also occurs in massive, granular, compact, and stalactitic habits. It is often white or colorless, but can be gray, greenish, or blue in color, as a result of inclusions, such as lead. The streak is white. Cerussite is transparent to translucent, and it has an adamantine, vitreous, or resinous luster.
• **FORMATION** Forms in the oxidized parts of mineral veins, with lead, copper, and zinc.
• **TESTS** Soluble in acids, in particular dilute nitric acid, when it produces effervescence. Sometimes it fluoresces in ultraviolet light.

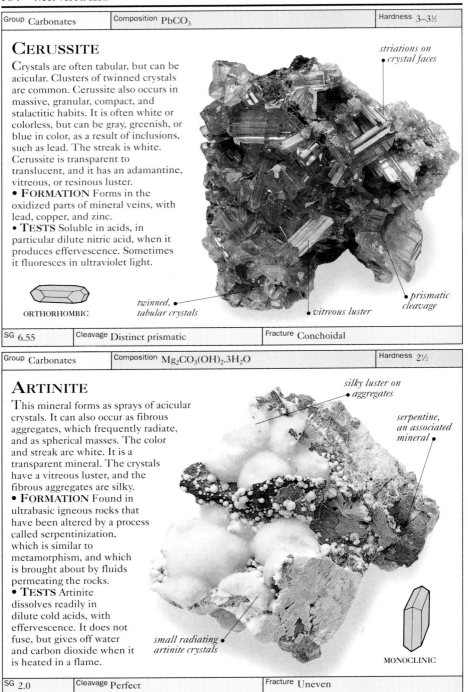

striations on crystal faces

ORTHORHOMBIC

twinned, tabular crystals

vitreous luster

prismatic cleavage

SG 6.55	Cleavage Distinct prismatic	Fracture Conchoidal

Group Carbonates	Composition $Mg_2CO_3(OH)_2.3H_2O$	Hardness 2½

ARTINITE

This mineral forms as sprays of acicular crystals. It can also occur as fibrous aggregates, which frequently radiate, and as spherical masses. The color and streak are white. It is a transparent mineral. The crystals have a vitreous luster, and the fibrous aggregates are silky.
• **FORMATION** Found in ultrabasic igneous rocks that have been altered by a process called serpentinization, which is similar to metamorphism, and which is brought about by fluids permeating the rocks.
• **TESTS** Artinite dissolves readily in dilute cold acids, with effervescence. It does not fuse, but gives off water and carbon dioxide when it is heated in a flame.

silky luster on aggregates

serpentine, an associated mineral

small radiating artinite crystals

MONOCLINIC

SG 2.0	Cleavage Perfect	Fracture Uneven

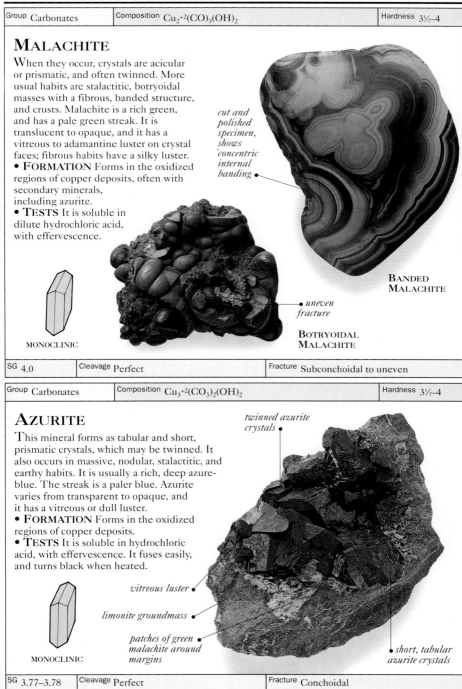

Group Carbonates	Composition $Cu_2^{+2}(CO)_3(OH)_2$	Hardness $3\frac{1}{2}$–4

MALACHITE

When they occur, crystals are acicular or prismatic, and often twinned. More usual habits are stalactitic, botryoidal masses with a fibrous, banded structure, and crusts. Malachite is a rich green, and has a pale green streak. It is translucent to opaque, and it has a vitreous to adamantine luster on crystal faces; fibrous habits have a silky luster.
• **FORMATION** Forms in the oxidized regions of copper deposits, often with secondary minerals, including azurite.
• **TESTS** It is soluble in dilute hydrochloric acid, with effervescence.

cut and polished specimen, shows concentric internal banding

BANDED MALACHITE

uneven fracture

BOTRYOIDAL MALACHITE

MONOCLINIC

SG 4.0	Cleavage Perfect	Fracture Subconchoidal to uneven

Group Carbonates	Composition $Cu_3^{+2}(CO_3)_2(OH)_2$	Hardness $3\frac{1}{2}$–4

AZURITE

This mineral forms as tabular and short, prismatic crystals, which may be twinned. It also occurs in massive, nodular, stalactitic, and earthy habits. It is usually a rich, deep azure-blue. The streak is a paler blue. Azurite varies from transparent to opaque, and it has a vitreous or dull luster.
• **FORMATION** Forms in the oxidized regions of copper deposits.
• **TESTS** It is soluble in hydrochloric acid, with effervescence. It fuses easily, and turns black when heated.

twinned azurite crystals

vitreous luster

limonite groundmass

patches of green malachite around margins

short, tabular azurite crystals

MONOCLINIC

SG 3.77–3.78	Cleavage Perfect	Fracture Conchoidal

Group Carbonates	Composition $(Zn,Cu^{+2})_5(CO_3)_2(OH)_6$	Hardness 1–2

AURICHALCITE

This mineral forms as acicular or slender, lath-shaped crystals. It also occurs as tufted aggregates and encrustations and is occasionally granular, columnar, or lamellar in habit. The color is pale green, greenish blue, or sky-blue, and the streak is pale blue-green. It is a transparent mineral, and it has a silky or pearly luster.

• **FORMATION** Forms in the altered and oxidized parts of copper and zinc veins with copper minerals, such as azurite and malachite.

• **TESTS** Aurichalcite is soluble in dilute hydrochloric acid, with effervescence. It colors a flame green as a result of its copper content, but it does not fuse.

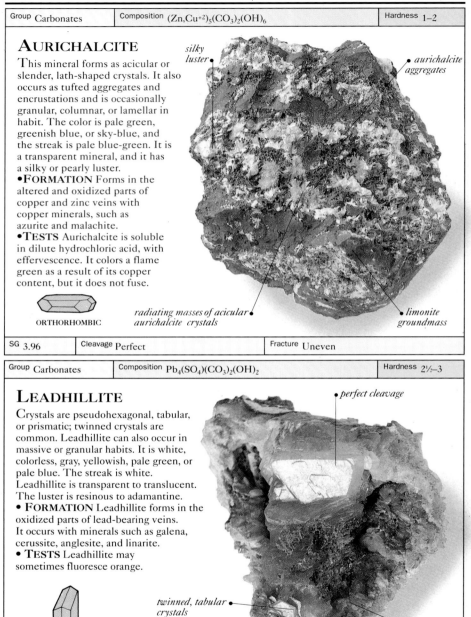

silky luster

aurichalcite aggregates

ORTHORHOMBIC

radiating masses of acicular aurichalcite crystals

limonite groundmass

SG 3.96	Cleavage Perfect	Fracture Uneven

Group Carbonates	Composition $Pb_4(SO_4)(CO_3)_2(OH)_2$	Hardness 2½–3

LEADHILLITE

Crystals are pseudohexagonal, tabular, or prismatic; twinned crystals are common. Leadhillite can also occur in massive or granular habits. It is white, colorless, gray, yellowish, pale green, or pale blue. The streak is white. Leadhillite is transparent to translucent. The luster is resinous to adamantine.

• **FORMATION** Leadhillite forms in the oxidized parts of lead-bearing veins. It occurs with minerals such as galena, cerussite, anglesite, and linarite.

• **TESTS** Leadhillite may sometimes fluoresce orange.

perfect cleavage

MONOCLINIC

twinned, tabular crystals

oxidized groundmass

resinous luster

SG 6.55	Cleavage Perfect basal	Fracture Conchoidal

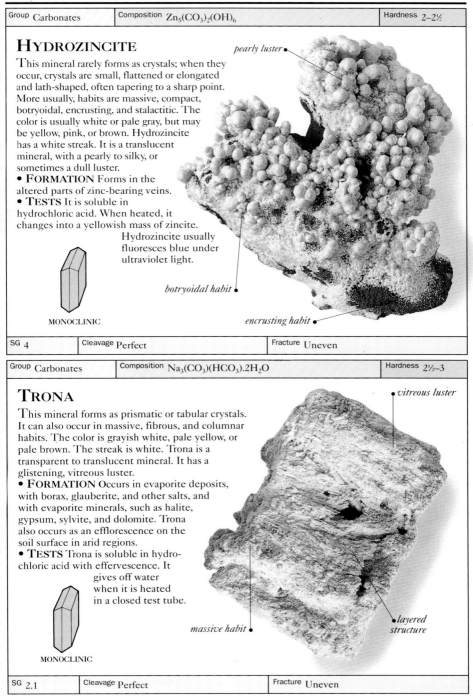

Group Carbonates	Composition $Zn_5(CO_3)_2(OH)_6$	Hardness 2–2½

HYDROZINCITE

This mineral rarely forms as crystals; when they occur, crystals are small, flattened or elongated and lath-shaped, often tapering to a sharp point. More usually, habits are massive, compact, botryoidal, encrusting, and stalactitic. The color is usually white or pale gray, but may be yellow, pink, or brown. Hydrozincite has a white streak. It is a translucent mineral, with a pearly to silky, or sometimes a dull luster.
• **FORMATION** Forms in the altered parts of zinc-bearing veins.
• **TESTS** It is soluble in hydrochloric acid. When heated, it changes into a yellowish mass of zincite. Hydrozincite usually fluoresces blue under ultraviolet light.

pearly luster

botryoidal habit

MONOCLINIC

encrusting habit

SG 4	Cleavage Perfect	Fracture Uneven

Group Carbonates	Composition $Na_3(CO_3)(HCO_3).2H_2O$	Hardness 2½–3

TRONA

This mineral forms as prismatic or tabular crystals. It can also occur in massive, fibrous, and columnar habits. The color is grayish white, pale yellow, or pale brown. The streak is white. Trona is a transparent to translucent mineral. It has a glistening, vitreous luster.
• **FORMATION** Occurs in evaporite deposits, with borax, glauberite, and other salts, and with evaporite minerals, such as halite, gypsum, sylvite, and dolomite. Trona also occurs as an efflorescence on the soil surface in arid regions.
• **TESTS** Trona is soluble in hydrochloric acid with effervescence. It gives off water when it is heated in a closed test tube.

vitreous luster

massive habit

layered structure

MONOCLINIC

SG 2.1	Cleavage Perfect	Fracture Uneven

Group Nitrates	Composition $NaNO_3$		Hardness 1½–2

NITRATINE

Crystals, which rarely occur, are rhombohedral in form, and often twinned. Nitratine more commonly occurs in massive or granular habits, and in crusts. White or colorless, it is frequently discolored by impurities, when it becomes gray, yellow, or brown. The streak is white. It is a transparent mineral, with a vitreous luster.

• **FORMATION** Occurs in arid areas as an efflorescent deposit on the surface, associated with gypsum. Nitratine often covers large areas of land. In the deserts of northern Chile, large deposits occur over a region about 450 miles (724 km) long, and from 10 to 50 miles (16 to 80 km) wide.

• **TESTS** It is easily soluble in water. It will dissolve in surface waters when in crusts on the ground. If placed in a flame, it fuses very easily, and colors the flame bright yellow. It is deliquescent, which means it takes in atmospheric moisture.

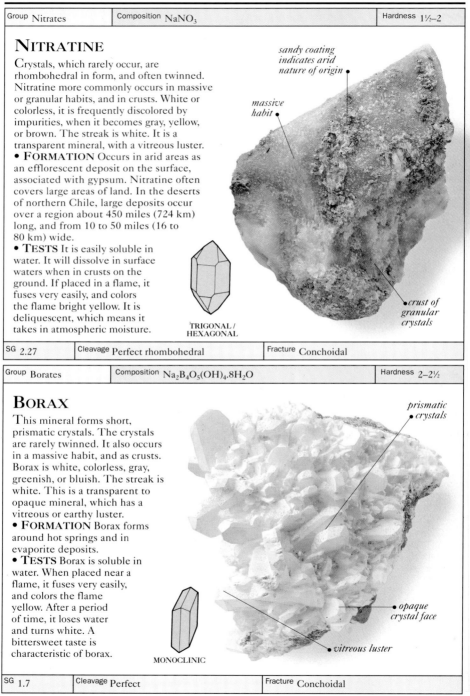

sandy coating indicates arid nature of origin

massive habit

crust of granular crystals

TRIGONAL / HEXAGONAL

SG 2.27	Cleavage Perfect rhombohedral	Fracture Conchoidal

Group Borates	Composition $Na_2B_4O_5(OH)_4.8H_2O$		Hardness 2–2½

BORAX

This mineral forms short, prismatic crystals. The crystals are rarely twinned. It also occurs in a massive habit, and as crusts. Borax is white, colorless, gray, greenish, or bluish. The streak is white. This is a transparent to opaque mineral, which has a vitreous or earthy luster.

• **FORMATION** Borax forms around hot springs and in evaporite deposits.

• **TESTS** Borax is soluble in water. When placed near a flame, it fuses very easily, and colors the flame yellow. After a period of time, it loses water and turns white. A bittersweet taste is characteristic of borax.

prismatic crystals

opaque crystal face

vitreous luster

MONOCLINIC

SG 1.7	Cleavage Perfect	Fracture Conchoidal

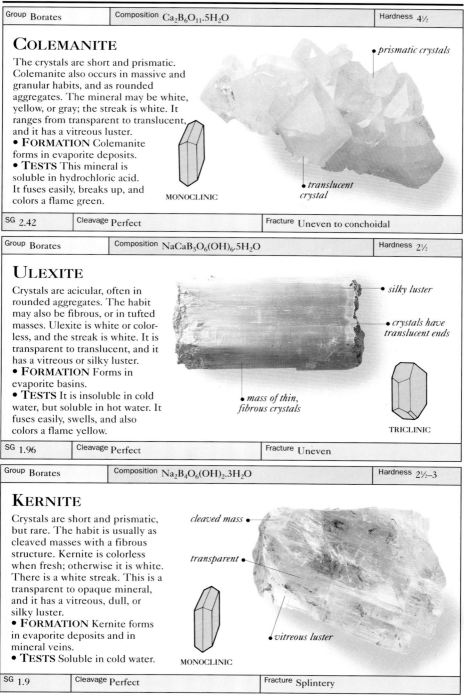

Group Borates	Composition $Ca_2B_6O_{11}.5H_2O$	Hardness $4\frac{1}{2}$

COLEMANITE

The crystals are short and prismatic. Colemanite also occurs in massive and granular habits, and as rounded aggregates. The mineral may be white, yellow, or gray; the streak is white. It ranges from transparent to translucent, and it has a vitreous luster.
• **FORMATION** Colemanite forms in evaporite deposits.
• **TESTS** This mineral is soluble in hydrochloric acid. It fuses easily, breaks up, and colors a flame green.

prismatic crystals

translucent crystal

MONOCLINIC

SG 2.42	Cleavage Perfect	Fracture Uneven to conchoidal

Group Borates	Composition $NaCaB_5O_6(OH)_6.5H_2O$	Hardness $2\frac{1}{2}$

ULEXITE

Crystals are acicular, often in rounded aggregates. The habit may also be fibrous, or in tufted masses. Ulexite is white or colorless, and the streak is white. It is transparent to translucent, and it has a vitreous or silky luster.
• **FORMATION** Forms in evaporite basins.
• **TESTS** It is insoluble in cold water, but soluble in hot water. It fuses easily, swells, and also colors a flame yellow.

silky luster

crystals have translucent ends

mass of thin, fibrous crystals

TRICLINIC

SG 1.96	Cleavage Perfect	Fracture Uneven

Group Borates	Composition $Na_2B_4O_6(OH)_2.3H_2O$	Hardness $2\frac{1}{2}–3$

KERNITE

Crystals are short and prismatic, but rare. The habit is usually as cleaved masses with a fibrous structure. Kernite is colorless when fresh; otherwise it is white. There is a white streak. This is a transparent to opaque mineral, and it has a vitreous, dull, or silky luster.
• **FORMATION** Kernite forms in evaporite deposits and in mineral veins.
• **TESTS** Soluble in cold water.

cleaved mass

transparent

vitreous luster

MONOCLINIC

SG 1.9	Cleavage Perfect	Fracture Splintery

SULFATES, CHROMATES,
MOLYBDATES, AND TUNGSTATES

SULFATES ARE compounds in which one or more metallic elements combine with the sulfate $(SO_4)^{-2}$ radical. Gypsum, the most abundant sulfate, occurs in evaporite deposits. Barite typically occurs in hydrothermal veins. Most sulfates are soft, light in color, and tend to have low densities. Chromates are compounds in which metallic elements combine with the chromate $(CrO_4)^{-2}$ radical. Chromates are small in number, and tend to be rare and brightly colored (e.g. crocoite). Molybdates and tungstates form when metallic elements combine with molybdate $(MoO_4)^{-2}$, and tungstate $(WO_4)^{-2}$ radicals. These are usually dense, brittle, and vividly colored minerals (e.g. wulfenite, lead molybdate, scheelite, and calcium tungstate).

Group Sulfates	Composition $CaSO_4.2H_2O$	Hardness 2

GYPSUM

Crystals are tabular, and diamond-shaped. Twinning is common. Gypsum also occurs in massive, granular (alabaster), and fibrous (satin spar), habits. Rosette-shaped masses are called desert roses, and radiating forms are termed daisy gypsum. It varies from colorless, to white, gray, greenish, yellowish, brownish, and reddish. The streak is white. It is transparent (selenite) to opaque, with a vitreous luster (pearly on cleavages); fibrous forms may be silky, massive forms are often dull.

• **FORMATION** Forms as an evaporite around hot springs, and in clay beds.

• **TESTS** Soluble in acids.

DESERT ROSE

rosette habit with sand grains

DAISY GYPSUM

SATIN SPAR

vitreous luster

transparent to translucent

transparent, diamond-shaped crystal

SELENITE

MONOCLINIC

radiating crystal mass

SG 2.32	Cleavage Perfect	Fracture Splintery

Group Sulfates	Composition $SrSO_4$		Hardness 3–3½

CELESTINE

The crystals form as tabular or prismatic specimens. Other habits are massive, fibrous, granular, or nodular. Celestine is colorless, white, gray, blue, green, yellowish, orange, reddish, or brown. The streak is white. It is transparent to translucent and has a vitreous luster (pearly on cleavages).
• **FORMATION** Forms in hydrothermal veins with minerals such as calcite and quartz, as well as in many sedimentary rocks, like limestones. Also found in some evaporite deposits, and some basic igneous rocks.
• **TESTS** Sometimes fluoresces under ultraviolet light. It is insoluble in acids, but slightly soluble in water. When heated, this mineral fuses easily, giving a milk-white globule and coloring the flame crimson.

prismatic celestine crystals

sulphur groundmass

ORTHORHOMBIC

SG 3.96–3.98	Cleavage Perfect	Fracture Uneven

Group Sulfates	Composition $CaSO_4$		Hardness 3–3½

ANHYDRITE

This mineral occurs as tabular or prismatic crystals, but usually forms in massive, granular, and fibrous habits. Anhydrite ranges from white, gray, or bluish, to pinkish, reddish, and brownish. A colorless form also occurs. There is a white streak. It is a transparent to translucent mineral, and it has a vitreous, pearly, or greasy luster.
• **FORMATION** It is commonly found as an evaporite with other evaporites, such as dolomite, gypsum, halite, sylvite, and calcite – often in salt domes. Very rarely, it occurs as a hydrothermal vein mineral, with quartz and calcite.
• **TESTS** When heated, it fuses easily and colors the flame brick-red.

massive habit

cleavage planes

ORTHORHOMBIC

SG 2.98	Cleavage Perfect	Fracture Uneven to splintery

Group Sulfates	Composition $BaSO_4$	Hardness 3–3½

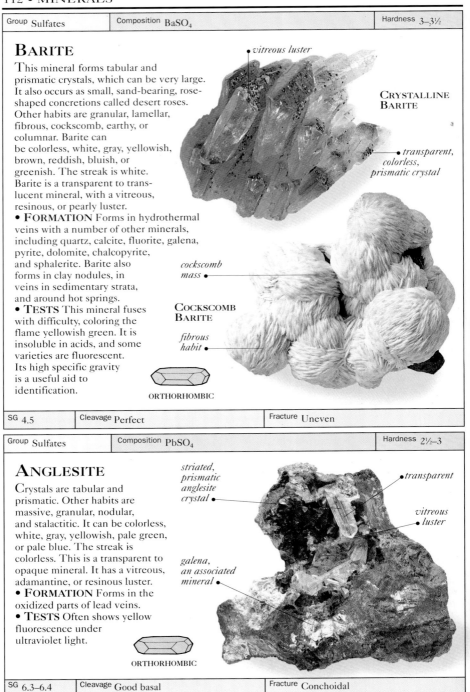

BARITE

This mineral forms tabular and prismatic crystals, which can be very large. It also occurs as small, sand-bearing, rose-shaped concretions called desert roses. Other habits are granular, lamellar, fibrous, cockscomb, earthy, or columnar. Barite can be colorless, white, gray, yellowish, brown, reddish, bluish, or greenish. The streak is white. Barite is a transparent to translucent mineral, with a vitreous, resinous, or pearly luster.
• **FORMATION** Forms in hydrothermal veins with a number of other minerals, including quartz, calcite, fluorite, galena, pyrite, dolomite, chalcopyrite, and sphalerite. Barite also forms in clay nodules, in veins in sedimentary strata, and around hot springs.
• **TESTS** This mineral fuses with difficulty, coloring the flame yellowish green. It is insoluble in acids, and some varieties are fluorescent. Its high specific gravity is a useful aid to identification.

vitreous luster

CRYSTALLINE
BARITE

transparent, colorless, prismatic crystal

cockscomb mass

COCKSCOMB
BARITE

fibrous habit

ORTHORHOMBIC

SG 4.5	Cleavage Perfect	Fracture Uneven

Group Sulfates	Composition $PbSO_4$	Hardness 2½–3

ANGLESITE

Crystals are tabular and prismatic. Other habits are massive, granular, nodular, and stalactitic. It can be colorless, white, gray, yellowish, pale green, or pale blue. The streak is colorless. This is a transparent to opaque mineral. It has a vitreous, adamantine, or resinous luster.
• **FORMATION** Forms in the oxidized parts of lead veins.
• **TESTS** Often shows yellow fluorescence under ultraviolet light.

striated, prismatic anglesite crystal

transparent

vitreous luster

galena, an associated mineral

ORTHORHOMBIC

SG 6.3–6.4	Cleavage Good basal	Fracture Conchoidal

Group Sulfates	Composition $Cu^{+2}SO_4.5H_2O$	Hardness $2\frac{1}{2}$

CHALCANTHITE

Short, prismatic, and thick, tabular crystals are formed by chalcanthite. Other habits exhibited are stalactitic, fibrous, massive, granular, compact, and encrusting. The color is sky-blue to dark blue, greenish blue, or greenish, and the streak is colorless. This is a transparent to translucent mineral. It has a vitreous to resinous luster.

• **FORMATION** Chalcanthite forms in oxidized parts of copper sulfide veins. This oxidization is usually brought about by waters circulating from above, which have their origin in rain (meteoritic). Hydrothermal fluids originating from deep underground, and rising under pressure, can also alter mineral veins. When water seeps through mine tunnels and shafts, chalcanthite crystallizes as crusts and stalactites on roofs and supports. It is found most frequently in areas of the world that have an arid climate.

• **TESTS** Chalcanthite is soluble in water. It gives off water when heated in a closed test tube. Its distinctive, sky-blue color is a valuable guide to identification, and it is poisonous.

kaolinite, an associated mineral

groundmass of rock

transparent to translucent

granular chalcanthite

TRICLINIC

SG 2.28	Cleavage Imperfect	Fracture Conchoidal

Group Sulfates	Composition $MgSO_4.7H_2O$	Hardness $2–2\frac{1}{2}$

EPSOMITE

Crystals rarely occur. Epsomite is usually massive, in acicular crusts, or stalactitic. Epsomite is white, pinkish, colorless, or greenish, and the streak is white. This is a transparent to translucent mineral. It has a vitreous to silky luster.

• **FORMATION** Forms on walls in mines, in limestone caverns, and on rock faces. Epsomite is also found in arid parts of the world, where it occurs in the oxidized parts of pyrite deposits.

• **TESTS** Epsomite is very soluble in water. It has a bitter, salty taste. Epsomite effloresces in dry air, and gives off water when it is heated in a test tube.

acicular masses and fibrous strands

silky to vitreous luster

ORTHORHOMBIC

SG 1.68	Cleavage Perfect	Fracture Conchoidal

Group Sulfates	Composition $KAl_3(SO_4)2(OH)_6$	Hardness $3\frac{1}{2}$–4

ALUNITE

This mineral forms rhom-
bohedral, often pseudo-
cubic, crystals, but usually
occurs in massive, granular, and
compact habits. It may also be fibrous.
The color is usually white, but may be
grayish, reddish, yellowish, or brown
with discoloration. The streak is
white. Alunite is transparent to
nearly opaque, with a vitreous or
pearly luster.
• **FORMATION** In volcanic
vents and as a vein mineral.
• **TESTS** It gives off water when
heated in a closed test tube.

pearly luster

compact habit

TRIGONAL/
HEXAGONAL

SG 2.6–2.9	Cleavage Distinct basal	Fracture Conchoidal

Group Sulfates	Composition $KFe_3^{+2}(SO_4)_2(OH)_6$	Hardness $2\frac{1}{2}$–$3\frac{1}{2}$

JAROSITE

Very small tabular or pseudo-cubic crystals are
formed by jarosite. Other habits are massive,
granular, fibrous, or earthy. The color varies
from yellowish brown to brown. The streak
is pale yellow. This mineral is translucent.
Jarosite may have a vitreous or resinous
luster on clean surfaces.
• **FORMATION** Forms in fissures
and layers within iron-rich deposits.
Jarosite occurs as a result of
secondary alteration of iron-rich
minerals. This is brought about
by the circulation of water and
other fluids through the upper
parts of the earth's crust.
• **TESTS** Jarosite's
distinctive pseudo-cubic
crystals are a useful aid
to identification.

mass of jarosite crystals

goethite, an associated mineral

vitreous luster

TRIGONAL/
HEXAGONAL

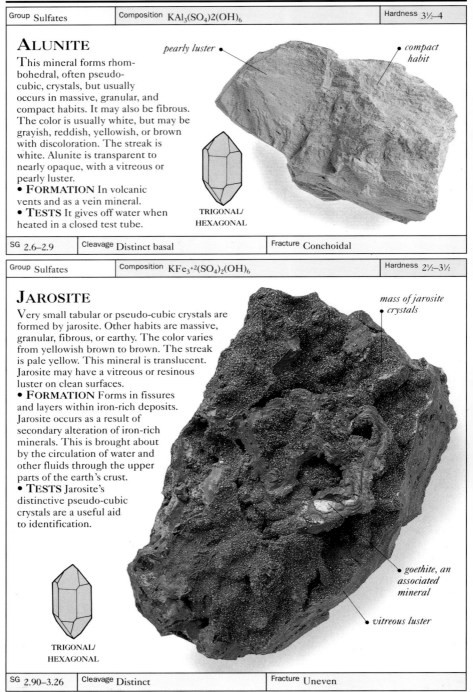

SG 2.90–3.26	Cleavage Distinct	Fracture Uneven

Group Sulfates	Composition $Na_2Ca(SO_4)_2$	Hardness $2\frac{1}{2}–3$

GLAUBERITE

This mineral forms tabular, prismatic, or dipyramidal crystals. The color may be colorless, gray, or yellowish, with a white streak. Glauberite is a transparent to translucent mineral. It has a vitreous luster, which changes to pearly on cleavage surfaces.
• **FORMATION** Glauberite forms in evaporite deposits. These deposits are formed when areas of saline water, salt lakes, or marine lagoons cut off from the main part of an ocean dry out.
• **TESTS** This mineral is partially soluble in water and soluble in hydrochloric acid.

composite crystal •

• vitreous luster

transparent to • translucent

MONOCLINIC

SG 2.8	Cleavage Perfect	Fracture Conchoidal

Group Sulfates	Composition Na_2SO_4	Hardness $2\frac{1}{2}–3$

THENARDITE

Crystals are tabular, dipyramidal, or prismatic, and commonly twinned. Thenardite also forms as crusts. It may be colorless, grayish white, yellowish, brownish, or reddish. Thenardite is a transparent to translucent mineral. It has a vitreous or resinous luster.
• **FORMATION** Forms in the deposits of salt lakes, as well as occurring on the soil surface in arid areas. When it occurs in salt lakes, thenardite may be associated with other evaporites, such as gypsum, halite, sylvite, and glauberite. Thenardite may also be found on the surface of recently erupted and cooled lava flows. It can occur around fumaroles, where it forms as a crustlike deposit.
• **TESTS** This mineral is highly soluble when placed in cold water. In common with several other evaporites, such as halite and sylvite, thenardite has a salty taste.

group of pyramidal crystals •

• resinous luster

transparent to • translucent

ORTHORHOMBIC

SG 2.66	Cleavage Perfect	Fracture Uneven

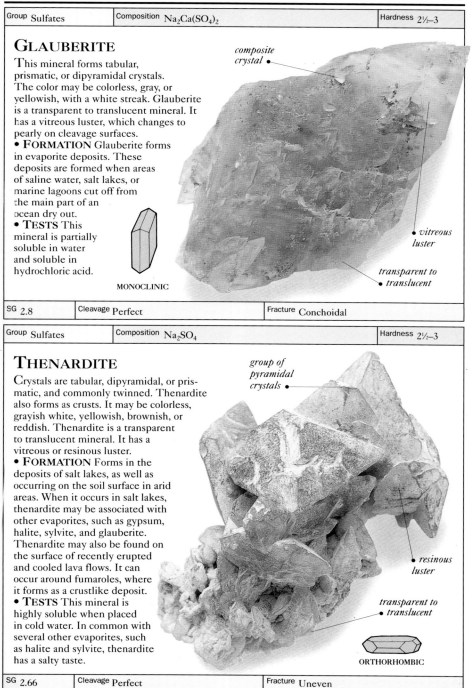

Group Sulfates	Composition $K_2Ca_2Mg(SO_4)_4.2H_2O$	Hardness 3½

POLYHALITE

This mineral rarely forms crystals; when they occur, crystals are small, highly modified, elongated, or tabular. Usually, the habit is as fibrous or foliated masses. Polyhalite is frequently flesh-pink to brick-red, as a result of iron oxide inclusions. When pure, it is colorless, white, or gray. It has a white streak. This is a transparent to translucent mineral; the luster is resinous or silky.
• **FORMATION** Forms in evaporite sequences of rocks, with minerals such as halite, gypsum, sylvite, carnallite, and anhydrite. Forms rarely from volcanic activity.
• **TESTS** Tastes salty, but more bitter than halite.

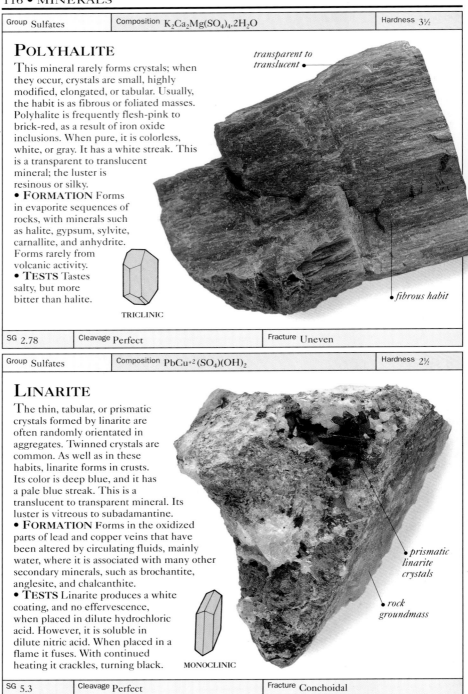

transparent to translucent

fibrous habit

TRICLINIC

SG 2.78	Cleavage Perfect	Fracture Uneven

Group Sulfates	Composition $PbCu^{+2}(SO_4)(OH)_2$	Hardness 2½

LINARITE

The thin, tabular, or prismatic crystals formed by linarite are often randomly orientated in aggregates. Twinned crystals are common. As well as in these habits, linarite forms in crusts. Its color is deep blue, and it has a pale blue streak. This is a translucent to transparent mineral. Its luster is vitreous to subadamantine.
• **FORMATION** Forms in the oxidized parts of lead and copper veins that have been altered by circulating fluids, mainly water, where it is associated with many other secondary minerals, such as brochantite, anglesite, and chalcanthite.
• **TESTS** Linarite produces a white coating, and no effervescence, when placed in dilute hydrochloric acid. However, it is soluble in dilute nitric acid. When placed in a flame it fuses. With continued heating it crackles, turning black.

prismatic linarite crystals

rock groundmass

MONOCLINIC

SG 5.3	Cleavage Perfect	Fracture Conchoidal

Group Sulfates	Composition $Fe^{+2}Fe_4^{+3}(SO_4)_6(OH)_2.2OH_2O$	Hardness $2\frac{1}{2}$–3

COPIAPITE

The usual habits of this mineral are as tabular crystals, crusts, and scaly aggregates, or masses. Copiapite is yellow, golden-yellow, or orange-yellow, though it may be greenish yellow to olive-green. It is transparent to translucent and has a pearly luster.
• **FORMATION** Copiapite forms when sulfides, such as iron pyrite, are oxidized.
• **TESTS** Soluble in water, producing a yellowish color. It fuses at very low temperatures.

TRICLINIC

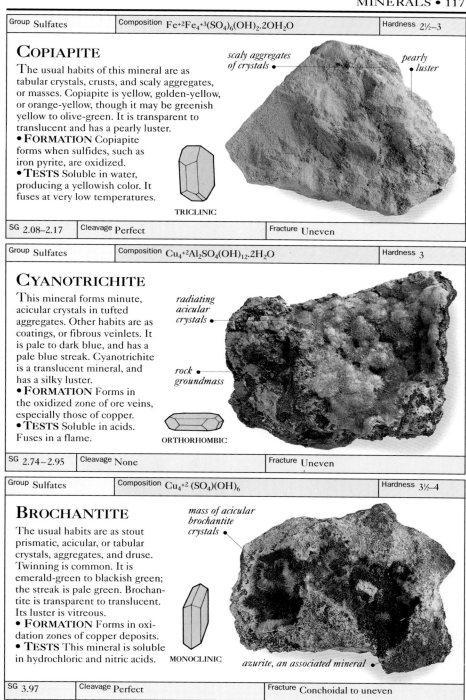

scaly aggregates of crystals

pearly luster

SG 2.08–2.17	Cleavage Perfect	Fracture Uneven

Group Sulfates	Composition $Cu_4^{+2}Al_2SO_4(OH)_{12}.2H_2O$	Hardness 3

CYANOTRICHITE

This mineral forms minute, acicular crystals in tufted aggregates. Other habits are as coatings, or fibrous veinlets. It is pale to dark blue, and has a pale blue streak. Cyanotrichite is a translucent mineral, and has a silky luster.
• **FORMATION** Forms in the oxidized zone of ore veins, especially those of copper.
• **TESTS** Soluble in acids. Fuses in a flame.

radiating acicular crystals

rock groundmass

ORTHORHOMBIC

SG 2.74–2.95	Cleavage None	Fracture Uneven

Group Sulfates	Composition $Cu_4^{+2}(SO_4)(OH)_6$	Hardness $3\frac{1}{2}$–4

BROCHANTITE

The usual habits are as stout prismatic, acicular, or tabular crystals, aggregates, and druse. Twinning is common. It is emerald-green to blackish green; the streak is pale green. Brochantite is transparent to translucent. Its luster is vitreous.
• **FORMATION** Forms in oxidation zones of copper deposits.
• **TESTS** This mineral is soluble in hydrochloric and nitric acids.

mass of acicular brochantite crystals

MONOCLINIC

azurite, an associated mineral

SG 3.97	Cleavage Perfect	Fracture Conchoidal to uneven

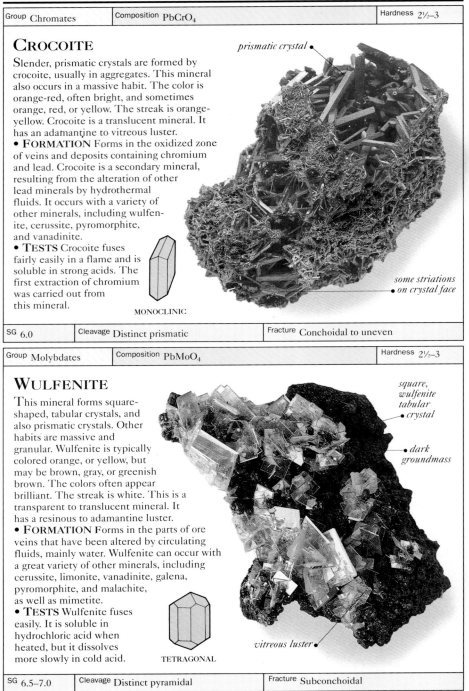

Group Chromates	Composition $PbCrO_4$		Hardness 2½–3

CROCOITE

prismatic crystal

Slender, prismatic crystals are formed by crocoite, usually in aggregates. This mineral also occurs in a massive habit. The color is orange-red, often bright, and sometimes orange, red, or yellow. The streak is orange-yellow. Crocoite is a translucent mineral. It has an adamantine to vitreous luster.
• **FORMATION** Forms in the oxidized zone of veins and deposits containing chromium and lead. Crocoite is a secondary mineral, resulting from the alteration of other lead minerals by hydrothermal fluids. It occurs with a variety of other minerals, including wulfenite, cerussite, pyromorphite, and vanadinite.
• **TESTS** Crocoite fuses fairly easily in a flame and is soluble in strong acids. The first extraction of chromium was carried out from this mineral.

MONOCLINIC

some striations on crystal face

SG 6.0	Cleavage Distinct prismatic	Fracture Conchoidal to uneven

Group Molybdates	Composition $PbMoO_4$		Hardness 2½–3

WULFENITE

square, wulfenite tabular crystal

This mineral forms square-shaped, tabular crystals, and also prismatic crystals. Other habits are massive and granular. Wulfenite is typically colored orange, or yellow, but may be brown, gray, or greenish brown. The colors often appear brilliant. The streak is white. This is a transparent to translucent mineral. It has a resinous to adamantine luster.
• **FORMATION** Forms in the parts of ore veins that have been altered by circulating fluids, mainly water. Wulfenite can occur with a great variety of other minerals, including cerussite, limonite, vanadinite, galena, pyromorphite, and malachite, as well as mimetite.
• **TESTS** Wulfenite fuses easily. It is soluble in hydrochloric acid when heated, but it dissolves more slowly in cold acid.

dark groundmass

TETRAGONAL

vitreous luster

SG 6.5–7.0	Cleavage Distinct pyramidal	Fracture Subconchoidal

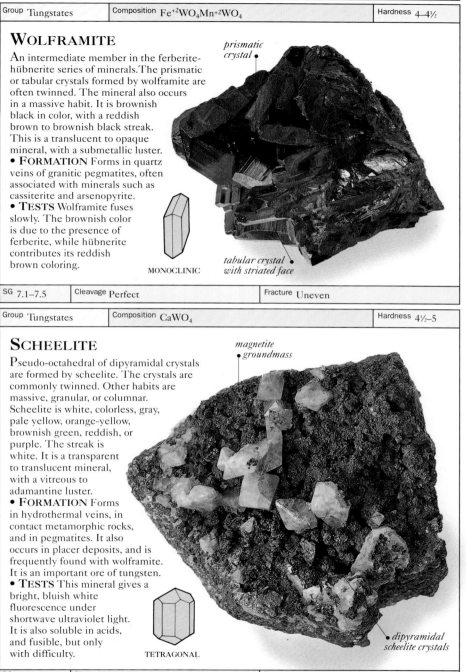

Group Tungstates	Composition $Fe^{+2}WO_4Mn^{+2}WO_4$		Hardness 4–4½

WOLFRAMITE

An intermediate member in the ferberite-hübnerite series of minerals. The prismatic or tabular crystals formed by wolframite are often twinned. The mineral also occurs in a massive habit. It is brownish black in color, with a reddish brown to brownish black streak. This is a translucent to opaque mineral, with a submetallic luster.

• **FORMATION** Forms in quartz veins of granitic pegmatites, often associated with minerals such as cassiterite and arsenopyrite.

• **TESTS** Wolframite fuses slowly. The brownish color is due to the presence of ferberite, while hübnerite contributes its reddish brown coloring.

prismatic crystal

MONOCLINIC

tabular crystal with striated face

SG 7.1–7.5	Cleavage Perfect	Fracture Uneven

Group Tungstates	Composition $CaWO_4$		Hardness 4½–5

SCHEELITE

Pseudo-octahedral of dipyramidal crystals are formed by scheelite. The crystals are commonly twinned. Other habits are massive, granular, or columnar. Scheelite is white, colorless, gray, pale yellow, orange-yellow, brownish green, reddish, or purple. The streak is white. It is a transparent to translucent mineral, with a vitreous to adamantine luster.

• **FORMATION** Forms in hydrothermal veins, in contact metamorphic rocks, and in pegmatites. It also occurs in placer deposits, and is frequently found with wolframite. It is an important ore of tungsten.

• **TESTS** This mineral gives a bright, bluish white fluorescence under shortwave ultraviolet light. It is also soluble in acids, and fusible, but only with difficulty.

magnetite groundmass

TETRAGONAL

dipyramidal scheelite crystals

SG 5.9–6.1	Cleavage Distinct	Fracture Subconchoidal to uneven

PHOSPHATES, ARSENATES, AND VANADATES

P HOSPHATES, arsenates, and vanadates are all compounds in which metallic elements combine with phosphate $(PO_4)^{-8}$; arsenate $(ASO_4)^{-8}$, $(ASO_3)^{-1}$; or vanadate $(VO_4)^{-3}$, $(VO_3)^{-1}$ radicals. Although several hundred phosphate, arsenate, and vanadate species are recognized, they are not abundant. Some phosphates, such as arsenic, are primary, but most members of the overall group form from the oxidation of primary sulfides. Their properties are variable, but generally they tend to be soft, brittle, very colorful, and well-crystallized. Phosphates include the radioactive minerals torbernite and autunite, lead-rich pyromorphite, bright blue lazulite, and turquoise, which gives its name to a shade of blue. The hardness of phosphates is particularly variable, ranging from 1½ in vivianite to 5–6 in turquoise. Many of the arsenates are highly sought after by collectors, particularly the well-crystallized and brightly-colored species – examples include adamite, erythrite, mimetite, and bayldonite. Arsenates tend to have a specific gravity of 3–5, apart from mimetite which, because it contains lead, has a specific gravity of 7–7.3. These minerals are usually found to be of low hardness.

———— • ————

Vanadinite is probably the best known and commonest of the vanadates. It occurs as beautiful red or orange hexagonal crystals.

Group Phosphates	Composition $(Li,Na)AlPO_4(F,OH)$		Hardness 5½–6

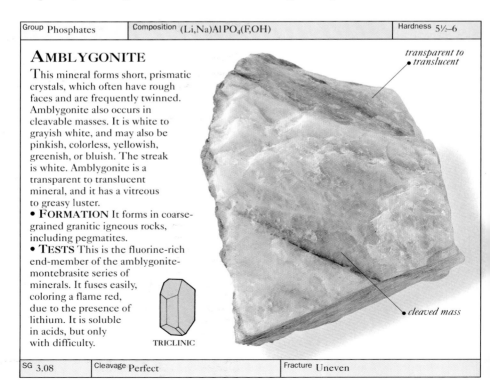

AMBLYGONITE

This mineral forms short, prismatic crystals, which often have rough faces and are frequently twinned. Amblygonite also occurs in cleavable masses. It is white to grayish white, and may also be pinkish, colorless, yellowish, greenish, or bluish. The streak is white. Amblygonite is a transparent to translucent mineral, and it has a vitreous to greasy luster.
• FORMATION It forms in coarse-grained granitic igneous rocks, including pegmatites.
• TESTS This is the fluorine-rich end-member of the amblygonite-montebrasite series of minerals. It fuses easily, coloring a flame red, due to the presence of lithium. It is soluble in acids, but only with difficulty.

TRICLINIC

transparent to translucent

cleaved mass

SG 3.08	Cleavage Perfect	Fracture Uneven

Group Phosphates	Composition $(Mg,Fe)Al_2(PO_4)_2(OH)_2$	Hardness $5\frac{1}{2}$–6

LAZULITE

Pseudo-dipyramidal crystals usually formed by lazulite, though tabular crystals also form. The crystals can be quite large, and are frequently twinned. Other habits in which this mineral commonly forms are massive, granular, and compact. Its color is blue, but ranges from a rich azure to light blue, or bluish green. The streak is white. This is a translucent to opaque mineral, with a vitreous to dull luster.

• **FORMATION** Lazulite forms in a variety of environments, including quartz veins, granitic pegmatites, and metamorphic rocks such as metaquartzite. Pegmatic lazulite typically occurs with andalusite and rutile. Metamorphic associates include quartz, garnet, kyanite, muscovite, pyrophyllite, sillimanite, and corundum.

• **TESTS** This mineral gives off water when heated in a closed test tube.

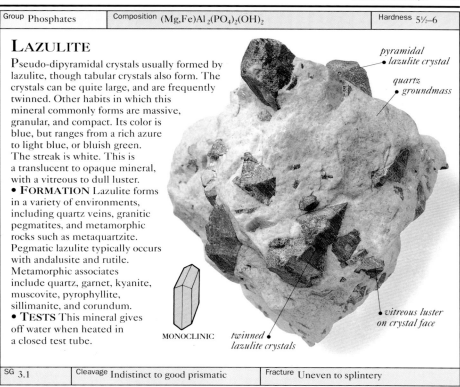

pyramidal lazulite crystal

quartz groundmass

vitreous luster on crystal face

MONOCLINIC

twinned lazulite crystals

SG 3.1	Cleavage Indistinct to good prismatic	Fracture Uneven to splintery

Group Phosphates	Composition $Pb_5(PO_4)_3Cl$	Hardness $3\frac{1}{2}$–4

PYROMORPHITE

This mineral usually forms short, hexagonal prisms, which are often barrel-shaped. It also occurs in globular, reniform, granular, earthy, botryoidal, and fibrous habits. It can be green, orange, gray, brown, or yellow in color. The streak is white. Pyromorphite is a transparent to translucent mineral. It has a resinous to adamantine luster.

• **FORMATION** Forms in the oxidation zone of lead veins, as a secondary mineral.

• **TESTS** Pyromorphite is soluble in certain acids.

limonite groundmass

aggregates of prismatic, hexagonal pyromorphite crystals

TRIGONAL / HEXAGONAL

SG 6.5–7.1	Cleavage Very poor prismatic	Fracture Uneven to subconchoidal

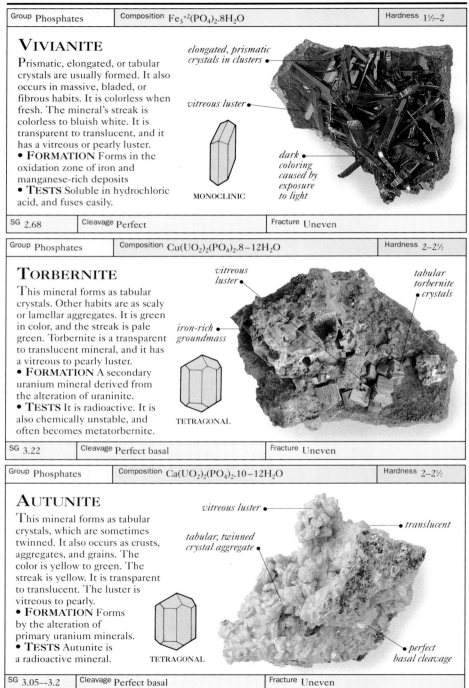

Group Phosphates	Composition $Fe_3^{+2}(PO_4)_2.8H_2O$	Hardness 1½–2

VIVIANITE

Prismatic, elongated, or tabular crystals are usually formed. It also occurs in massive, bladed, or fibrous habits. It is colorless when fresh. The mineral's streak is colorless to bluish white. It is transparent to translucent, and it has a vitreous or pearly luster.
• **FORMATION** Forms in the oxidation zone of iron and manganese-rich deposits
• **TESTS** Soluble in hydrochloric acid, and fuses easily.

elongated, prismatic crystals in clusters

vitreous luster

MONOCLINIC

dark coloring caused by exposure to light

SG 2.68	Cleavage Perfect	Fracture Uneven

Group Phosphates	Composition $Cu(UO_2)_2(PO_4)_2.8–12H_2O$	Hardness 2–2½

TORBERNITE

This mineral forms as tabular crystals. Other habits are as scaly or lamellar aggregates. It is green in color, and the streak is pale green. Torbernite is a transparent to translucent mineral, and it has a vitreous to pearly luster.
• **FORMATION** A secondary uranium mineral derived from the alteration of uraninite.
• **TESTS** It is radioactive. It is also chemically unstable, and often becomes metatorbernite.

vitreous luster

iron-rich groundmass

TETRAGONAL

tabular torbernite crystals

SG 3.22	Cleavage Perfect basal	Fracture Uneven

Group Phosphates	Composition $Ca(UO_2)_2(PO_4)_2.10–12H_2O$	Hardness 2–2½

AUTUNITE

This mineral forms as tabular crystals, which are sometimes twinned. It also occurs as crusts, aggregates, and grains. The color is yellow to green. The streak is yellow. It is transparent to translucent. The luster is vitreous to pearly.
• **FORMATION** Forms by the alteration of primary uranium minerals.
• **TESTS** Autunite is a radioactive mineral.

vitreous luster

tabular, twinned crystal aggregate

translucent

TETRAGONAL

perfect basal cleavage

SG 3.05––3.2	Cleavage Perfect basal	Fracture Uneven

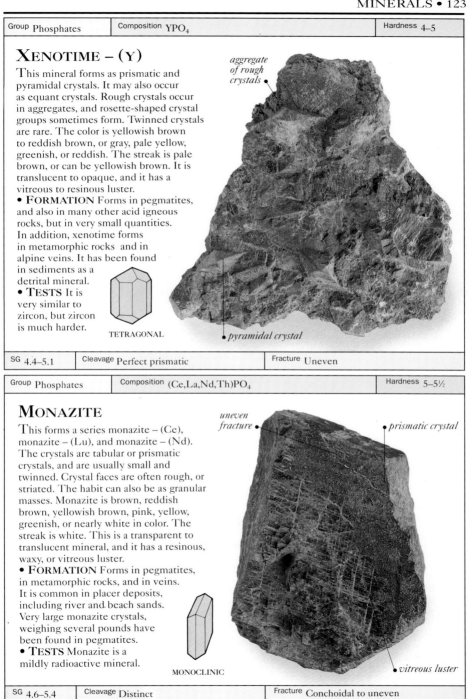

Group Phosphates	Composition YPO_4		Hardness 4–5

XENOTIME – (Y)

This mineral forms as prismatic and pyramidal crystals. It may also occur as equant crystals. Rough crystals occur in aggregates, and rosette-shaped crystal groups sometimes form. Twinned crystals are rare. The color is yellowish brown to reddish brown, or gray, pale yellow, greenish, or reddish. The streak is pale brown, or can be yellowish brown. It is translucent to opaque, and it has a vitreous to resinous luster.
• **FORMATION** Forms in pegmatites, and also in many other acid igneous rocks, but in very small quantities. In addition, xenotime forms in metamorphic rocks and in alpine veins. It has been found in sediments as a detrital mineral.
• **TESTS** It is very similar to zircon, but zircon is much harder.

aggregate of rough crystals

TETRAGONAL

pyramidal crystal

SG 4.4–5.1	Cleavage Perfect prismatic	Fracture Uneven

Group Phosphates	Composition $(Ce,La,Nd,Th)PO_4$		Hardness 5–5½

MONAZITE

This forms a series monazite – (Ce), monazite – (Lu), and monazite – (Nd). The crystals are tabular or prismatic crystals, and are usually small and twinned. Crystal faces are often rough, or striated. The habit can also be as granular masses. Monazite is brown, reddish brown, yellowish brown, pink, yellow, greenish, or nearly white in color. The streak is white. This is a transparent to translucent mineral, and it has a resinous, waxy, or vitreous luster.
• **FORMATION** Forms in pegmatites, in metamorphic rocks, and in veins. It is common in placer deposits, including river and beach sands. Very large monazite crystals, weighing several pounds have been found in pegmatites.
• **TESTS** Monazite is a mildly radioactive mineral.

uneven fracture

prismatic crystal

MONOCLINIC

vitreous luster

SG 4.6–5.4	Cleavage Distinct	Fracture Conchoidal to uneven

Group Phosphates	Composition $CuAl_6(PO_4)_4(OH)_8 \cdot 4H_2O$	Hardness 5–6

TURQUOISE

This mineral rarely forms crystals, but when they occur, it is as small, short, prismatic specimens. The more common habits are massive, granular, cryptocrystalline, stalactitic, and concretionary; it also forms in crusts, and veinlets. Turquoise is bright blue to pale blue, greenish blue, green, and gray. It has a white or pale green streak. The crystals are transparent and have a vitreous luster; massive forms are opaque, with a waxy or dull luster.

• **FORMATION** Forms in aluminum-rich igneous and sedimentary rocks that have been altered, often by surface water.

• **TESTS** Turquoise is soluble in hydrochloric acid.

TRICLINIC

crust of turquoise

rock groundmass

SG 2.6–2.8	Cleavage Good	Fracture Conchoidal

Group Phosphates	Composition $Al_3(PO_4)_2(OH,F)_3 \cdot 5H_2O$	Hardness 3½–4

WAVELLITE

This mineral occurs occasionally as minute, prismatic crystals. It also forms as acicular, radiating aggregates, which are often spherical. Additionally, it forms crusts. The color is white to greenish white, and green; also yellowish green to yellow, and yellowish brown. There is a white streak. Wavellite is a transparent to translucent mineral, and has a vitreous, resinous or pearly luster.

• **FORMATION** Forms on rock fracture and joint surfaces as a secondary mineral.

• **TESTS** This mineral dissolves in most acids, and is infusible. It gives off water when heated in a closed test tube.

radiating acicular wavellite crystals

rock groundmass

ORTHORHOMBIC

SG 2.36	Cleavage Perfect	Fracture Subconchoidal to uneven

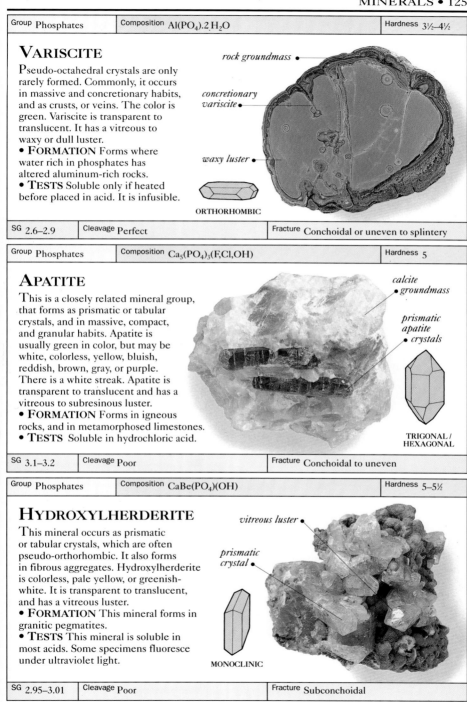

| Group Phosphates | Composition Al(PO₄).2 H₂O | | Hardness 3½–4½ |

$Al(PO_4) \cdot 2H_2O$

VARISCITE

Pseudo-octahedral crystals are only rarely formed. Commonly, it occurs in massive and concretionary habits, and as crusts, or veins. The color is green. Variscite is transparent to translucent. It has a vitreous to waxy or dull luster.
• **FORMATION** Forms where water rich in phosphates has altered aluminum-rich rocks.
• **TESTS** Soluble only if heated before placed in acid. It is infusible.

rock groundmass

concretionary variscite

waxy luster

ORTHORHOMBIC

| SG 2.6–2.9 | Cleavage Perfect | Fracture Conchoidal or uneven to splintery |

| Group Phosphates | Composition Ca₅(PO₄)₃(F,Cl,OH) | | Hardness 5 |

$Ca_5(PO_4)_3(F,Cl,OH)$

APATITE

This is a closely related mineral group, that forms as prismatic or tabular crystals, and in massive, compact, and granular habits. Apatite is usually green in color, but may be white, colorless, yellow, bluish, reddish, brown, gray, or purple. There is a white streak. Apatite is transparent to translucent and has a vitreous to subresinous luster.
• **FORMATION** Forms in igneous rocks, and in metamorphosed limestones.
• **TESTS** Soluble in hydrochloric acid.

calcite groundmass

prismatic apatite crystals

TRIGONAL / HEXAGONAL

| SG 3.1–3.2 | Cleavage Poor | Fracture Conchoidal to uneven |

| Group Phosphates | Composition CaBe(PO₄)(OH) | | Hardness 5–5½ |

$CaBe(PO_4)(OH)$

HYDROXYLHERDERITE

This mineral occurs as prismatic or tabular crystals, which are often pseudo-orthorhombic. It also forms in fibrous aggregates. Hydroxylherderite is colorless, pale yellow, or greenish-white. It is transparent to translucent, and has a vitreous luster.
• **FORMATION** This mineral forms in granitic pegmatites.
• **TESTS** This mineral is soluble in most acids. Some specimens fluoresce under ultraviolet light.

vitreous luster

prismatic crystal

MONOCLINIC

| SG 2.95–3.01 | Cleavage Poor | Fracture Subconchoidal |

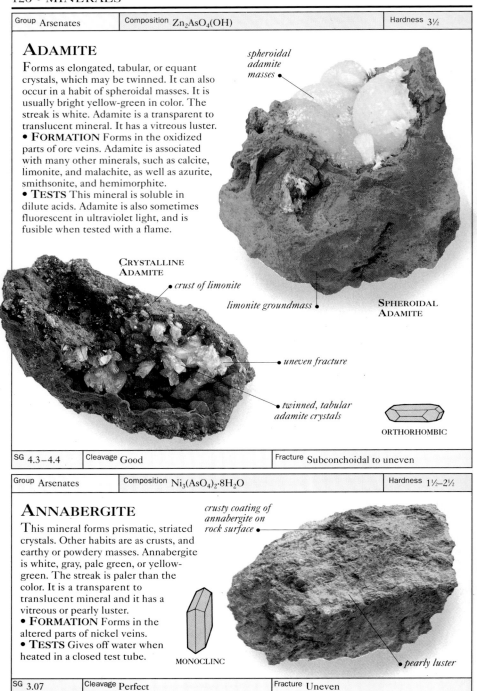

Group Arsenates	Composition $Zn_2AsO_4(OH)$	Hardness $3\frac{1}{2}$

ADAMITE

Forms as elongated, tabular, or equant crystals, which may be twinned. It can also occur in a habit of spheroidal masses. It is usually bright yellow-green in color. The streak is white. Adamite is a transparent to translucent mineral. It has a vitreous luster.
• **FORMATION** Forms in the oxidized parts of ore veins. Adamite is associated with many other minerals, such as calcite, limonite, and malachite, as well as azurite, smithsonite, and hemimorphite.
• **TESTS** This mineral is soluble in dilute acids. Adamite is also sometimes fluorescent in ultraviolet light, and is fusible when tested with a flame.

spheroidal adamite masses •

CRYSTALLINE ADAMITE

• crust of limonite

limonite groundmass •

SPHEROIDAL ADAMITE

• uneven fracture

• twinned, tabular adamite crystals

ORTHORHOMBIC

SG $4.3-4.4$	Cleavage Good	Fracture Subconchoidal to uneven

Group Arsenates	Composition $Ni_3(AsO_4)_2 \cdot 8H_2O$	Hardness $1\frac{1}{2}-2\frac{1}{2}$

ANNABERGITE

This mineral forms prismatic, striated crystals. Other habits are as crusts, and earthy or powdery masses. Annabergite is white, gray, pale green, or yellow-green. The streak is paler than the color. It is a transparent to translucent mineral and it has a vitreous or pearly luster.
• **FORMATION** Forms in the altered parts of nickel veins.
• **TESTS** Gives off water when heated in a closed test tube.

crusty coating of annabergite on rock surface •

MONOCLINIC

• pearly luster

SG 3.07	Cleavage Perfect	Fracture Uneven

Group Arsenates	Composition $Cu_3^{+2}(AsO_4)(OH)_3$	Hardness $2\frac{1}{2}$–3

CLINOCLASE

The crystals form as elongated or tabular shapes, and may have a rhombohedral appearance, in which case they are described as pseudorhombohedral. Crystals occur either isolated or as rosettes. This mineral is dark greenish blue to greenish black in color, and has a bluish green streak. Clinoclase is transparent to translucent. It has a vitreous luster on crystal faces, which becomes pearly on the cleavage surfaces.
• **FORMATION** Forms as a secondary mineral in the oxidation zone of copper sulfide deposits, both on and beneath the earth's surface. Clinoclase is frequently associated with olivenite, a member of the same mineral group.
• **TESTS** Clinoclase is soluble in acids and produces a garlic smell when heated.

broken clinoclase rosette, with internal, radiating structure

uneven fracture

olivenite, an associated mineral

vitreous luster

MONOCLINIC

SG 4.33	Cleavage Perfect	Fracture Uneven

Group Arsenates	Composition $Co_3(AsO_4)_2.8H_2O$	Hardness $1\frac{1}{2}$–$2\frac{1}{2}$

ERYTHRITE

The prismatic to acicular crystals formed by this mineral are often striated, or in bladed aggregates. Erythrite also occurs in a habit of earthy masses. In color, it is deep purple to pale pink. The streak is just a shade paler than the color. This mineral ranges from transparent to translucent, and it has an adamantine to vitreous or pearly luster.
• **FORMATION** Forms in the parts of cobalt veins that have been altered by circulating fluid, and where oxidation has occurred.
• **TESTS** Soluble in hydrochloric acid.

bladed aggregates of crystals in striated acicular habit

vitreous luster

MONOCLINIC

SG 3.18	Cleavage Perfect	Fracture Uneven

Group Arsenates	Composition $Pb_5(AsO_4)_3Cl$	Hardness $3\frac{1}{2}$–4

MIMETITE

This mineral forms acicular to slender prismatic crystals; sometimes, these crystals can be barrel-shaped, in which case they are called campylite crystals. Other habits include botryoidal, reniform, and granular. Mimetite ranges in color from yellow, orange, and brown, to white, colorless, and greenish. It has a white streak. This is a transparent to translucent mineral, and it has a vitreous to resinous luster.

• **FORMATION** Forms in the oxidation zone of lead deposits that have been altered by circulating hydro-thermal fluids. It is often found with pyromorphite, vanadinite, galena, anglesite, hemimorphite, and arsenopyrite.

• **TESTS** Soluble in hydrochloric acid. It will fuse easily if put in a flame, when a very strong smell, which is reminiscent of garlic, is produced.

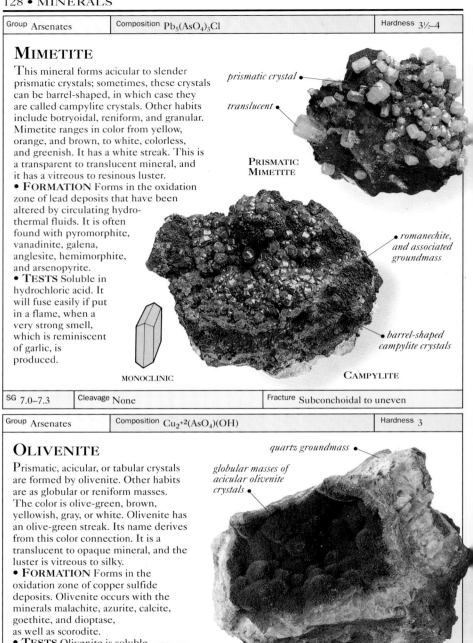

prismatic crystal

translucent

PRISMATIC MIMETITE

romanechite, and associated groundmass

barrel-shaped campylite crystals

MONOCLINIC

CAMPYLITE

SG 7.0–7.3	Cleavage None	Fracture Subconchoidal to uneven

Group Arsenates	Composition $Cu_2^{+2}(AsO_4)(OH)$	Hardness 3

OLIVENITE

Prismatic, acicular, or tabular crystals are formed by olivenite. Other habits are as globular or reniform masses. The color is olive-green, brown, yellowish, gray, or white. Olivenite has an olive-green streak. Its name derives from this color connection. It is a translucent to opaque mineral, and the luster is vitreous to silky.

• **FORMATION** Forms in the oxidation zone of copper sulfide deposits. Olivenite occurs with the minerals malachite, azurite, calcite, goethite, and dioptase, as well as scorodite.

• **TESTS** Olivenite is soluble in acids, and produces a garlic smell when heated.

quartz groundmass

globular masses of acicular olivenite crystals

ORTHORHOMBIC

SG 4.4	Cleavage Indistinct	Fracture Uneven to conchoidal

Group Arsenates	Composition $Fe^{+3}AsO_4.2H_2O$	Hardness $3\frac{1}{2}$–4

SCORODITE

The crystals formed by scorodite are pyramidal, prismatic, and tabular. Scorodite also occurs in massive and earthy habits. It is pale green, grayish green, bluish green, blue, brownish, colorless, yellowish, or violet. The streak is white. This is a transparent to translucent mineral. Its luster is vitreous to resinous, or dull.
• **FORMATION** Forms in the oxidation zone of arsenic deposits.
• **TESTS** This mineral is soluble in hydrochloric, as well as nitric acids. When heated, a smell that is reminiscent of garlic is produced. If heated in a closed test tube, water is given off.

pyramidal scorodite crystal

rock groundmass

ORTHORHOMBIC

vitreous luster

SG 3.28	Cleavage Imperfect	Fracture Subconchoidal

Group Arsenates	Composition $(Cu,Zn)_3Pb(AsO_4)_2(OH)_2.H_2O$	Hardness $4\frac{1}{2}$

BAYLDONITE

Usually forms in a massive habit but also in granular, and powdery, habits. The latter habits may occur on rock surfaces and it is difficult to detect any crystal form unless a high magnification is used. This mineral also occurs as crusts, and rounded concretions, which may have a fibrous, threadlike, internal structure. The color is often bright grass-green, but can be yellowish or dark green. No streak has been determined. Light hardly passes through crystalline specimens, so bayldonite is described as subtranslucent. The luster is resinous, and the surface is almost sticky in appearance.
• **FORMATION** Balydonite forms in the oxidation zone of copper-bearing deposits. It is associated with many minerals, including olivenite, azurite, malachite, and mimetite.
• **TESTS** Balydonite gives off water when heated in a closed test tube.

crust of bayldonite on quartz groundmass

resinous luster

MONOCLINIC

SG 5.5	Cleavage None	Fracture Uneven

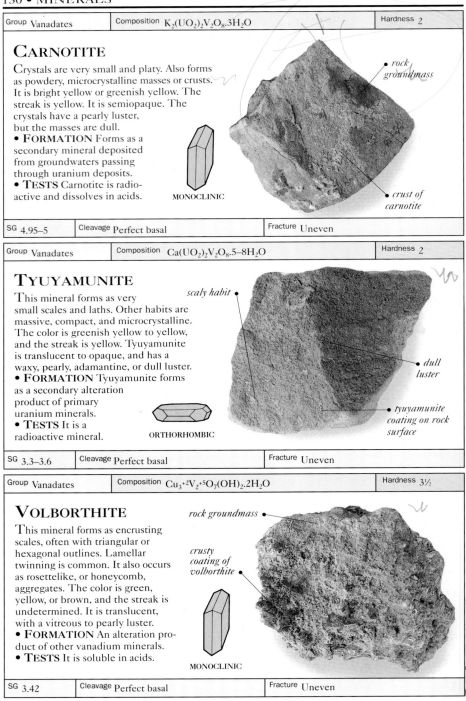

Group Vanadates	Composition $K_2(UO_2)_2V_2O_8.3H_2O$	Hardness 2

CARNOTITE

Crystals are very small and platy. Also forms as powdery, microcrystalline masses or crusts. It is bright yellow or greenish yellow. The streak is yellow. It is semiopaque. The crystals have a pearly luster, but the masses are dull.
• **FORMATION** Forms as a secondary mineral deposited from groundwaters passing through uranium deposits.
• **TESTS** Carnotite is radioactive and dissolves in acids.

rock groundmass

MONOCLINIC

crust of carnotite

SG 4.95–5	Cleavage Perfect basal	Fracture Uneven

Group Vanadates	Composition $Ca(UO_2)_2V_2O_8.5–8H_2O$	Hardness 2

TYUYAMUNITE

This mineral forms as very small scales and laths. Other habits are massive, compact, and microcrystalline. The color is greenish yellow to yellow, and the streak is yellow. Tyuyamunite is translucent to opaque, and has a waxy, pearly, adamantine, or dull luster.
• **FORMATION** Tyuyamunite forms as a secondary alteration product of primary uranium minerals.
• **TESTS** It is a radioactive mineral.

scaly habit

ORTHORHOMBIC

dull luster

tyuyamunite coating on rock surface

SG 3.3–3.6	Cleavage Perfect basal	Fracture Uneven

Group Vanadates	Composition $Cu_3^{+2}V_2^{+5}O_7(OH)_2.2H_2O$	Hardness 3½

VOLBORTHITE

This mineral forms as encrusting scales, often with triangular or hexagonal outlines. Lamellar twinning is common. It also occurs as rosettelike, or honeycomb, aggregates. The color is green, yellow, or brown, and the streak is undetermined. It is translucent, with a vitreous to pearly luster.
• **FORMATION** An alteration product of other vanadium minerals.
• **TESTS** It is soluble in acids.

rock groundmass

crusty coating of volborthite

MONOCLINIC

SG 3.42	Cleavage Perfect basal	Fracture Uneven

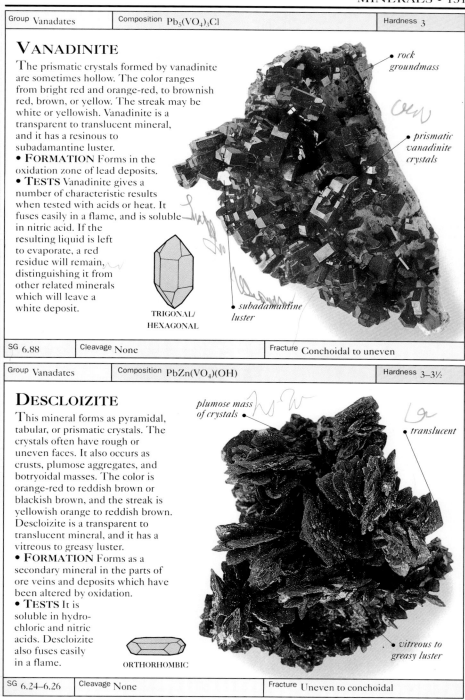

Group Vanadates	Composition $Pb_5(VO_4)_3Cl$	Hardness 3

VANADINITE

The prismatic crystals formed by vanadinite are sometimes hollow. The color ranges from bright red and orange-red, to brownish red, brown, or yellow. The streak may be white or yellowish. Vanadinite is a transparent to translucent mineral, and it has a resinous to subadamantine luster.

• **FORMATION** Forms in the oxidation zone of lead deposits.

• **TESTS** Vanadinite gives a number of characteristic results when tested with acids or heat. It fuses easily in a flame, and is soluble in nitric acid. If the resulting liquid is left to evaporate, a red residue will remain, distinguishing it from other related minerals which will leave a white deposit.

TRIGONAL/
HEXAGONAL

rock
groundmass

prismatic
vanadinite
crystals

subadamantine
luster

SG 6.88	Cleavage None	Fracture Conchoidal to uneven

Group Vanadates	Composition $PbZn(VO_4)(OH)$	Hardness 3–3½

DESCLOIZITE

This mineral forms as pyramidal, tabular, or prismatic crystals. The crystals often have rough or uneven faces. It also occurs as crusts, plumose aggregates, and botryoidal masses. The color is orange-red to reddish brown or blackish brown, and the streak is yellowish orange to reddish brown. Descloizite is a transparent to translucent mineral, and it has a vitreous to greasy luster.

• **FORMATION** Forms as a secondary mineral in the parts of ore veins and deposits which have been altered by oxidation.

• **TESTS** It is soluble in hydro-chloric and nitric acids. Descloizite also fuses easily in a flame.

ORTHORHOMBIC

plumose mass
of crystals

translucent

vitreous to
greasy luster

SG 6.24–6.26	Cleavage None	Fracture Uneven to conchoidal

SILICATES

SILICATES ARE compounds in which metallic elements combine with either single or linked Si-O tetrahedra $(SiO_4)^{-4}$. Structurally, silicates are divided into six classes: Neosilicates have isolated $(SiO_4)^{-4}$ tetrahedra linked by a non-silicon cation; Sorosilicates feature two tetrahedra joined and sharing one common oxygen ion; Cyclosilicates have tetrahedra joined into rings; Inosilicates have tetrahedra joined into either single or double-chains; Phylosilicates have sheetlike structures formed by the sharing of three oxygen ions by each adjacent tetrahedron; Tectosilicates are "framework" silicates in which every silicon atom shares all four of its oxygen ions with neighboring silicon atoms.

Silicates are the largest and most abundant class of minerals, while primary silicates are the main constituents of igneous and metamorphic rocks. Silicates tend to be hard, transparent to translucent, and of average density.

Group Silicates	Composition $Mg_2SiO_4–Fe_2SiO_4$	Hardness 6½–7

OLIVINE

This group of minerals forms thick, tabular crystals, frequently with wedge-shaped terminations. Other habits are massive, compact, and granular. The color is green, greenish yellow, yellowish brown, brown, and white, and the streak is colorless. These are transparent to translucent minerals, and they have a vitreous luster. The gem variety of forsteritic olivine is called peridot.
• **FORMATION** An end-member of the olivine group of minerals, forsterite forms in basic and ultrabasic igneous rocks, and is also found in marbles. It is rich in magnesium. Fayalite, the other end-member, is rich in iron, and forms in acid igneous rocks, which have cooled rapidly.
• **TESTS** Olivine is soluble in hydrochloric acid, with gelatinization.

transparent

striated crystal

PERIDOT

vitreous luster

tabular forsterite crystals

altered limestone groundmass

FORSTERITE

ORTHORHOMBIC

SG 3.27–4.32	Cleavage Imperfect	Fracture Conchoidal

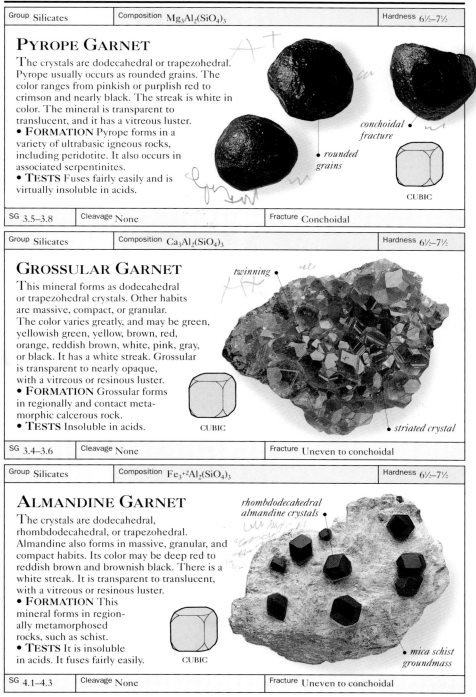

Group Silicates	Composition $Mg_3Al_2(SiO_4)_3$	Hardness 6½–7½

PYROPE GARNET

The crystals are dodecahedral or trapezohedral. Pyrope usually occurs as rounded grains. The color ranges from pinkish or purplish red to crimson and nearly black. The streak is white in color. The mineral is transparent to translucent, and it has a vitreous luster.
• **FORMATION** Pyrope forms in a variety of ultrabasic igneous rocks, including peridotite. It also occurs in associated serpentinites.
• **TESTS** Fuses fairly easily and is virtually insoluble in acids.

conchoidal fracture

rounded grains

CUBIC

SG 3.5–3.8	Cleavage None	Fracture Conchoidal

Group Silicates	Composition $Ca_3Al_2(SiO_4)_3$	Hardness 6½–7½

GROSSULAR GARNET

This mineral forms as dodecahedral or trapezohedral crystals. Other habits are massive, compact, or granular. The color varies greatly, and may be green, yellowish green, yellow, brown, red, orange, reddish brown, white, pink, gray, or black. It has a white streak. Grossular is transparent to nearly opaque, with a vitreous or resinous luster.
• **FORMATION** Grossular forms in regionally and contact meta-morphic calcerous rock.
• **TESTS** Insoluble in acids.

twinning

CUBIC

striated crystal

SG 3.4–3.6	Cleavage None	Fracture Uneven to conchoidal

Group Silicates	Composition $Fe_3^{+2}Al_2(SiO_4)_3$	Hardness 6½–7½

ALMANDINE GARNET

The crystals are dodecahedral, rhombdodecahedral, or trapezohedral. Almandine also forms in massive, granular, and compact habits. Its color may be deep red to reddish brown and brownish black. There is a white streak. It is transparent to translucent, with a vitreous or resinous luster.
• **FORMATION** This mineral forms in region-ally metamorphosed rocks, such as schist.
• **TESTS** It is insoluble in acids. It fuses fairly easily.

rhombdodecahedral almandine crystals

CUBIC

mica schist groundmass

SG 4.1–4.3	Cleavage None	Fracture Uneven to conchoidal

Group Silicates	Composition $(Mg,Fe^{+2})_7(SiO_4)_3(F,OH)_2$	Hardness 6

HUMITE

Small, stubby crystals with a varied, often highly modified, habit are formed by this mineral. The color is white, yellow, dark orange, or brown. Humite is transparent to translucent, and it has a vitreous luster on fresh crystal surfaces.
• **FORMATION** Occurs in contact metamorphosed limestones and in some mineral veins. It also occurs with numerous minerals, including calcite, graphite, spinel, diopside, vesuvianite, garnet, and other types of minerals typical of metamorphosed limestones. The humite group consists of humite, clinohumite, norbergite, and chondrodite.
• **TESTS** No further tests are required to identify it.

ORTHORHOMBIC

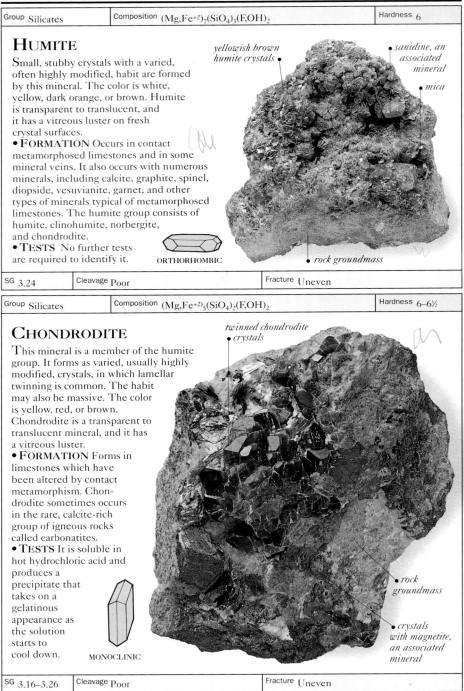

yellowish brown humite crystals

sanidine, an associated mineral

mica

rock groundmass

SG 3.24	Cleavage Poor		Fracture Uneven

Group Silicates	Composition $(Mg,Fe^{+2})_5(SiO_4)_2(F,OH)_2$	Hardness 6–6½

CHONDRODITE

This mineral is a member of the humite group. It forms as varied, usually highly modified, crystals, in which lamellar twinning is common. The habit may also be massive. The color is yellow, red, or brown. Chondrodite is a transparent to translucent mineral, and it has a vitreous luster.
• **FORMATION** Forms in limestones which have been altered by contact metamorphism. Chondrodite sometimes occurs in the rare, calcite-rich group of igneous rocks called carbonatites.
• **TESTS** It is soluble in hot hydrochloric acid and produces a precipitate that takes on a gelatinous appearance as the solution starts to cool down.

MONOCLINIC

twinned chondrodite crystals

rock groundmass

crystals with magnetite, an associated mineral

SG 3.16–3.26	Cleavage Poor		Fracture Uneven

Group Silicates	Composition $Al_2SiO_4(F,OH)_2$	Hardness 8

TOPAZ

This mineral occurs as well-formed prismatic crystals, which can be of great size, and may weigh over 220 pounds (100 kg). Topaz can also form in massive, granular, and columnar habits. The color of this mineral is very variable: it may be white, colorless, gray, yellow, orange, brown, bluish, greenish, purple, or pink. The streak is colorless. Topaz is a transparent to translucent mineral, and it has a vitreous luster.

•**FORMATION** Forms most commonly in pegmatites. Topaz can also form in veins and cavities in granitic rocks. Topaz occurs with a variety of minerals, including quartz.

•**TESTS** Insoluble in acids; infusible when flame heated.

prismatic topaz crystal

crystals in pegmatite

ORTHORHOMBIC

SG 3.49–3.57	Cleavage Perfect	Fracture Subconchoidal to uneven

Group Silicates	Composition Zn_2SiO_4	Hardness 5½

WILLEMITE

Hexagonal prismatic crystals, which are frequently terminated by rhombohedra, are formed by this mineral. It may also occur in massive, fibrous, compact, and granular habits. Willemite may be white, colorless, gray, green, yellow, brown, or reddish. The streak is colorless. Willemite is transparent to translucent, and it has a vitreous or resinous luster.

•**FORMATION** Forms in the oxidized zone of zinc ore deposits, in veins, by secondary alteration, and in metamorphosed limestone rocks.

•**TESTS** It can be very phosphorescent. It is soluble in hydrochloric acid. Also exhibits bright green fluorescence under ultraviolet light.

vitreous to resinous luster

franklinite, an associated mineral

prismatic willemite crystals

rock groundmass

TRIGONAL /
HEXAGONAL

SG 3.89–4.19	Cleavage Basal	Fracture Uneven

Group Silicates	Composition $(Fe^{+2},Mg,Zn)_2Al_9(Si,Al)_4O_{22}(OH)_2$	Hardness 7–7½

STAUROLITE

This mineral forms short, prismatic crystals, often as cruciform twins. The color is dark brown, reddish brown, yellowish brown, or brownish black. The streak is colorless to grayish. Staurolite is translucent to nearly opaque and has a vitreous to resinous luster.
• **FORMATION** Forms deep in the earth's crust, in regionally metamorphosed rocks that have been formed by extremes of temperature and pressure. Such rocks include gneisses and mica schists. Staurolite is associated with such metamorphic minerals as kyanite, muscovite, garnet, and quartz.
• **TESTS** Some varieties have manganese traces, in which case they will fuse.

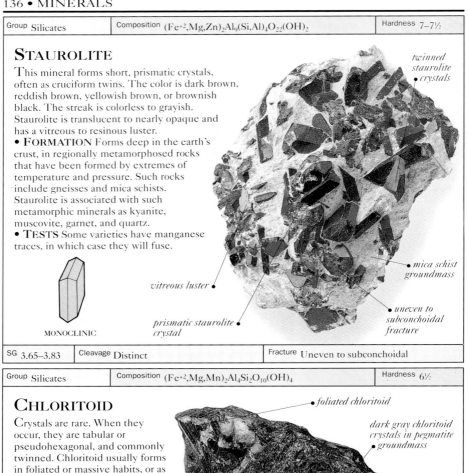

twinned staurolite crystals

mica schist groundmass

vitreous luster

uneven to subconchoidal fracture

MONOCLINIC

prismatic staurolite crystal

SG 3.65–3.83	Cleavage Distinct	Fracture Uneven to subconchoidal

Group Silicates	Composition $(Fe^{+2},Mg,Mn)_2Al_4Si_2O_{10}(OH)_4$	Hardness 6½

CHLORITOID

Crystals are rare. When they occur, they are tabular or pseudohexagonal, and commonly twinned. Chloritoid usually forms in foliated or massive habits, or as scales or plates. It is dark gray, or greenish to greenish black in color. No streak has been determined. This is a translucent mineral. It has a pearly luster on cleavage surfaces.
• **FORMATION** Forms in rocks such as schist and phyllite which have been regionally metamorphosed. Chloritoid also forms in pegmatites. Associated minerals are muscovite, chlorite, garnet, staurolite (above), as well as kyanite.
• **TESTS** Chloritoid is soluble in concentrated sulphuric acid, but not in hydrochloric acid. It fuses, but only with some difficulty.

foliated chloritoid

dark gray chloritoid crystals in pegmatite groundmass

pearly luster on cleavage surfaces

TRICLINIC / MONOCLINIC

SG 3.6	Cleavage Perfect	Fracture Uneven

Group Silicates	Composition $ZrSiO_4$		Hardness $7\frac{1}{2}$

ZIRCON

This mineral forms as prismatic crystals with bipyramidal terminations, and also as radiating fibrous aggregates. Twinned crystals are common. Other habits include irregular grains. It is colorless, red, brown, yellow, green, or gray. Zircon is a transparent to opaque mineral and its luster may be vitreous, adamantine, or greasy.

• **FORMATION** Forms in igneous rocks such as syenite, and in certain metamorphic rocks. Zircon also occurs in many detrital sedimentary rocks, where it is a product of weathering and erosion of primary, zircon-bearing rocks.

• **TESTS** Zircon is often a radioactive mineral, because it can contain small amounts of uranium and thorium.

zircon crystals set in syenite groundmass

prismatic zircon

TETRAGONAL

vitreous luster

SG 4.6–4.7	Cleavage Imperfect	Fracture Uneven to conchoidal

Group Silicates	Composition Al_2SiO_5		Hardness $6\frac{1}{2}$–$7\frac{1}{2}$

ANDALUSITE

This mineral forms prismatic crystals, with an almost square cross-section. (Chiastolite is a variety of andalusite with a cruciform cross-section.) Andalusite also occurs in massive, fibrous, or columnar habits. The color is pink, reddish, brownish, whitish, grayish, or greenish, and the streak is colorless. This is a transparent to nearly opaque mineral. Its luster is vitreous.

• **FORMATION** Forms in granites, and pegmatites, and in many metamorphosed rocks. It occurs with kyanite, cordierite, sillimanite, and corundum.

• **TESTS** This mineral is insoluble in any fluids, and infusible when heated with a flame.

prismatic andalusite crystal

quartz groundmass

uneven fracture

ORTHORHOMBIC

distinct cleavage

SG 3.13–3.16	Cleavage Distinct prismatic	Fracture Uneven to subconchoidal

Group Silicates	Composition Al_2SiO_5	Hardness 6½–7½

SILLIMANITE

Long prismatic crystals, with an almost square cross-section, are formed by sillimanite. It can occur in fibrous masses. It may be white, colorless, gray, yellowish, brownish, greenish, or bluish. The streak is colorless. It is a transparent to translucent mineral, and it has a vitreous to silky luster.
• **FORMATION** Forms in high-temperature regional metamorphic rocks, and in some igneous pegmatites.
• **TESTS** This mineral is infusible and insoluble in acids.

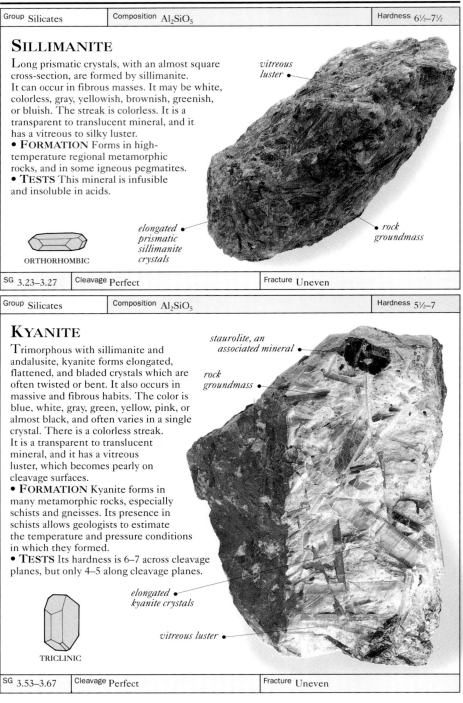

vitreous luster •

ORTHORHOMBIC

elongated • *prismatic sillimanite crystals*

• *rock groundmass*

SG 3.23–3.27	Cleavage Perfect	Fracture Uneven

Group Silicates	Composition Al_2SiO_5	Hardness 5½–7

KYANITE

Trimorphous with sillimanite and andalusite, kyanite forms elongated, flattened, and bladed crystals which are often twisted or bent. It also occurs in massive and fibrous habits. The color is blue, white, gray, green, yellow, pink, or almost black, and often varies in a single crystal. There is a colorless streak. It is a transparent to translucent mineral, and it has a vitreous luster, which becomes pearly on cleavage surfaces.
• **FORMATION** Kyanite forms in many metamorphic rocks, especially schists and gneisses. Its presence in schists allows geologists to estimate the temperature and pressure conditions in which they formed.
• **TESTS** Its hardness is 6–7 across cleavage planes, but only 4–5 along cleavage planes.

staurolite, an associated mineral •

rock groundmass •

elongated • *kyanite crystals*

TRICLINIC

vitreous luster •

SG 3.53–3.67	Cleavage Perfect	Fracture Uneven

Group Silicates	Composition $CaTiSiO_5$	Hardness 5–5½

TITANITE (SPHENE)

The crystals formed by titanite are wedge-shaped or prismatic, and commonly twinned. This mineral also occurs in massive, lamellar, and compact habits. Titanite varies and may be brown, yellow, green, colorless, gray, red, or black, and often varies within a single crystal. The streak is white. It is a transparent to nearly opaque mineral, and it has an adamantine to resinous luster.

• **FORMATION**
Titanite occurs in many igneous rocks as an accessory mineral.

• **TESTS**
It is soluble in sulfuric acid.

MONOCLINIC

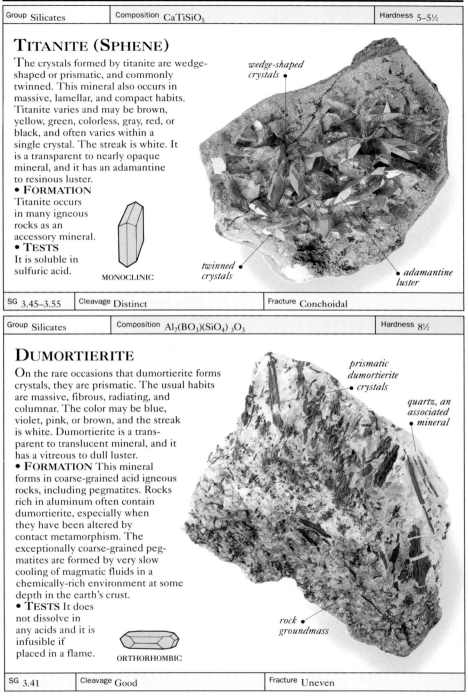

wedge-shaped crystals •

twinned • crystals

• adamantine luster

SG 3.45–3.55	Cleavage Distinct	Fracture Conchoidal

Group Silicates	Composition $Al_7(BO_3)(SiO_4)_3O_3$	Hardness 8½

DUMORTIERITE

On the rare occasions that dumortierite forms crystals, they are prismatic. The usual habits are massive, fibrous, radiating, and columnar. The color may be blue, violet, pink, or brown, and the streak is white. Dumortierite is a transparent to translucent mineral, and it has a vitreous to dull luster.

• **FORMATION** This mineral forms in coarse-grained acid igneous rocks, including pegmatites. Rocks rich in aluminum often contain dumortierite, especially when they have been altered by contact metamorphism. The exceptionally coarse-grained pegmatites are formed by very slow cooling of magmatic fluids in a chemically-rich environment at some depth in the earth's crust.

• **TESTS** It does not dissolve in any acids and it is infusible if placed in a flame.

ORTHORHOMBIC

prismatic dumortierite • crystals

quartz, an associated • mineral

rock • groundmass

SG 3.41	Cleavage Good	Fracture Uneven

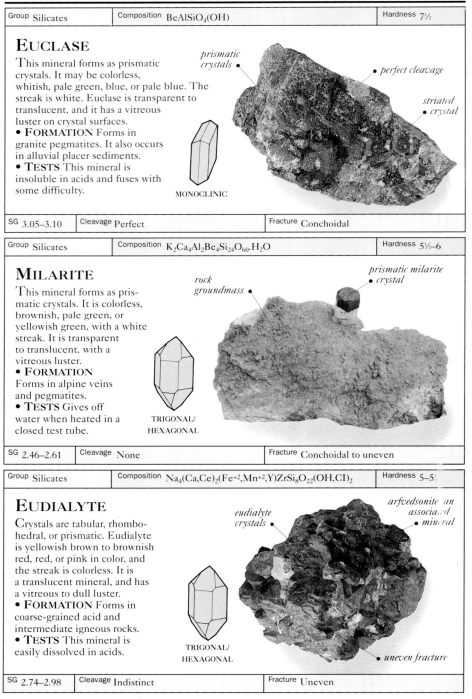

Group Silicates	Composition BeAlSiO$_4$(OH)		Hardness 7½

EUCLASE

This mineral forms as prismatic crystals. It may be colorless, whitish, pale green, blue, or pale blue. The streak is white. Euclase is transparent to translucent, and it has a vitreous luster on crystal surfaces.
• **FORMATION** Forms in granite pegmatites. It also occurs in alluvial placer sediments.
• **TESTS** This mineral is insoluble in acids and fuses with some difficulty.

prismatic crystals
perfect cleavage
striated crystal

MONOCLINIC

SG 3.05–3.10	Cleavage Perfect	Fracture Conchoidal

Group Silicates	Composition K$_2$Ca$_4$Al$_2$Be$_4$Si$_{24}$O$_{60}$·H$_2$O		Hardness 5½–6

MILARITE

This mineral forms as prismatic crystals. It is colorless, brownish, pale green, or yellowish green, with a white streak. It is transparent to translucent, with a vitreous luster.
• **FORMATION** Forms in alpine veins and pegmatites.
• **TESTS** Gives off water when heated in a closed test tube.

rock groundmass
prismatic milarite crystal

TRIGONAL/ HEXAGONAL

SG 2.46–2.61	Cleavage None	Fracture Conchoidal to uneven

Group Silicates	Composition Na$_4$(Ca,Ce)$_2$(Fe^{+2},Mn^{+2},Y)ZrSi$_8$O$_{22}$(OH,Cl)$_2$		Hardness 5–5½

EUDIALYTE

Crystals are tabular, rhombohedral, or prismatic. Eudialyte is yellowish brown to brownish red, red, or pink in color, and the streak is colorless. It is a translucent mineral, and has a vitreous to dull luster.
• **FORMATION** Forms in coarse-grained acid and intermediate igneous rocks.
• **TESTS** This mineral is easily dissolved in acids.

eudialyte crystals
arfvedsonite an associated mineral
uneven fracture

TRIGONAL/ HEXAGONAL

SG 2.74–2.98	Cleavage Indistinct	Fracture Uneven

Group Silicates	Composition $CaBSiO_4(OH)$		Hardness 5–5½

DATOLITE

This mineral forms as short, prismatic, very variable, crystals, and also as granular or compact masses. It is colorless, white, pale yellow, pale green, or tinted pink, reddish, or brown by impurities. The streak is colorless. Datolite is a transparent to translucent mineral, with a vitreous luster.
• **FORMATION** This mineral forms in veins and cavities in basaltic igneous rocks. It also occurs with calcite, quartz, and some zeolite minerals.
• **TESTS** It is soluble in acids and turns a flame green.

short prismatic crystals

uneven fracture

vitreous luster

MONOCLINIC

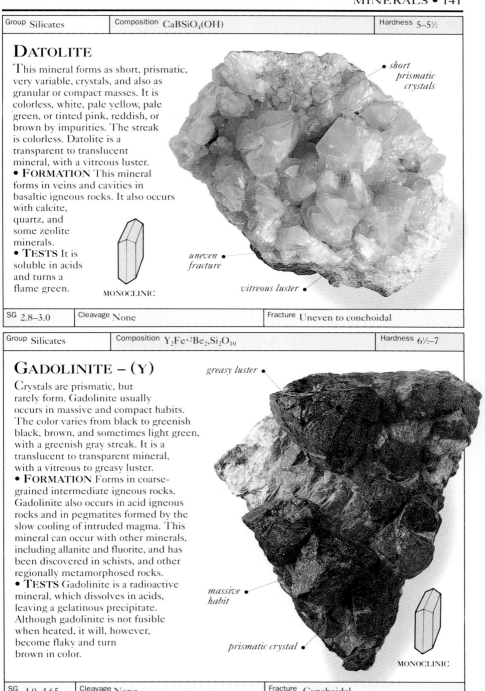

SG 2.8–3.0	Cleavage None	Fracture Uneven to conchoidal

Group Silicates	Composition $Y_2Fe^{+2}Be_2Si_2O_{10}$		Hardness 6½–7

GADOLINITE – (Y)

Crystals are prismatic, but rarely form. Gadolinite usually occurs in massive and compact habits. The color varies from black to greenish black, brown, and sometimes light green, with a greenish gray streak. It is a translucent to transparent mineral, with a vitreous to greasy luster.
• **FORMATION** Forms in coarse-grained intermediate igneous rocks. Gadolinite also occurs in acid igneous rocks and in pegmatites formed by the slow cooling of intruded magma. This mineral can occur with other minerals, including allanite and fluorite, and has been discovered in schists, and other regionally metamorphosed rocks.
• **TESTS** Gadolinite is a radioactive mineral, which dissolves in acids, leaving a gelatinous precipitate. Although gadolinite is not fusible when heated, it will, however, become flaky and turn brown in color.

greasy luster

massive habit

prismatic crystal

MONOCLINIC

SG 4.0–4.65	Cleavage None	Fracture Conchoidal

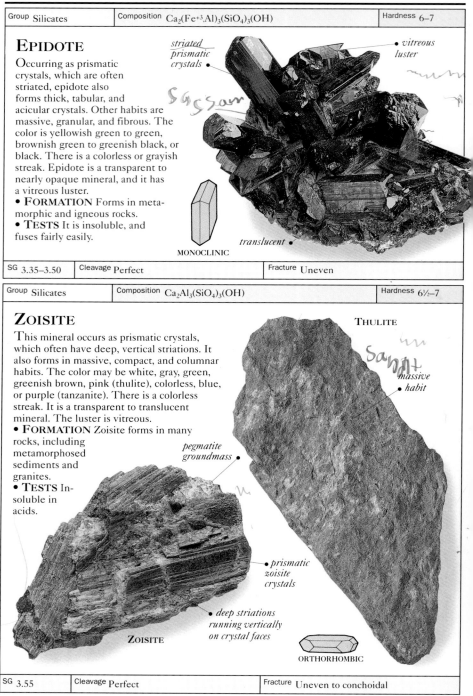

Group Silicates	Composition $Ca_2(Fe^{+3},Al)_3(SiO_4)_3(OH)$	Hardness 6–7

EPIDOTE

Occurring as prismatic crystals, which are often striated, epidote also forms thick, tabular, and acicular crystals. Other habits are massive, granular, and fibrous. The color is yellowish green to green, brownish green to greenish black, or black. There is a colorless or grayish streak. Epidote is a transparent to nearly opaque mineral, and it has a vitreous luster.
• **FORMATION** Forms in metamorphic and igneous rocks.
• **TESTS** It is insoluble, and fuses fairly easily.

striated prismatic crystals

vitreous luster

MONOCLINIC

translucent

SG 3.35–3.50	Cleavage Perfect	Fracture Uneven

Group Silicates	Composition $Ca_2Al_3(SiO_4)_3(OH)$	Hardness 6½–7

ZOISITE

THULITE

This mineral occurs as prismatic crystals, which often have deep, vertical striations. It also forms in massive, compact, and columnar habits. The color may be white, gray, green, greenish brown, pink (thulite), colorless, blue, or purple (tanzanite). There is a colorless streak. It is a transparent to translucent mineral. The luster is vitreous.
• **FORMATION** Zoisite forms in many rocks, including metamorphosed sediments and granites.
• **TESTS** Insoluble in acids.

massive habit

pegmatite groundmass

prismatic zoisite crystals

deep striations running vertically on crystal faces

ZOISITE

ORTHORHOMBIC

SG 3.55	Cleavage Perfect	Fracture Uneven to conchoidal

Group Silicates	Composition $Ca_2Al_3(SiO_4)_3(OH)$		Hardness $6\frac{1}{2}$

CLINOZOISITE

Crystals are prismatic and often deeply striated. Clinozoisite can also form as acicular crystals and in massive, granular, or fibrous habits. It may be gray, yellow, pale green, pink, or colorless. The streak is colorless or grayish. It is a transparent to translucent mineral and has a vitreous luster.
• **FORMATION** Forms in contact metamorphosed limestones and regionally metamorphosed rocks.
• **TESTS** Insoluble in acids.

mass of radiating acicular crystals

MONOCLINIC

vitreous luster

SG 3.21–3.38	Cleavage Perfect	Fracture Uneven

Group Silicates	Composition $Ca_2Al(Si,Al)O_7$		Hardness 5–6

GEHLENITE

A member of the melilite group, gehlenite occurs as short, prismatic crystals and also in massive and granular habits. It can be grayish green, brown, yellow, or colorless. The streak is undetermined. It is transparent to translucent, with a vitreous to resinous luster.
• **FORMATION** Gehlenite forms in basaltic lavas and contact metamorphosed limestones.
• **TESTS** Soluble in strong acids.

massive habit

short gehlenite prismatic crystals

calcite an associated mineral

uneven fracture   TETRAGONAL

SG 3.04	Cleavage Distinct	Fracture Uneven to conchoidal

Group Silicates	Composition $Ca_2MgSi_2O_7$		Hardness 5–6

AKERMANITE

This mineral forms prismatic crystals, which may be twinned. It can occur in massive and granular habits. It varies from colorless to grayish, brown, and green. It is transparent to translucent, with a vitreous to resinous luster.
• **FORMATION** Forms in thermally metamorphosed impure limestones.
• **TESTS** It is soluble in strong acids with gelatization.

prismatic crystal

TETRAGONAL

SG 2.94	Cleavage Distinct	Fracture Uneven to conchoidal

Group Silicates	Composition $Zn_4Si_2O_7(OH)_2.H_2O$	Hardness $4\frac{1}{2}$–5

HEMIMORPHITE

This mineral forms as thin tabular crystals with vertical striations. The crystals have different terminations at each end, which are termed hemimorphic. Hemimorphite also occurs in massive, compact, granular, botryoidal, stalactitic, fibrous, and encrusting habits. The color is white, colorless, blue, greenish, gray, yellowish or brown, and the streak is colorless. It is transparent to translucent, with a vitreous or silky luster.

• **FORMATION** Forms where zinc veins have been altered by oxidation. It commonly occurs in mineral veins along with many other minerals, including smithsonite, galena, calcite, anglesite, sphalerite, cerussite, and aurichalcite.

• **TESTS** It gives off water when heated in a closed tube. It is soluble in acids with gelatinization, and fuses only with great difficulty.

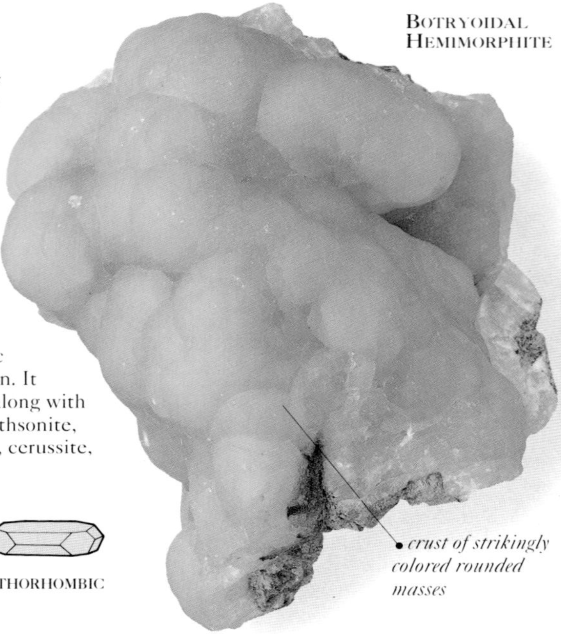

ORTHORHOMBIC

BOTRYOIDAL
HEMIMORPHITE

crust of strikingly
colored rounded
masses

rock
ground-
mass

clusters of
crystals

translucent
crystals

GREEN
HEMIMORPHITE

vitreous
luster

CRYSTALLINE
HEMIMORPHITE

rounded
masses

SG 3.4–3.5	Cleavage Perfect	Fracture Uneven to conchoidal

Group Silicates	Composition $Ca_{10}Mg_2Al_4(SiO_4)_5(Si_2O_7)_2(OH)_4$	Hardness 6–7

VESUVIANITE

Also known as idocrase, this mineral forms short prismatic and pyramidal crystals. It can occur in massive, granular, columnar, and compact habits. Idocrase is green, brown, white, yellow, red, or purple. A blue variety is called cyprine, and californite is white or yellow. It is transparent to translucent and the luster is vitreous to resinous. A semiprecious gemstone when transparent, vesuvianite was discovered at Mount Vesuvius, Italy.

• **FORMATION** This mineral forms in impure limestones that have been altered by contact metamorphism. It also occurs in some igneous rocks, including nepheline syenite. Vesuvianite is found with many minerals, including diopside, epidote, garnets, calcite, phlogopite, and wollastonite.

• **TESTS** This mineral is virtually insoluble in acids.

prismatic crystals

TETRAGONAL

VESUVIANITE

• *vitreous luster on crystal faces*

columnar crystals

• *resinous luster*

• *massive habit*

thulite, an associated mineral

CYPRINE

• *resinous luster*

CALIFORNITE

SG 3.33–3.45	Cleavage Indistinct	Fracture Uneven to conchoidal

Group Silicates	Composition $Be_3Al_2Si_6O_{18}$	Hardness 7–8

BERYL

This mineral occurs as prismatic crystals which are sometimes terminated with small pyramids. The crystals are often striated parallel to their length, and may be of vast size; specimens up to 18 feet (5.5 m) long have been recorded. It also forms in massive, compact, and columnar habits. The color varies greatly and gives rise to named varieties. It may be colorless, white, green (emerald), yellow (heliodor), pink (morganite), red, and blue (aquamarine). The streak is white. Beryl is transparent to translucent, with a vitreous luster.

• **FORMATION** Forms in pegmatites and granites and in some regionally metamorphosed rocks.

• **TESTS** It fuses with difficulty, rounding the edges of small fragments.

transparent

prismatic crystal

rock groundmass

BERYL

rock groundmass

perfect prismatic crystal

transparent

HELIODOR

vitreous luster

EMERALD

transparent to translucent

MORGANITE

vitreous luster

AQUAMARINE

TRIGONAL/ HEXAGONAL

SG 2.6–2.9	Cleavage Indistinct	Fracture Uneven to conchoidal

Group Silicates	Composition $Na(Mg,Fe,Li,Mn,Al)_3Al_6(BO_3)_3Si_6.O_{18}(OH,F)_4$	Hardness 7–7½

TOURMALINE

The prismatic crystals formed by this group are often vertically striated. These crystals may be rounded triangular in cross-section. It also forms in massive and compact habits. Seven distinct species make up the tourmaline group: elbaite (multi-hued), schorl (black), buergerite and dravite (brown), rubellite (pink), chromdravite (green), and uvite (black, brown, yellowy green). Crystals are often pink at one end and green at the other, and may be of considerable size. There is a colorless streak. Tourmaline is transparent to opaque, and has a vitreous luster.

- **FORMATION** Forms in granites and pegmatites, as well as in some metamorphic rocks. Tourmaline may be found with a wide range of minerals, including beryl, zircon, quartz, and feldspar.
- **TESTS** This group is insoluble in acids. The darker minerals tend to fuse with more difficulty than the red and green varieties.

vertically striated crystal

RUBELLITE

ELBAITE

vitreous luster

prismatic crystal

feldspar groundmass

quartz, an associated mineral

transparent bicolored crystal

TOURMALINE

vitreous luster

schorl crystal

SCHORL

TRIGONAL/ HEXAGONAL

SG 3.0–3.2	Cleavage Very indistinct	Fracture Uneven to conchoidal

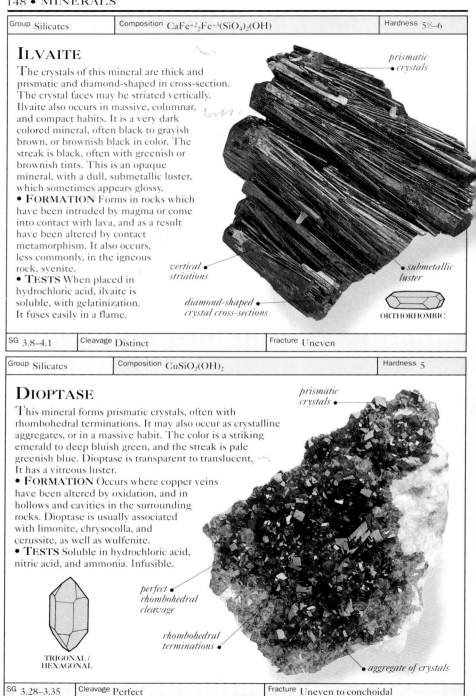

Group Silicates	Composition $CaFe^{+2}_2Fe^{+3}(SiO_4)_2(OH)$	Hardness 5½–6

ILVAITE

The crystals of this mineral are thick and prismatic and diamond-shaped in cross-section. The crystal faces may be striated vertically. Ilvaite also occurs in massive, columnar, and compact habits. It is a very dark colored mineral, often black to grayish brown, or brownish black in color. The streak is black, often with greenish or brownish tints. This is an opaque mineral, with a dull, submetallic luster, which sometimes appears glossy.
• **FORMATION** Forms in rocks which have been intruded by magma or come into contact with lava, and as a result have been altered by contact metamorphism. It also occurs, less commonly, in the igneous rock, syenite.
• **TESTS** When placed in hydrochloric acid, ilvaite is soluble, with gelatinization. It fuses easily in a flame.

prismatic crystals

vertical striations

submetallic luster

diamond-shaped crystal cross-sections

ORTHORHOMBIC

SG 3.8–4.1	Cleavage Distinct		Fracture Uneven

Group Silicates	Composition $CuSiO_2(OH)_2$	Hardness 5

DIOPTASE

This mineral forms prismatic crystals, often with rhombohedral terminations. It may also occur as crystalline aggregates, or in a massive habit. The color is a striking emerald to deep bluish green, and the streak is pale greenish blue. Dioptase is transparent to translucent. It has a vitreous luster.
• **FORMATION** Occurs where copper veins have been altered by oxidation, and in hollows and cavities in the surrounding rocks. Dioptase is usually associated with limonite, chrysocolla, and cerussite, as well as wulfenite.
• **TESTS** Soluble in hydrochloric acid, nitric acid, and ammonia. Infusible.

prismatic crystals

perfect rhombohedral cleavage

rhombohedral terminations

TRIGONAL / HEXAGONAL

aggregate of crystals

SG 3.28–3.35	Cleavage Perfect		Fracture Uneven to conchoidal

Group Silicates	Composition $Mg_2Al_4Si_5O_{18}$	Hardness 7–7½

CORDIERITE

Crystals are short and prismatic, and twinning is common. Other habits are massive and granular. It is blue, but can be greenish, yellowish, gray, or brown, and is often strongly pleochroic. The streak is colorless. Cordierite is transparent to translucent, with a vitreous luster.
• **FORMATION** Cordierite forms in igneous and contact metamorphic rocks.
• **TESTS** Fusible on thin edges in flames.

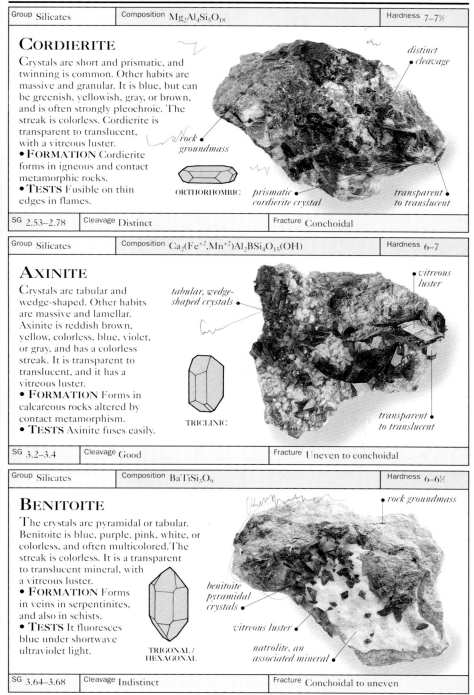

distinct cleavage

rock groundmass

ORTHORHOMBIC

prismatic cordierite crystal

transparent to translucent

SG 2.53–2.78	Cleavage Distinct	Fracture Conchoidal

Group Silicates	Composition $Ca_2(Fe^{+2},Mn^{+2})Al_2BSi_4O_{15}(OH)$	Hardness 6–7

AXINITE

Crystals are tabular and wedge-shaped. Other habits are massive and lamellar. Axinite is reddish brown, yellow, colorless, blue, violet, or gray, and has a colorless streak. It is transparent to translucent, and it has a vitreous luster.
• **FORMATION** Forms in calcareous rocks altered by contact metamorphism.
• **TESTS** Axinite fuses easily.

tabular, wedge-shaped crystals

vitreous luster

TRICLINIC

transparent to translucent

SG 3.2–3.4	Cleavage Good	Fracture Uneven to conchoidal

Group Silicates	Composition $BaTiSi_3O_9$	Hardness 6–6½

BENITOITE

The crystals are pyramidal or tabular. Benitoite is blue, purple, pink, white, or colorless, and often multicolored. The streak is colorless. It is a transparent to translucent mineral, with a vitreous luster.
• **FORMATION** Forms in veins in serpentinites, and also in schists.
• **TESTS** It fluoresces blue under shortwave ultraviolet light.

rock groundmass

benitoite pyramidal crystals

vitreous luster

TRIGONAL / HEXAGONAL

natrolite, an associated mineral

SG 3.64–3.68	Cleavage Indistinct	Fracture Conchoidal to uneven

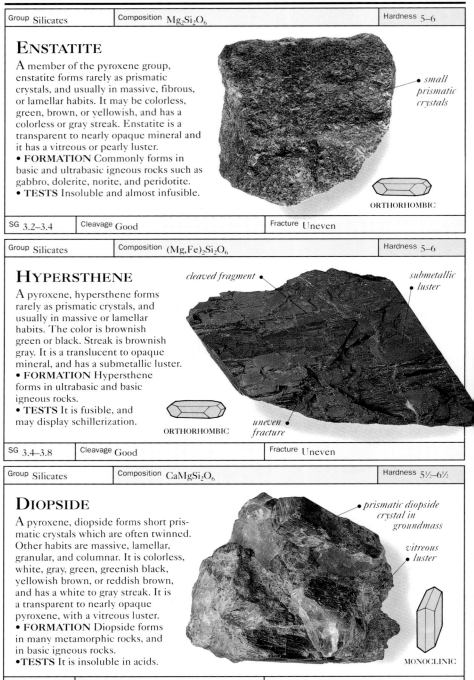

Group Silicates	Composition $Mg_2Si_2O_6$		Hardness 5–6

ENSTATITE

A member of the pyroxene group, enstatite forms rarely as prismatic crystals, and usually in massive, fibrous, or lamellar habits. It may be colorless, green, brown, or yellowish, and has a colorless or gray streak. Enstatite is a transparent to nearly opaque mineral and it has a vitreous or pearly luster.
• FORMATION Commonly forms in basic and ultrabasic igneous rocks such as gabbro, dolerite, norite, and peridotite.
• TESTS Insoluble and almost infusible.

small prismatic crystals

ORTHORHOMBIC

SG 3.2–3.4	Cleavage Good	Fracture Uneven

Group Silicates	Composition $(Mg,Fe)_2Si_2O_6$		Hardness 5–6

HYPERSTHENE

A pyroxene, hypersthene forms rarely as prismatic crystals, and usually in massive or lamellar habits. The color is brownish green or black. Streak is brownish gray. It is a translucent to opaque mineral, and has a submetallic luster.
• FORMATION Hypersthene forms in ultrabasic and basic igneous rocks.
• TESTS It is fusible, and may display schillerization.

cleaved fragment

submetallic luster

ORTHORHOMBIC

uneven fracture

SG 3.4–3.8	Cleavage Good	Fracture Uneven

Group Silicates	Composition $CaMgSi_2O_6$		Hardness 5½–6½

DIOPSIDE

A pyroxene, diopside forms short prismatic crystals which are often twinned. Other habits are massive, lamellar, granular, and columnar. It is colorless, white, gray, green, greenish black, yellowish brown, or reddish brown, and has a white to gray streak. It is a transparent to nearly opaque pyroxene, with a vitreous luster.
• FORMATION Diopside forms in many metamorphic rocks, and in basic igneous rocks.
•TESTS It is insoluble in acids.

prismatic diopside crystal in groundmass

vitreous luster

MONOCLINIC

SG 3.22–3.38	Cleavage Good	Fracture Uneven

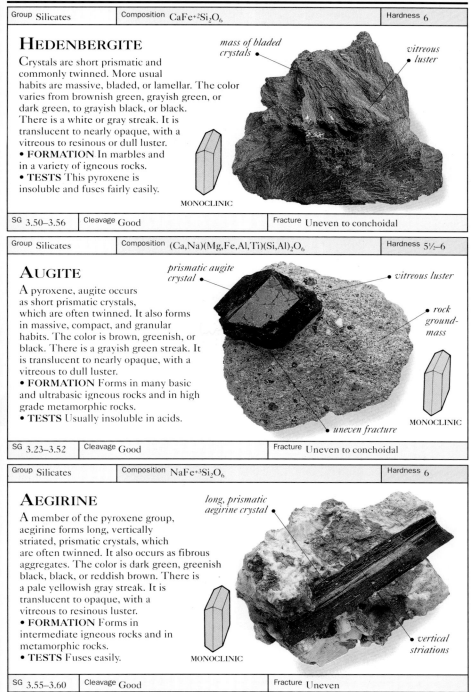

Group Silicates	Composition $CaFe^{+2}Si_2O_6$		Hardness 6

HEDENBERGITE

Crystals are short prismatic and commonly twinned. More usual habits are massive, bladed, or lamellar. The color varies from brownish green, grayish green, or dark green, to grayish black, or black. There is a white or gray streak. It is translucent to nearly opaque, with a vitreous to resinous or dull luster.
• FORMATION In marbles and in a variety of igneous rocks.
• TESTS This pyroxene is insoluble and fuses fairly easily.

mass of bladed crystals

vitreous luster

MONOCLINIC

SG 3.50–3.56	Cleavage Good	Fracture Uneven to conchoidal

Group Silicates	Composition $(Ca,Na)(Mg,Fe,Al,Ti)(Si,Al)_2O_6$		Hardness 5½–6

AUGITE

A pyroxene, augite occurs as short prismatic crystals, which are often twinned. It also forms in massive, compact, and granular habits. The color is brown, greenish, or black. There is a grayish green streak. It is translucent to nearly opaque, with a vitreous to dull luster.
• FORMATION Forms in many basic and ultrabasic igneous rocks and in high grade metamorphic rocks.
• TESTS Usually insoluble in acids.

prismatic augite crystal

vitreous luster

rock ground-mass

uneven fracture

MONOCLINIC

SG 3.23–3.52	Cleavage Good	Fracture Uneven to conchoidal

Group Silicates	Composition $NaFe^{+3}Si_2O_6$		Hardness 6

AEGIRINE

A member of the pyroxene group, aegirine forms long, vertically striated, prismatic crystals, which are often twinned. It also occurs as fibrous aggregates. The color is dark green, greenish black, black, or reddish brown. There is a pale yellowish gray streak. It is translucent to opaque, with a vitreous to resinous luster.
• FORMATION Forms in intermediate igneous rocks and in metamorphic rocks.
• TESTS Fuses easily.

long, prismatic aegirine crystal

vertical striations

MONOCLINIC

SG 3.55–3.60	Cleavage Good	Fracture Uneven

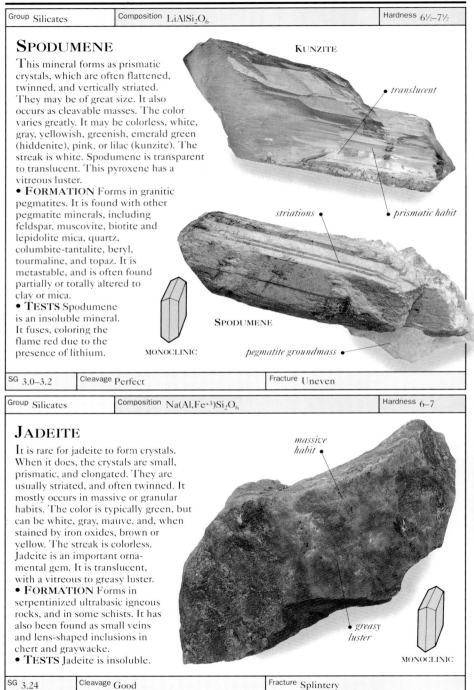

Group Silicates	Composition $LiAlSi_2O_6$	Hardness $6\frac{1}{2}$–$7\frac{1}{2}$

SPODUMENE

This mineral forms as prismatic crystals, which are often flattened, twinned, and vertically striated. They may be of great size. It also occurs as cleavable masses. The color varies greatly. It may be colorless, white, gray, yellowish, greenish, emerald green (hiddenite), pink, or lilac (kunzite). The streak is white. Spodumene is transparent to translucent. This pyroxene has a vitreous luster.

• **FORMATION** Forms in granitic pegmatites. It is found with other pegmatite minerals, including feldspar, muscovite, biotite and lepidolite mica, quartz, columbite-tantalite, beryl, tourmaline, and topaz. It is metastable, and is often found partially or totally altered to clay or mica.

• **TESTS** Spodumene is an insoluble mineral. It fuses, coloring the flame red due to the presence of lithium.

KUNZITE

• *translucent*

striations •

• *prismatic habit*

SPODUMENE

MONOCLINIC

pegmatite groundmass •

SG 3.0–3.2	Cleavage Perfect	Fracture Uneven

Group Silicates	Composition $Na(Al,Fe^{+3})Si_2O_6$	Hardness 6–7

JADEITE

It is rare for jadeite to form crystals. When it does, the crystals are small, prismatic, and elongated. They are usually striated, and often twinned. It mostly occurs in massive or granular habits. The color is typically green, but can be white, gray, mauve, and, when stained by iron oxides, brown or yellow. The streak is colorless. Jadeite is an important ornamental gem. It is translucent, with a vitreous to greasy luster.

• **FORMATION** Forms in serpentinized ultrabasic igneous rocks, and in some schists. It has also been found as small veins and lens-shaped inclusions in chert and graywacke.

• **TESTS** Jadeite is insoluble.

massive habit •

• *greasy luster*

MONOCLINIC

SG 3.24	Cleavage Good	Fracture Splintery

Group Silicates	Composition $Ca_2(Mg,Fe)_4Al(Si_7Al)O_{22}(OH,F)_2$	Hardness 5–6

HORNBLENDE

This amphibole group forms prismatic crystals, often hexagonal in cross-section, and frequently twinned. It also occurs in massive, compact, granular, columnar, bladed, and fibrous habits. It is green, greenish brown, or black. The streak is white or gray. It is translucent to opaque. The luster is vitreous. There is an angle of 60° or 120° between cleavage planes.
• **FORMATION** In igneous rocks, and also found in the metamorphic rock, amphibolite.
• **TESTS** Insoluble. Fuses with difficulty.

• *prismatic hornblende crystals*

• *twinned crystals*

MONOCLINIC

SG 3.28–3.41	Cleavage Perfect	Fracture Uneven

Group Silicates	Composition $(Mg,Fe^{+2})_7Si_8O_{22}(OH)_2$	Hardness 5½–6

ANTHOPHYLLITE

This amphibole forms prismatic crystals, but it is rare for it to do so. It occurs in massive, fibrous, or lamellar habits. The color is white to gray, greenish, brownish green, and brown. There is a colorless or gray streak. This mineral is transparent to almost opaque. It has a vitreous luster.
•**FORMATION** Forms in crystalline schists and gneisses.
• **TESTS** Insoluble, but fuses with difficulty.

• *mass of fibrous, radiating crystals*

• *vitreous luster*

ORTHORHOMBIC

• *radiating aggregate*

SG 2.85–3.57	Cleavage Perfect	Fracture Uneven

Group Silicates	Composition $(Fe^{+2},Mg)_7Si_8O_{22}(OH)_2$	Hardness 5–6

GRUNERITE

An end member of the cummingtonite–grunerite amphibole series, grunerite forms as fibrous or lamellar crystals, which are often in radiating aggregates. They are very commonly twinned. It is gray, dark green, or brown. Grunerite is translucent to nearly opaque, and has a silky luster.
• **FORMATION** In rocks which have undergone contact metamorphism.
• **TESTS** It is insoluble.

• *opaque*

• *fibrous habit*

silky luster

MONOCLINIC

SG 3.44–3.60	Cleavage Good	Fracture Uneven

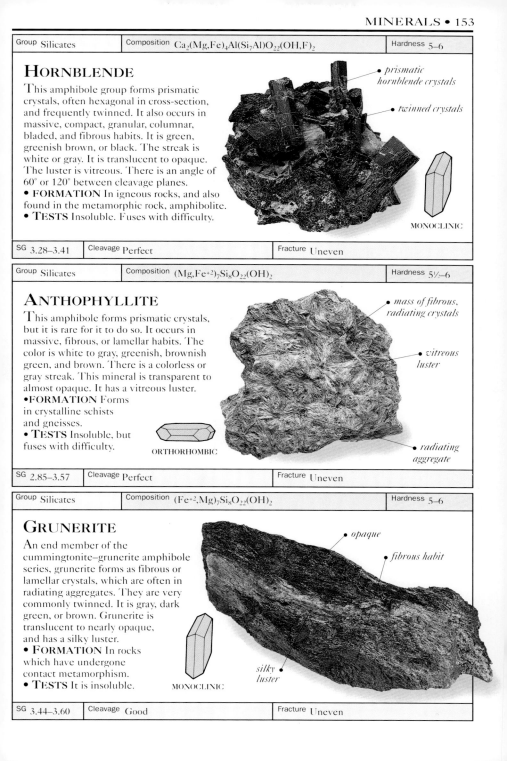

Group Silicates	Composition $Na_2(Mg,Fe^{+2})_3Al_2Si_8O_{22}(OH)_2$	Hardness 6

GLAUCOPHANE

A member of the amphibole group, it forms as slender, prismatic crystals. Other habits are massive, fibrous, and granular. It is gray, blue, bluish black, or lavender-blue. The streak is a grayish blue. Glaucophane is a translucent mineral, and has a vitreous to dull or pearly luster.
• **FORMATION** Forms in metamorphic rocks, chiefly those subjected to low temperature and high pressure conditions.
• **TESTS** It is insoluble in acids, and fuses readily to a green-colored glass.

prismatic glaucophane crystals with chlorite

pearly luster

MONOCLINIC

SG 3.08–3.15	Cleavage Perfect	Fracture Uneven to conchoidal

Group Silicates	Composition $Na_2(Fe^{+2},Mg,Fe^{+3})_5Si_8O_{22}(OH)_2$	Hardness 5

RIEBECKITE

Long, prismatic crystals with parallel striations occur in this mineral. It may also be massive, fibrous, and asbestiform (crocidolite). The color is dark blue to black. No streak has been determined. Riebeckite is translucent, and it has a vitreous or silky luster.
• **FORMATION** Forms in many igneous rocks, and in schists.
• **TESTS** Fuses easily.

group of prismatic crystals

vitreous luster

MONOCLINIC

SG 3.32–3.38	Cleavage Perfect	Fracture Uneven

Group Silicates	Composition $Ca_2(Mg,Fe^{+2})_5Si_8O_{22}(OH)_2$	Hardness 5–6

ACTINOLITE

The crystals form as long, bladed specimens, commonly twinned. Actinolite may be in lamellar and columnar aggregates, often radiating, and in massive, fibrous, or granular habits. The color is light to blackish green. The streak is white. Actinolite is transparent to nearly opaque and has a vitreous luster. A compact variety is called nephrite, a form of jade.
• **FORMATION** Forms in schists and amphibolites, commonly from the metamorphism of basic igneous rocks.
• **TESTS** Insoluble in hydrochloric acid.

prismatic crystals

vitreous luster

talc groundmass

thin prisms

MONOCLINIC

SG 3.0–3.44	Cleavage Good	Fracture Uneven to subconchoidal

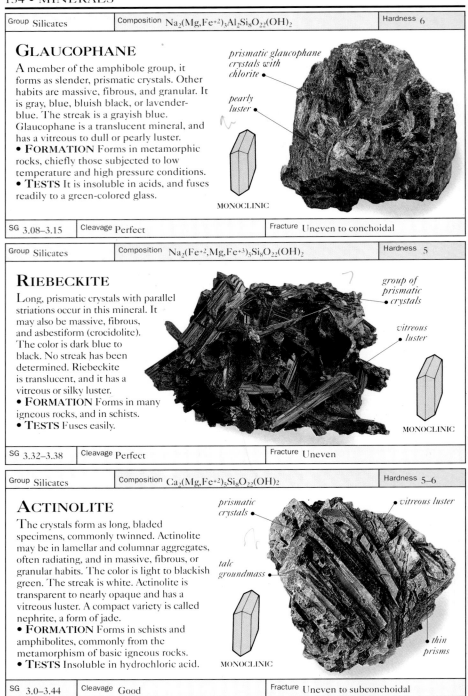

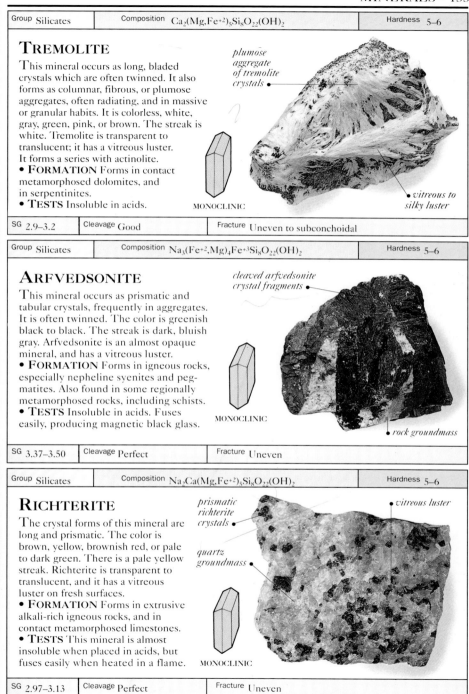

Group Silicates	Composition $Ca_2(Mg,Fe^{+2})_5Si_8O_{22}(OH)_2$	Hardness 5–6

TREMOLITE

This mineral occurs as long, bladed crystals which are often twinned. It also forms as columnar, fibrous, or plumose aggregates, often radiating, and in massive or granular habits. It is colorless, white, gray, green, pink, or brown. The streak is white. Tremolite is transparent to translucent; it has a vitreous luster. It forms a series with actinolite.
• **FORMATION** Forms in contact metamorphosed dolomites, and in serpentinites.
• **TESTS** Insoluble in acids.

plumose aggregate of tremolite crystals •

MONOCLINIC

• vitreous to silky luster

SG 2.9–3.2	Cleavage Good	Fracture Uneven to subconchoidal

Group Silicates	Composition $Na_3(Fe^{+2},Mg)_4Fe^{+3}Si_8O_{22}(OH)_2$	Hardness 5–6

ARFVEDSONITE

This mineral occurs as prismatic and tabular crystals, frequently in aggregates. It is often twinned. The color is greenish black to black. The streak is dark, bluish gray. Arfvedsonite is an almost opaque mineral, and has a vitreous luster.
• **FORMATION** Forms in igneous rocks, especially nepheline syenites and pegmatites. Also found in some regionally metamorphosed rocks, including schists.
• **TESTS** Insoluble in acids. Fuses easily, producing magnetic black glass.

cleaved arfvedsonite crystal fragments •

MONOCLINIC

• rock groundmass

SG 3.37–3.50	Cleavage Perfect	Fracture Uneven

Group Silicates	Composition $Na_2Ca(Mg,Fe^{+2})_5Si_8O_{22}(OH)_2$	Hardness 5–6

RICHTERITE

The crystal forms of this mineral are long and prismatic. The color is brown, yellow, brownish red, or pale to dark green. There is a pale yellow streak. Richterite is transparent to translucent, and it has a vitreous luster on fresh surfaces.
• **FORMATION** Forms in extrusive alkali-rich igneous rocks, and in contact metamorphosed limestones.
• **TESTS** This mineral is almost insoluble when placed in acids, but fuses easily when heated in a flame.

prismatic richterite crystals •

• vitreous luster

quartz groundmass •

MONOCLINIC

SG 2.97–3.13	Cleavage Perfect	Fracture Uneven

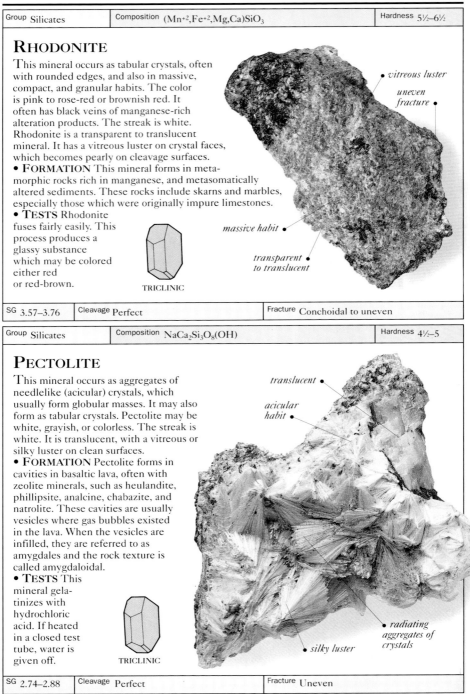

Group Silicates	Composition $(Mn^{+2},Fe^{+2},Mg,Ca)SiO_3$	Hardness 5½–6½

RHODONITE

This mineral occurs as tabular crystals, often with rounded edges, and also in massive, compact, and granular habits. The color is pink to rose-red or brownish red. It often has black veins of manganese-rich alteration products. The streak is white. Rhodonite is a transparent to translucent mineral. It has a vitreous luster on crystal faces, which becomes pearly on cleavage surfaces.
• **FORMATION** This mineral forms in metamorphic rocks rich in manganese, and metasomatically altered sediments. These rocks include skarns and marbles, especially those which were originally impure limestones.
• **TESTS** Rhodonite fuses fairly easily. This process produces a glassy substance which may be colored either red or red-brown.

vitreous luster

uneven fracture

massive habit

transparent to translucent

TRICLINIC

SG 3.57–3.76	Cleavage Perfect	Fracture Conchoidal to uneven

Group Silicates	Composition $NaCa_2Si_3O_8(OH)$	Hardness 4½–5

PECTOLITE

This mineral occurs as aggregates of needlelike (acicular) crystals, which usually form globular masses. It may also form as tabular crystals. Pectolite may be white, grayish, or colorless. The streak is white. It is translucent, with a vitreous or silky luster on clean surfaces.
• **FORMATION** Pectolite forms in cavities in basaltic lava, often with zeolite minerals, such as heulandite, phillipsite, analcine, chabazite, and natrolite. These cavities are usually vesicles where gas bubbles existed in the lava. When the vesicles are infilled, they are referred to as amygdales and the rock texture is called amygdaloidal.
• **TESTS** This mineral gelatinizes with hydrochloric acid. If heated in a closed test tube, water is given off.

translucent

acicular habit

radiating aggregates of crystals

silky luster

TRICLINIC

SG 2.74–2.88	Cleavage Perfect	Fracture Uneven

Group Silicates	Composition $CaSiO_3$	Hardness $4\frac{1}{2}$–5

WOLLASTONITE

Crystals are tabular, and frequently twinned. Wollastonite also forms in massive, fibrous, granular, and compact habits. The color is white to grayish, and sometimes very pale green, or colorless. There is a white streak. This is a transparent to translucent mineral, and it has a vitreous to pearly luster on fresh faces.

• **FORMATION** Forms by the metamorphism of impure limestones. When this occurs, wollastonite may be associated with brucite and epidote. These minerals often produce the brightly colored veins in marble. Wollastonite also occurs in some igneous rocks, and in regionally metamorphosed slates, phyllites, and schists.

• **TESTS** It is soluble in acids, producing a separation of the silica in its composition. This mineral also fuses fairly easily.

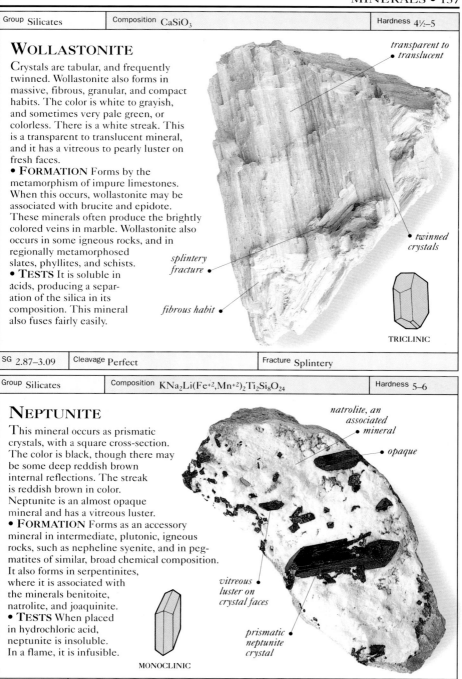

transparent to translucent

twinned crystals

splintery fracture

fibrous habit

TRICLINIC

SG 2.87–3.09	Cleavage Perfect		Fracture Splintery

Group Silicates	Composition $KNa_2Li(Fe^{+2},Mn^{+2})_2Ti_2Si_8O_{24}$	Hardness 5–6

NEPTUNITE

This mineral occurs as prismatic crystals, with a square cross-section. The color is black, though there may be some deep reddish brown internal reflections. The streak is reddish brown in color. Neptunite is an almost opaque mineral and has a vitreous luster.

• **FORMATION** Forms as an accessory mineral in intermediate, plutonic, igneous rocks, such as nepheline syenite, and in pegmatites of similar, broad chemical composition. It also forms in serpentinites, where it is associated with the minerals benitoite, natrolite, and joaquinite.

• **TESTS** When placed in hydrochloric acid, neptunite is insoluble. In a flame, it is infusible.

natrolite, an associated mineral

opaque

vitreous luster on crystal faces

prismatic neptunite crystal

MONOCLINIC

SG 3.19–3.23	Cleavage Perfect		Fracture Conchoidal

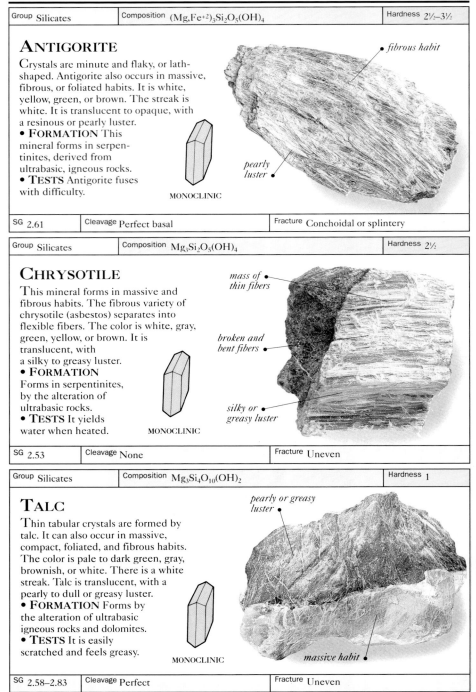

Group Silicates	Composition $(Mg,Fe^{+2})_3Si_2O_5(OH)_4$		Hardness $2\frac{1}{2}$–$3\frac{1}{2}$

ANTIGORITE

Crystals are minute and flaky, or lath-shaped. Antigorite also occurs in massive, fibrous, or foliated habits. It is white, yellow, green, or brown. The streak is white. It is translucent to opaque, with a resinous or pearly luster.
• **FORMATION** This mineral forms in serpentinites, derived from ultrabasic, igneous rocks.
• **TESTS** Antigorite fuses with difficulty.

fibrous habit

pearly luster

MONOCLINIC

SG 2.61	Cleavage Perfect basal	Fracture Conchoidal or splintery

Group Silicates	Composition $Mg_3Si_2O_5(OH)_4$	Hardness $2\frac{1}{2}$

CHRYSOTILE

This mineral forms in massive and fibrous habits. The fibrous variety of chrysotile (asbestos) separates into flexible fibers. The color is white, gray, green, yellow, or brown. It is translucent, with a silky to greasy luster.
• **FORMATION** Forms in serpentinites, by the alteration of ultrabasic rocks.
• **TESTS** It yields water when heated.

mass of thin fibers

broken and bent fibers

silky or greasy luster

MONOCLINIC

SG 2.53	Cleavage None	Fracture Uneven

Group Silicates	Composition $Mg_3Si_4O_{10}(OH)_2$	Hardness 1

TALC

Thin tabular crystals are formed by talc. It can also occur in massive, compact, foliated, and fibrous habits. The color is pale to dark green, gray, brownish, or white. There is a white streak. Talc is translucent, with a pearly to dull or greasy luster.
• **FORMATION** Forms by the alteration of ultrabasic igneous rocks and dolomites.
• **TESTS** It is easily scratched and feels greasy.

pearly or greasy luster

massive habit

MONOCLINIC

SG 2.58–2.83	Cleavage Perfect	Fracture Uneven

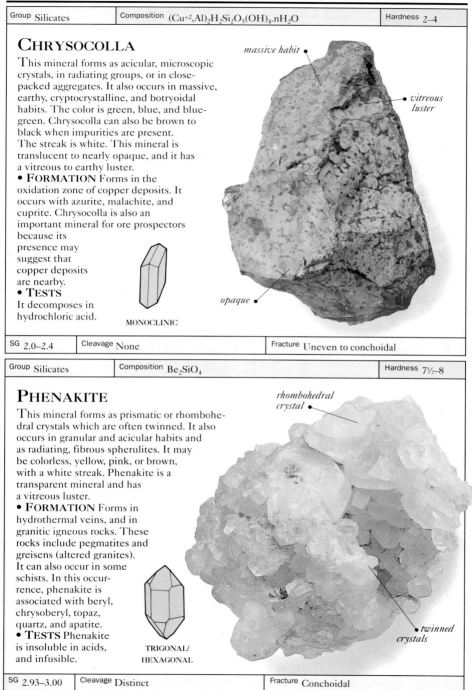

| Group Silicates | Composition $(Cu^{+2},Al)_2H_2Si_2O_5(OH)_4 \cdot nH_2O$ | | Hardness 2–4 |

CHRYSOCOLLA

This mineral forms as acicular, microscopic crystals, in radiating groups, or in close-packed aggregates. It also occurs in massive, earthy, cryptocrystalline, and botryoidal habits. The color is green, blue, and blue-green. Chrysocolla can also be brown to black when impurities are present. The streak is white. This mineral is translucent to nearly opaque, and it has a vitreous to earthy luster.
• **FORMATION** Forms in the oxidation zone of copper deposits. It occurs with azurite, malachite, and cuprite. Chrysocolla is also an important mineral for ore prospectors because its presence may suggest that copper deposits are nearby.
• **TESTS** It decomposes in hydrochloric acid.

massive habit

vitreous luster

opaque

MONOCLINIC

| SG 2.0–2.4 | Cleavage None | | Fracture Uneven to conchoidal |

| Group Silicates | Composition Be_2SiO_4 | | Hardness 7½–8 |

PHENAKITE

This mineral forms as prismatic or rhombohe-dral crystals which are often twinned. It also occurs in granular and acicular habits and as radiating, fibrous spherulites. It may be colorless, yellow, pink, or brown, with a white streak. Phenakite is a transparent mineral and has a vitreous luster.
• **FORMATION** Forms in hydrothermal veins, and in granitic igneous rocks. These rocks include pegmatites and greisens (altered granites). It can also occur in some schists. In this occur-rence, phenakite is associated with beryl, chrysoberyl, topaz, quartz, and apatite.
• **TESTS** Phenakite is insoluble in acids, and infusible.

rhombohedral crystal

TRIGONAL/ HEXAGONAL

twinned crystals

| SG 2.93–3.00 | Cleavage Distinct | | Fracture Conchoidal |

Group Silicates	Composition $KAl_2(Si_3Al)O_{10}(OH,F)_2$	Hardness $2\frac{1}{2}–4$

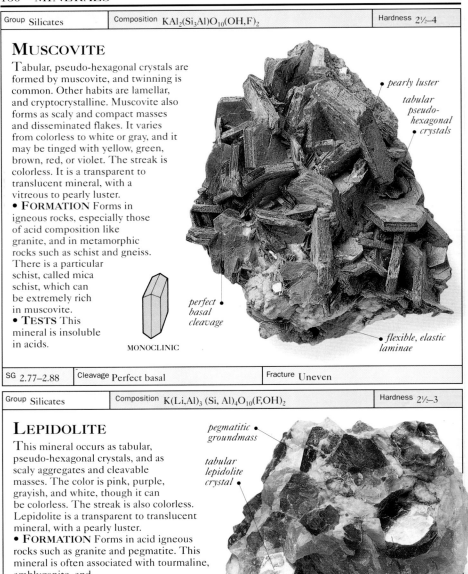

MUSCOVITE

Tabular, pseudo-hexagonal crystals are formed by muscovite, and twinning is common. Other habits are lamellar, and cryptocrystalline. Muscovite also forms as scaly and compact masses and disseminated flakes. It varies from colorless to white or gray, and it may be tinged with yellow, green, brown, red, or violet. The streak is colorless. It is a transparent to translucent mineral, with a vitreous to pearly luster.

• **FORMATION** Forms in igneous rocks, especially those of acid composition like granite, and in metamorphic rocks such as schist and gneiss. There is a particular schist, called mica schist, which can be extremely rich in muscovite.

• **TESTS** This mineral is insoluble in acids.

MONOCLINIC

pearly luster

tabular pseudo-hexagonal crystals

perfect basal cleavage

flexible, elastic laminae

SG 2.77–2.88	Cleavage Perfect basal	Fracture Uneven

Group Silicates	Composition $K(Li,Al)_3(Si, Al)_4O_{10}(F,OH)_2$	Hardness $2\frac{1}{2}–3$

LEPIDOLITE

This mineral occurs as tabular, pseudo-hexagonal crystals, and as scaly aggregates and cleavable masses. The color is pink, purple, grayish, and white, though it can be colorless. The streak is also colorless. Lepidolite is a transparent to translucent mineral, with a pearly luster.

• **FORMATION** Forms in acid igneous rocks such as granite and pegmatite. This mineral is often associated with tourmaline, amblygonite, and spodumene. Lepidolite can be found in mineral veins that are rich in tin.

• **TESTS** It colors a flame red and is insoluble in acids.

MONOCLINIC

pegmatitic groundmass

tabular lepidolite crystal

vitreous luster

SG 2.8–3.3	Cleavage Perfect basal	Fracture Uneven

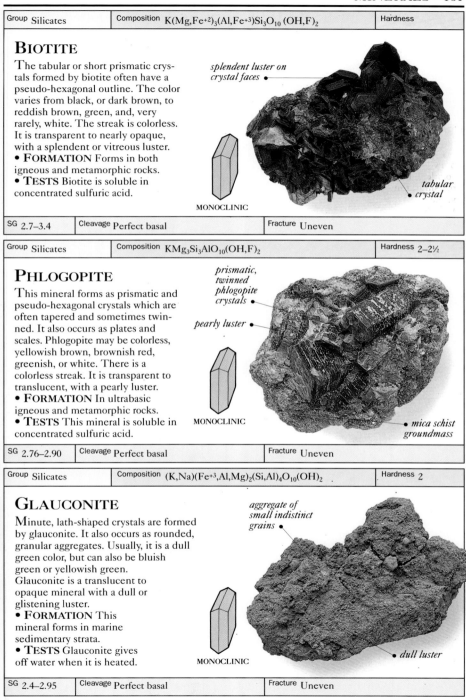

Group Silicates	Composition $K(Mg,Fe^{+2})_3(Al,Fe^{+3})Si_3O_{10}(OH,F)_2$	Hardness

BIOTITE

The tabular or short prismatic crystals formed by biotite often have a pseudo-hexagonal outline. The color varies from black, or dark brown, to reddish brown, green, and, very rarely, white. The streak is colorless. It is transparent to nearly opaque, with a splendent or vitreous luster.
• **FORMATION** Forms in both igneous and metamorphic rocks.
• **TESTS** Biotite is soluble in concentrated sulfuric acid.

splendent luster on crystal faces •

tabular crystal

MONOCLINIC

SG 2.7–3.4	Cleavage Perfect basal	Fracture Uneven

Group Silicates	Composition $KMg_3Si_3AlO_{10}(OH,F)_2$	Hardness 2–2½

PHLOGOPITE

This mineral forms as prismatic and pseudo-hexagonal crystals which are often tapered and sometimes twinned. It also occurs as plates and scales. Phlogopite may be colorless, yellowish brown, brownish red, greenish, or white. There is a colorless streak. It is transparent to translucent, with a pearly luster.
• **FORMATION** In ultrabasic igneous and metamorphic rocks.
• **TESTS** This mineral is soluble in concentrated sulfuric acid.

prismatic, twinned phlogopite crystals •

pearly luster •

MONOCLINIC

mica schist groundmass

SG 2.76–2.90	Cleavage Perfect basal	Fracture Uneven

Group Silicates	Composition $(K,Na)(Fe^{+3},Al,Mg)_2(Si,Al)_4O_{10}(OH)_2$	Hardness 2

GLAUCONITE

Minute, lath-shaped crystals are formed by glauconite. It also occurs as rounded, granular aggregates. Usually, it is a dull green color, but can also be bluish green or yellowish green. Glauconite is a translucent to opaque mineral with a dull or glistening luster.
• **FORMATION** This mineral forms in marine sedimentary strata.
• **TESTS** Glauconite gives off water when it is heated.

aggregate of small indistinct grains •

MONOCLINIC

dull luster

SG 2.4–2.95	Cleavage Perfect basal	Fracture Uneven

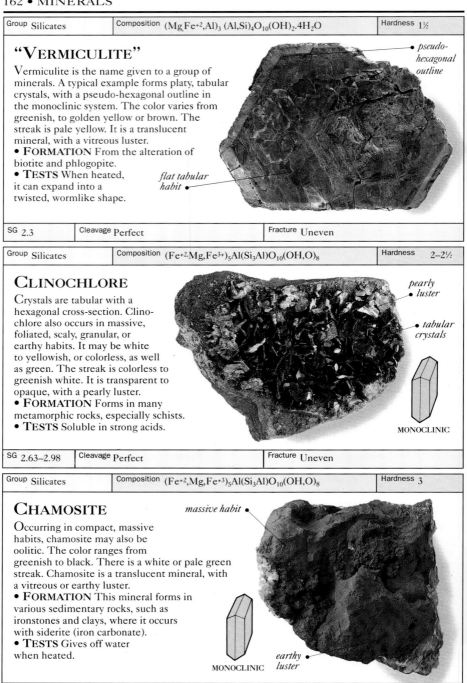

Group Silicates	Composition $(Mg,Fe^{+2},Al)_3 (Al,Si)_4O_{10}(OH)_2.4H_2O$	Hardness 1½

"VERMICULITE"

Vermiculite is the name given to a group of
minerals. A typical example forms platy, tabular
crystals, with a pseudo-hexagonal outline in
the monoclinic system. The color varies from
greenish, to golden yellow or brown. The
streak is pale yellow. It is a translucent
mineral, with a vitreous luster.
• **FORMATION** From the alteration of
biotite and phlogopite.
• **TESTS** When heated,
it can expand into a
twisted, wormlike shape.

pseudo-hexagonal outline

flat tabular habit

SG 2.3	Cleavage Perfect	Fracture Uneven

Group Silicates	Composition $(Fe^{+2},Mg,Fe^{3+})_5Al(Si_3Al)O_{10}(OH,O)_8$	Hardness 2–2½

CLINOCHLORE

Crystals are tabular with a
hexagonal cross-section. Clino-
chlore also occurs in massive,
foliated, scaly, granular, or
earthy habits. It may be white
to yellowish, or colorless, as well
as green. The streak is colorless to
greenish white. It is transparent to
opaque, with a pearly luster.
• **FORMATION** Forms in many
metamorphic rocks, especially schists.
• **TESTS** Soluble in strong acids.

pearly luster

tabular crystals

MONOCLINIC

SG 2.63–2.98	Cleavage Perfect	Fracture Uneven

Group Silicates	Composition $(Fe^{+2},Mg,Fe^{+3})_5Al(Si_3Al)O_{10}(OH,O)_8$	Hardness 3

CHAMOSITE

massive habit

Occurring in compact, massive
habits, chamosite may also be
oolitic. The color ranges from
greenish to black. There is a white or pale green
streak. Chamosite is a translucent mineral, with
a vitreous or earthy luster.
• **FORMATION** This mineral forms in
various sedimentary rocks, such as
ironstones and clays, where it occurs
with siderite (iron carbonate).
• **TESTS** Gives off water
when heated.

MONOCLINIC

earthy luster

SG 3–3.4	Cleavage Not determined	Fracture Uneven

Group Silicates	Composition $Al_2Si_2O_5(OH)_4$	Hardness $2-2\frac{1}{2}$

KAOLINITE

This group of minerals, which includes kaolinite, nacrite, and halloysite, forms very small pseudo-hexagonal platelets or scales. It may also occur in massive, compact habits, and in earthy or clayey masses. Kaolinite varies from white and colorless, to yellowish, brownish, reddish, or bluish. There is a white streak. The kaolinite group is transparent to translucent, with a pearly to dull or earthy luster.

• **FORMATION** Forms by the alteration of feldspars and other aluminum-rich silicate minerals. This can be brought about by weathering, especially in humid regions, or, on a much larger scale, by hydrothermal fluids rising from depth through rocks. When this occurs, granite is reduced to an unconsolidated mass of quartz and mica sand, with white, kaolinite clay.

• **TESTS** These minerals are plastic when moist, and lose water when heated in a closed tube. Special optical tests are needed to tell kaolinite minerals apart.

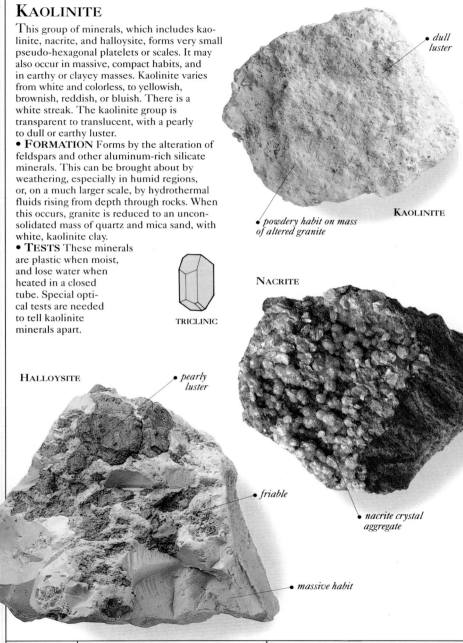

dull luster

KAOLINITE

powdery habit on mass of altered granite

NACRITE

TRICLINIC

HALLOYSITE

pearly luster

friable

nacrite crystal aggregate

massive habit

SG 2.6–2.63	Cleavage Perfect basal	Fracture Uneven

Group Silicates	Composition $Ca_2Al_2Si_3O_{10}(OH)_2$		Hardness 6–6½

PREHNITE

This mineral can form prismatic, tabular, or pyramidal crystals, but usually occurs in botryoidal, reniform, stalactitic, granular, or compact habits. It is usually green in color, but may be white, colorless, yellow, or gray. It has a colorless streak. Prehnite is transparent to translucent, with a vitreous to pearly luster.
• **FORMATION** Forms in cavities in basaltic lavas.
• **TESTS** This mineral gives off water when it is heated.

ORTHORHOMBIC

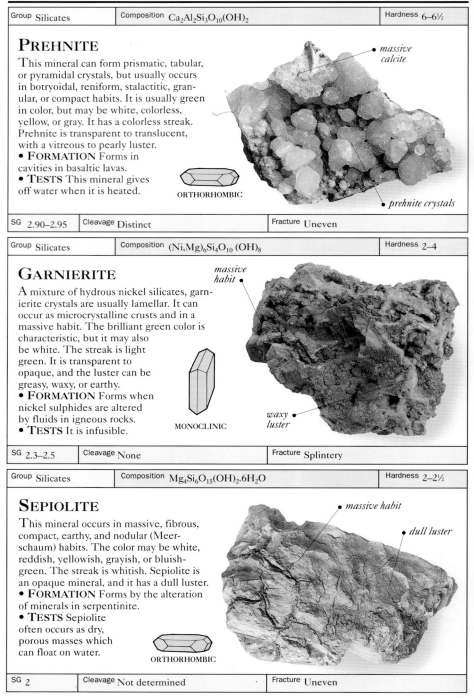

massive calcite

prehnite crystals

SG 2.90–2.95	Cleavage Distinct		Fracture Uneven

Group Silicates	Composition $(Ni,Mg)_6Si_4O_{10}(OH)_8$		Hardness 2–4

GARNIERITE

A mixture of hydrous nickel silicates, garnierite crystals are usually lamellar. It can occur as microcrystalline crusts and in a massive habit. The brilliant green color is characteristic, but it may also be white. The streak is light green. It is transparent to opaque, and the luster can be greasy, waxy, or earthy.
• **FORMATION** Forms when nickel sulphides are altered by fluids in igneous rocks.
• **TESTS** It is infusible.

MONOCLINIC

massive habit

waxy luster

SG 2.3–2.5	Cleavage None		Fracture Splintery

Group Silicates	Composition $Mg_4Si_6O_{15}(OH)_2.6H_2O$		Hardness 2–2½

SEPIOLITE

This mineral occurs in massive, fibrous, compact, earthy, and nodular (Meerschaum) habits. The color may be white, reddish, yellowish, grayish, or bluish-green. The streak is whitish. Sepiolite is an opaque mineral, and it has a dull luster.
• **FORMATION** Forms by the alteration of minerals in serpentinite.
• **TESTS** Sepiolite often occurs as dry, porous masses which can float on water.

ORTHORHOMBIC

massive habit

dull luster

SG 2	Cleavage Not determined	.	Fracture Uneven

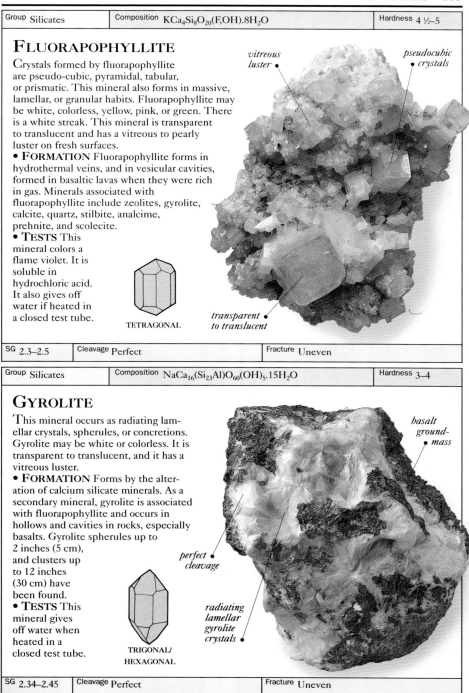

Group Silicates	Composition $KCa_4Si_8O_{20}(F,OH).8H_2O$	Hardness 4 ½–5

FLUORAPOPHYLLITE

Crystals formed by fluorapophyllite are pseudo-cubic, pyramidal, tabular, or prismatic. This mineral also forms in massive, lamellar, or granular habits. Fluorapophyllite may be white, colorless, yellow, pink, or green. There is a white streak. This mineral is transparent to translucent and has a vitreous to pearly luster on fresh surfaces.

• **FORMATION** Fluorapophyllite forms in hydrothermal veins, and in vesicular cavities, formed in basaltic lavas when they were rich in gas. Minerals associated with fluorapophyllite include zeolites, gyrolite, calcite, quartz, stilbite, analcime, prehnite, and scolecite.

• **TESTS** This mineral colors a flame violet. It is soluble in hydrochloric acid. It also gives off water if heated in a closed test tube.

vitreous luster

pseudocubic crystals

TETRAGONAL

transparent to translucent

SG 2.3–2.5	Cleavage Perfect		Fracture Uneven

Group Silicates	Composition $NaCa_{16}(Si_{23}Al)O_{60}(OH)_5.15H_2O$	Hardness 3–4

GYROLITE

This mineral occurs as radiating lamellar crystals, spherules, or concretions. Gyrolite may be white or colorless. It is transparent to translucent, and it has a vitreous luster.

• **FORMATION** Forms by the alteration of calcium silicate minerals. As a secondary mineral, gyrolite is associated with fluorapophyllite and occurs in hollows and cavities in rocks, especially basalts. Gyrolite spherules up to 2 inches (5 cm), and clusters up to 12 inches (30 cm) have been found.

• **TESTS** This mineral gives off water when heated in a closed test tube.

basalt ground-mass

perfect cleavage

radiating lamellar gyrolite crystals

TRIGONAL/HEXAGONAL

SG 2.34–2.45	Cleavage Perfect		Fracture Uneven

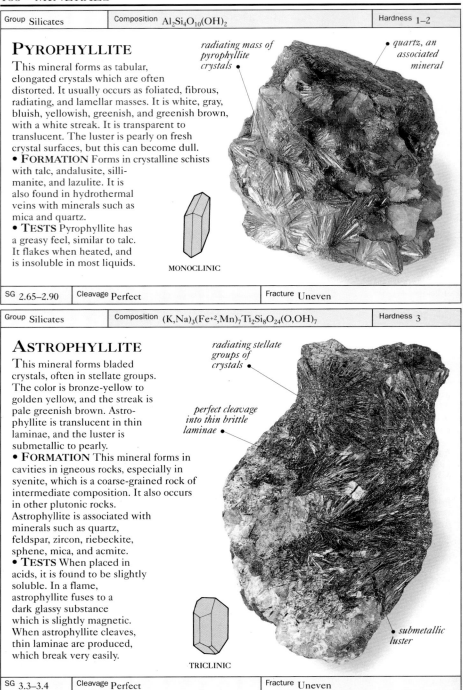

Group Silicates	Composition $Al_2Si_4O_{10}(OH)_2$	Hardness 1–2

PYROPHYLLITE

This mineral forms as tabular, elongated crystals which are often distorted. It usually occurs as foliated, fibrous, radiating, and lamellar masses. It is white, gray, bluish, yellowish, greenish, and greenish brown, with a white streak. It is transparent to translucent. The luster is pearly on fresh crystal surfaces, but this can become dull.
• **FORMATION** Forms in crystalline schists with talc, andalusite, silli-manite, and lazulite. It is also found in hydrothermal veins with minerals such as mica and quartz.
• **TESTS** Pyrophyllite has a greasy feel, similar to talc. It flakes when heated, and is insoluble in most liquids.

radiating mass of pyrophyllite crystals

quartz, an associated mineral

MONOCLINIC

SG 2.65–2.90	Cleavage Perfect	Fracture Uneven

Group Silicates	Composition $(K,Na)_3(Fe^{+2},Mn)_7Ti_2Si_8O_{24}(O,OH)_7$	Hardness 3

ASTROPHYLLITE

This mineral forms bladed crystals, often in stellate groups. The color is bronze-yellow to golden yellow, and the streak is pale greenish brown. Astro-phyllite is translucent in thin laminae, and the luster is submetallic to pearly.
• **FORMATION** This mineral forms in cavities in igneous rocks, especially in syenite, which is a coarse-grained rock of intermediate composition. It also occurs in other plutonic rocks. Astrophyllite is associated with minerals such as quartz, feldspar, zircon, riebeckite, sphene, mica, and acmite.
• **TESTS** When placed in acids, it is found to be slightly soluble. In a flame, astrophyllite fuses to a dark glassy substance which is slightly magnetic. When astrophyllite cleaves, thin laminae are produced, which break very easily.

radiating stellate groups of crystals

perfect cleavage into thin brittle laminae

submetallic luster

TRICLINIC

SG 3.3–3.4	Cleavage Perfect	Fracture Uneven

Group Silicates	Composition $(Na,K) AlSi_3O_8$	Hardness $6–6\frac{1}{2}$

ANORTHOCLASE

Belonging to the alkali feldspar series, this mineral forms as short prismatic or tabular crystals, with common twinning. It may occur as massive, lamellar, granular, or cryptocrystalline specimens. It is yellowish, colorless, reddish, white, gray, or greenish. It has a white streak, and is transparent to translucent, with a vitreous luster.
• **FORMATION** Forms mainly in volcanic igneous rocks.
• **TESTS** It is insoluble in acids.

TRICLINIC

vitreous luster

a single prismatic crystal

SG $2.56–2.62$	Cleavage Perfect	Fracture Uneven

Group Silicates	Composition $KAlSi_3O_8$	Hardness $6–6\frac{1}{2}$

MICROCLINE

AMAZONSTONE

This mineral is an alkali feldspar and forms tabular or, more frequently, short prismatic crystals, which are very commonly twinned. It also occurs in a massive habit. The color may be gray, white, yellowish, reddish, or pink. There is also a green-colored form of microcline, which is usually known as amazonstone. The streak is white. This is a transparent to translucent mineral, with a luster that is vitreous, or pearly on cleavage surfaces.
• **FORMATION** Commonly forms in igneous rocks, especially granites, pegmatites, and syenites. It also occurs in certain metamorphic rocks, particularly schists. In addition, microcline can be found in hydrothermal veins and areas of contact metamorphism. It is often associated with quartz and albite when it forms in pegmatites.
• **TESTS** It is insoluble in acids except hydrofluoric acid, which should be used with care. It is infusible in a flame.

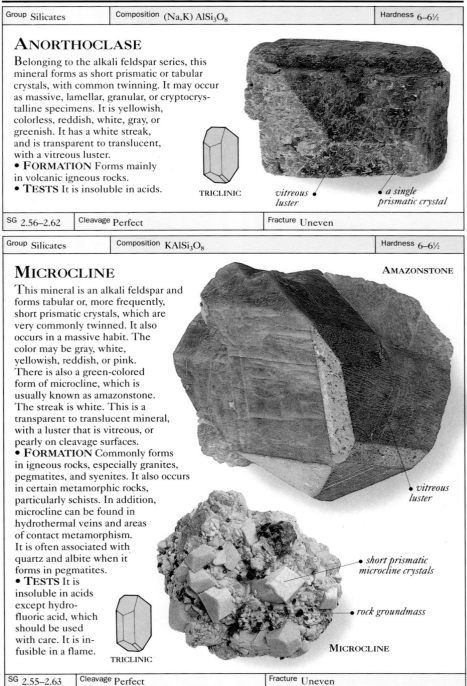

vitreous luster

short prismatic microcline crystals

rock groundmass

MICROCLINE

TRICLINIC

SG $2.55–2.63$	Cleavage Perfect	Fracture Uneven

Group Silicates	Composition $KAlSi_3O_8$	Hardness 6

SANIDINE

A member of the alkali feldspar group, sanidine occurs as prismatic or tabular crystals, which are often twinned. It is whitish or colorless. There is a white streak. It is a translucent mineral with a vitreous luster on crystal faces.
• FORMATION Forms in a variety of volcanic rocks, including trachyte and rhyolite. Sanidine can also be found in several varieties of contact metamorphosed rocks.
• TESTS Sanidine is insoluble in most acids, but will dissolve completely when placed in hydrofluoric acid. Great care, however, should be taken when using this acid.

MONOCLINIC

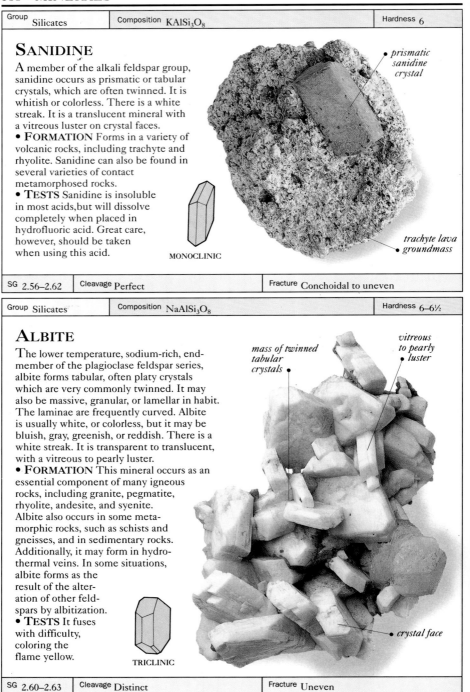

prismatic sanidine crystal

trachyte lava groundmass

SG 2.56–2.62	Cleavage Perfect	Fracture Conchoidal to uneven

Group Silicates	Composition $NaAlSi_3O_8$	Hardness 6–6½

ALBITE

The lower temperature, sodium-rich, end-member of the plagioclase feldspar series, albite forms tabular, often platy crystals which are very commonly twinned. It may also be massive, granular, or lamellar in habit. The laminae are frequently curved. Albite is usually white, or colorless, but it may be bluish, gray, greenish, or reddish. There is a white streak. It is transparent to translucent, with a vitreous to pearly luster.
• FORMATION This mineral occurs as an essential component of many igneous rocks, including granite, pegmatite, rhyolite, andesite, and syenite. Albite also occurs in some metamorphic rocks, such as schists and gneisses, and in sedimentary rocks. Additionally, it may form in hydrothermal veins. In some situations, albite forms as the result of the alteration of other feldspars by albitization.
• TESTS It fuses with difficulty, coloring the flame yellow.

mass of twinned tabular crystals

vitreous to pearly luster

crystal face

TRICLINIC

SG 2.60–2.63	Cleavage Distinct	Fracture Uneven

Group Silicates	Composition $(Na,Ca)Al_{1-2}Si_{3-2}O_8$	Hardness 6–6½

LABRADORITE

An intermediate member of the plagioclase feldspar series, labradorite rarely forms crystals; when crystals do occur, they are tabular and often twinned. Other habits are massive, granular, or compact. Labradorite is blue, gray, white, or colorless, and frequently exhibits a rich play of colors on cleavage surfaces. The streak is white. It is translucent with a vitreous luster.
• **FORMATION** This mineral is an important constituent of certain igneous and metamorphic rocks. These include basalt, gabbro, diorite, andesite, norite, and amphibolite. Labradorite is common in intermediate and basic rocks, but rare in granitic rocks.
• **TESTS** The schillerization, or play of colors on broken surfaces, is very characteristic of labradorite. It is also soluble in acid when powdered.

TRICLINIC

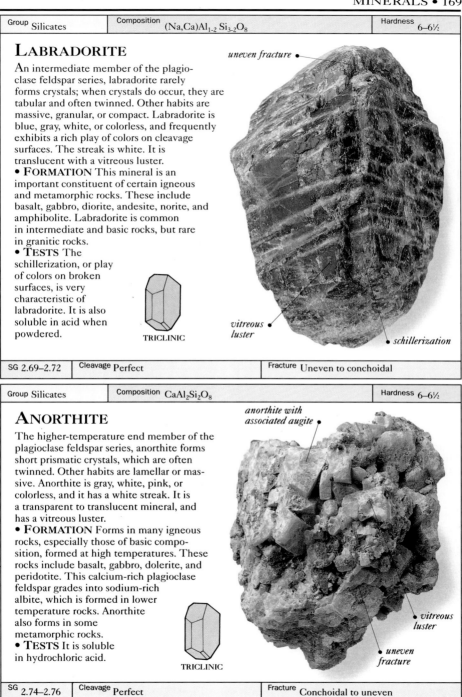

uneven fracture •

vitreous luster •

• *schillerization*

SG 2.69–2.72	Cleavage Perfect	Fracture Uneven to conchoidal

Group Silicates	Composition $CaAl_2Si_2O_8$	Hardness 6–6½

ANORTHITE

The higher-temperature end member of the plagioclase feldspar series, anorthite forms short prismatic crystals, which are often twinned. Other habits are lamellar or massive. Anorthite is gray, white, pink, or colorless, and it has a white streak. It is a transparent to translucent mineral, and has a vitreous luster.
• **FORMATION** Forms in many igneous rocks, especially those of basic composition, formed at high temperatures. These rocks include basalt, gabbro, dolerite, and peridotite. This calcium-rich plagioclase feldspar grades into sodium-rich albite, which is formed in lower temperature rocks. Anorthite also forms in some metamorphic rocks.
• **TESTS** It is soluble in hydrochloric acid.

TRICLINIC

anorthite with associated augite •

• *vitreous luster*

• *uneven fracture*

SG 2.74–2.76	Cleavage Perfect	Fracture Conchoidal to uneven

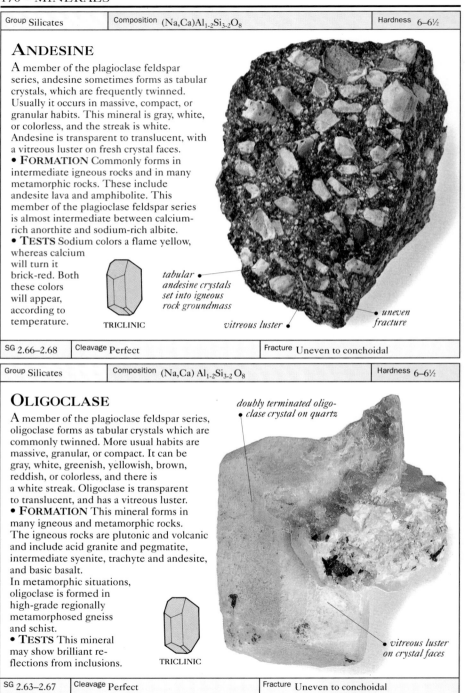

Group Silicates	Composition $(Na,Ca)Al_{1-2}Si_{3-2}O_8$	Hardness 6–6½

ANDESINE

A member of the plagioclase feldspar series, andesine sometimes forms as tabular crystals, which are frequently twinned. Usually it occurs in massive, compact, or granular habits. This mineral is gray, white, or colorless, and the streak is white. Andesine is transparent to translucent, with a vitreous luster on fresh crystal faces.
• **FORMATION** Commonly forms in intermediate igneous rocks and in many metamorphic rocks. These include andesite lava and amphibolite. This member of the plagioclase feldspar series is almost intermediate between calcium-rich anorthite and sodium-rich albite.
• **TESTS** Sodium colors a flame yellow, whereas calcium will turn it brick-red. Both these colors will appear, according to temperature.

TRICLINIC

tabular andesine crystals set into igneous rock groundmass

vitreous luster

uneven fracture

SG 2.66–2.68	Cleavage Perfect	Fracture Uneven to conchoidal

Group Silicates	Composition $(Na,Ca) Al_{1-2}Si_{3-2}O_8$	Hardness 6–6½

OLIGOCLASE

A member of the plagioclase feldspar series, oligoclase forms as tabular crystals which are commonly twinned. More usual habits are massive, granular, or compact. It can be gray, white, greenish, yellowish, brown, reddish, or colorless, and there is a white streak. Oligoclase is transparent to translucent, and has a vitreous luster.
• **FORMATION** This mineral forms in many igneous and metamorphic rocks. The igneous rocks are plutonic and volcanic and include acid granite and pegmatite, intermediate syenite, trachyte and andesite, and basic basalt. In metamorphic situations, oligoclase is formed in high-grade regionally metamorphosed gneiss and schist.
• **TESTS** This mineral may show brilliant reflections from inclusions.

doubly terminated oligoclase crystal on quartz

TRICLINIC

vitreous luster on crystal faces

SG 2.63–2.67	Cleavage Perfect	Fracture Uneven to conchoidal

Group Silicates	Composition $KAlSi_3O_8$	Hardness $6-6\frac{1}{2}$

ORTHOCLASE

An important rock-forming mineral, orthoclase feldspar forms as prismatic or tabular crystals which are often twinned. Other habits are massive, lamellar, and granular. It is white, reddish, colorless, yellow, gray, or green, and has a white streak. Orthoclase is a transparent to translucent mineral, with a vitreous to pearly luster.
• **FORMATION** Forms in many igneous and metamorphic rocks. The igneous rocks include granite, pegmatite, rhyolite, trachyte, and syenite; metamorphic examples include gneisses and schists. This mineral can also occur in some sedimentary rocks.
• **TESTS** Orthoclase is insoluble in acids and is almost infusible.

MONOCLINIC

prismatic orthoclase crystals

quartz, an associated mineral

SG 2.55–2.63	Cleavage Perfect	Fracture Uneven to conchoidal

Group Silicates	Composition $(Na,Ca) Al_{1-2} Si_{3-2}O_8$	Hardness $6-6\frac{1}{2}$

BYTOWNITE

A calcic member of the plagioclase feldspar series, bytownite forms as tabular crystals which are commonly twinned. More often, it occurs in massive, compact, and granular habits. It is white, gray, brownish, or colorless, and has a white streak. It is transparent to translucent and there is a vitreous luster.
• **FORMATION** Forms as an essential component of many igneous rocks, such as dolerite, basalt, gabbro, norite, and anorthosite. It is also found in some metamorphic rocks, including gneiss and schist, formed by regional metamorphism.
• **TESTS** In common with other members of the plagioclase feldspar series, bytownite shows multiple twinning. This helps distinguish it from orthoclase, which has simple twinning.

TRICLINIC

vitreous luster

perfect cleavage

uneven fracture

SG 2.72–2.74	Cleavage Perfect	Fracture Uneven to conchoidal

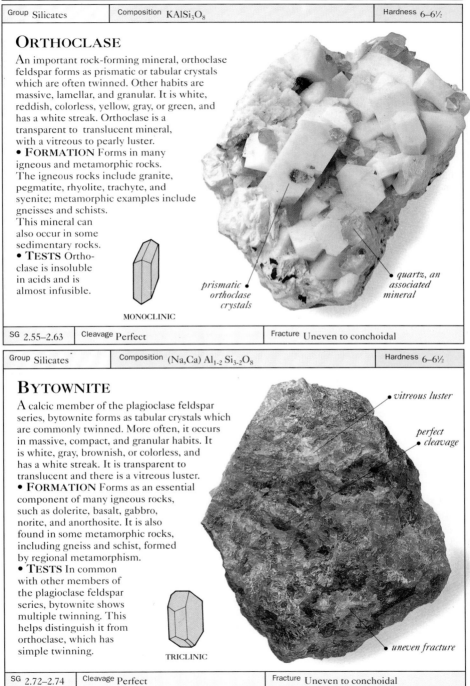

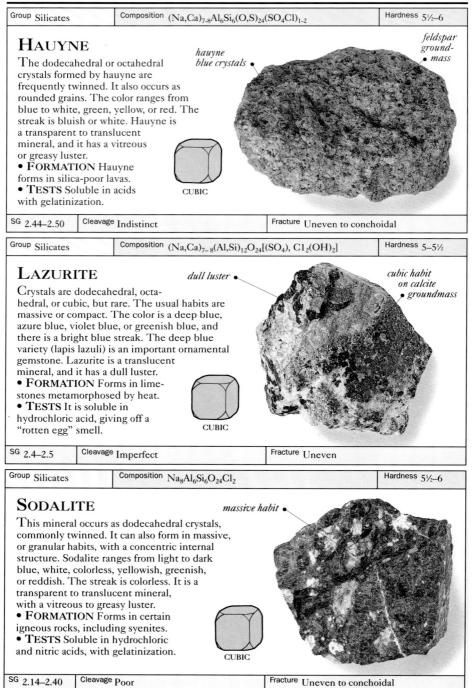

Group Silicates	Composition $(Na,Ca)_{7-8}Al_6Si_6(O,S)_{24}(SO_4Cl)_{1-2}$	Hardness $5\frac{1}{2}$–6

HAUYNE

The dodecahedral or octahedral crystals formed by hauyne are frequently twinned. It also occurs as rounded grains. The color ranges from blue to white, green, yellow, or red. The streak is bluish or white. Hauyne is a transparent to translucent mineral, and it has a vitreous or greasy luster.
• **FORMATION** Hauyne forms in silica-poor lavas.
• **TESTS** Soluble in acids with gelatinization.

hauyne blue crystals •

feldspar ground-• mass

CUBIC

SG 2.44–2.50	Cleavage Indistinct	Fracture Uneven to conchoidal

Group Silicates	Composition $(Na,Ca)_{7-8}(Al,Si)_{12}O_{24}[(SO_4), Cl_2(OH)_2]$	Hardness 5–$5\frac{1}{2}$

LAZURITE

Crystals are dodecahedral, octahedral, or cubic, but rare. The usual habits are massive or compact. The color is a deep blue, azure blue, violet blue, or greenish blue, and there is a bright blue streak. The deep blue variety (lapis lazuli) is an important ornamental gemstone. Lazurite is a translucent mineral, and it has a dull luster.
• **FORMATION** Forms in lime-stones metamorphosed by heat.
• **TESTS** It is soluble in hydrochloric acid, giving off a "rotten egg" smell.

dull luster •

cubic habit on calcite • groundmass

CUBIC

SG 2.4–2.5	Cleavage Imperfect	Fracture Uneven

Group Silicates	Composition $Na_8Al_6Si_6O_{24}Cl_2$	Hardness $5\frac{1}{2}$–6

SODALITE

This mineral occurs as dodecahedral crystals, commonly twinned. It can also form in massive, or granular habits, with a concentric internal structure. Sodalite ranges from light to dark blue, white, colorless, yellowish, greenish, or reddish. The streak is colorless. It is a transparent to translucent mineral, with a vitreous to greasy luster.
• **FORMATION** Forms in certain igneous rocks, including syenites.
• **TESTS** Soluble in hydrochloric and nitric acids, with gelatinization.

massive habit •

CUBIC

SG 2.14–2.40	Cleavage Poor	Fracture Uneven to conchoidal

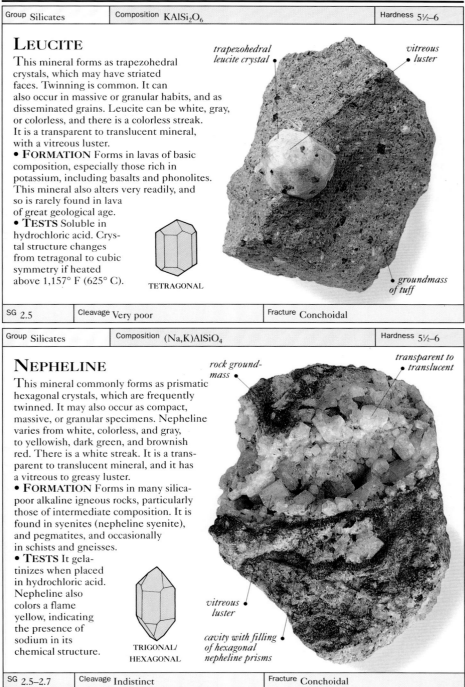

Group Silicates	Composition $KAlSi_2O_6$	Hardness 5½–6

LEUCITE

This mineral forms as trapezohedral crystals, which may have striated faces. Twinning is common. It can also occur in massive or granular habits, and as disseminated grains. Leucite can be white, gray, or colorless, and there is a colorless streak. It is a transparent to translucent mineral, with a vitreous luster.

• **FORMATION** Forms in lavas of basic composition, especially those rich in potassium, including basalts and phonolites. This mineral also alters very readily, and so is rarely found in lava of great geological age.

• **TESTS** Soluble in hydrochloric acid. Crystal structure changes from tetragonal to cubic symmetry if heated above 1,157° F (625° C).

trapezohedral leucite crystal

vitreous luster

TETRAGONAL

groundmass of tuff

SG 2.5	Cleavage Very poor	Fracture Conchoidal

Group Silicates	Composition $(Na,K)AlSiO_4$	Hardness 5½–6

NEPHELINE

This mineral commonly forms as prismatic hexagonal crystals, which are frequently twinned. It may also occur as compact, massive, or granular specimens. Nepheline varies from white, colorless, and gray, to yellowish, dark green, and brownish red. There is a white streak. It is a transparent to translucent mineral, and it has a vitreous to greasy luster.

• **FORMATION** Forms in many silica-poor alkaline igneous rocks, particularly those of intermediate composition. It is found in syenites (nepheline syenite), and pegmatites, and occasionally in schists and gneisses.

• **TESTS** It gelatinizes when placed in hydrochloric acid. Nepheline also colors a flame yellow, indicating the presence of sodium in its chemical structure.

rock groundmass

transparent to translucent

vitreous luster

cavity with filling of hexagonal nepheline prisms

TRIGONAL/ HEXAGONAL

SG 2.5–2.7	Cleavage Indistinct	Fracture Conchoidal

Group Silicates	Composition $Na_8Al_6Si_6O_{24}(SO_4)$	Hardness $5\frac{1}{2}$–6

NOSEAN

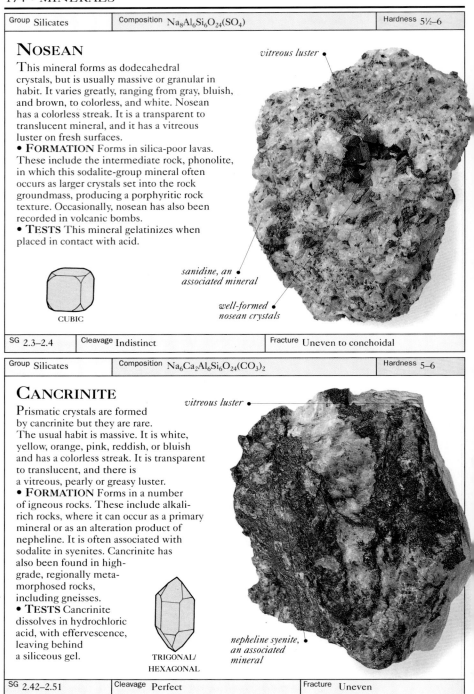

vitreous luster

This mineral forms as dodecahedral crystals, but is usually massive or granular in habit. It varies greatly, ranging from gray, bluish, and brown, to colorless, and white. Nosean has a colorless streak. It is a transparent to translucent mineral, and it has a vitreous luster on fresh surfaces.
• **FORMATION** Forms in silica-poor lavas. These include the intermediate rock, phonolite, in which this sodalite-group mineral often occurs as larger crystals set into the rock groundmass, producing a porphyritic rock texture. Occasionally, nosean has also been recorded in volcanic bombs.
• **TESTS** This mineral gelatinizes when placed in contact with acid.

CUBIC

sanidine, an associated mineral

well-formed nosean crystals

SG 2.3–2.4	Cleavage Indistinct	Fracture Uneven to conchoidal

Group Silicates	Composition $Na_6Ca_2Al_6Si_6O_{24}(CO_3)_2$	Hardness 5–6

CANCRINITE

vitreous luster

Prismatic crystals are formed by cancrinite but they are rare. The usual habit is massive. It is white, yellow, orange, pink, reddish, or bluish and has a colorless streak. It is transparent to translucent, and there is a vitreous, pearly or greasy luster.
• **FORMATION** Forms in a number of igneous rocks. These include alkali-rich rocks, where it can occur as a primary mineral or as an alteration product of nepheline. It is often associated with sodalite in syenites. Cancrinite has also been found in high-grade, regionally meta-morphosed rocks, including gneisses.
• **TESTS** Cancrinite dissolves in hydrochloric acid, with effervescence, leaving behind a siliceous gel.

TRIGONAL/
HEXAGONAL

nepheline syenite, an associated mineral

SG 2.42–2.51	Cleavage Perfect	Fracture Uneven

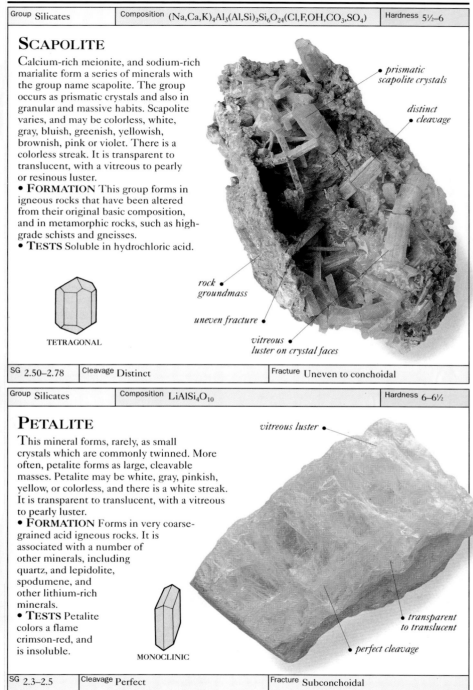

Group Silicates	Composition $(Na,Ca,K)_4Al_3(Al,Si)_3Si_6O_{24}(Cl,F,OH,CO_3,SO_4)$	Hardness $5\frac{1}{2}$–6

SCAPOLITE

Calcium-rich meionite, and sodium-rich marialite form a series of minerals with the group name scapolite. The group occurs as prismatic crystals and also in granular and massive habits. Scapolite varies, and may be colorless, white, gray, bluish, greenish, yellowish, brownish, pink or violet. There is a colorless streak. It is transparent to translucent, with a vitreous to pearly or resinous luster.

• **FORMATION** This group forms in igneous rocks that have been altered from their original basic composition, and in metamorphic rocks, such as high-grade schists and gneisses.

• **TESTS** Soluble in hydrochloric acid.

prismatic scapolite crystals

distinct cleavage

rock groundmass

uneven fracture

TETRAGONAL

vitreous luster on crystal faces

SG 2.50–2.78	Cleavage Distinct	Fracture Uneven to conchoidal

Group Silicates	Composition $LiAlSi_4O_{10}$	Hardness 6–$6\frac{1}{2}$

PETALITE

vitreous luster

This mineral forms, rarely, as small crystals which are commonly twinned. More often, petalite forms as large, cleavable masses. Petalite may be white, gray, pinkish, yellow, or colorless, and there is a white streak. It is transparent to translucent, with a vitreous to pearly luster.

• **FORMATION** Forms in very coarse-grained acid igneous rocks. It is associated with a number of other minerals, including quartz, and lepidolite, spodumene, and other lithium-rich minerals.

• **TESTS** Petalite colors a flame crimson-red, and is insoluble.

MONOCLINIC

transparent to translucent

perfect cleavage

SG 2.3–2.5	Cleavage Perfect	Fracture Subconchoidal

Group Silicates	Composition $NaAlSi_2O_6.H_2O$	Hardness 5–5½

ANALCIME

A zeolite mineral that occurs as well-formed trapezohedra, icositetrahedra, and modified cubes, analcime also forms in massive, granular, and compact habits. It may be white, colorless, gray, pink, yellowish, or greenish, with a white streak. Analcime is a transparent to translucent mineral, with a vitreous luster.
• **FORMATION** Occurs in basaltic igneous rocks and may be formed by the alteration of sodalite and nepheline. Analcime is also found in some detrital sediments, with other zeolites and calcite.
• **TESTS** When heated, it fuses and colors the flame yellow. This mineral is soluble in acids. It will yield water when heated in a closed test tube.

icositetrahedral crystal in cavity in groundmass •

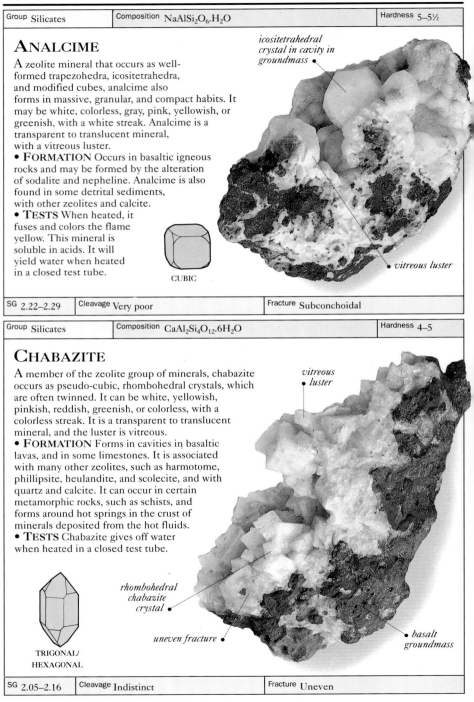

• vitreous luster

CUBIC

SG 2.22–2.29	Cleavage Very poor	Fracture Subconchoidal

Group Silicates	Composition $CaAl_2Si_4O_{12}.6H_2O$	Hardness 4–5

CHABAZITE

A member of the zeolite group of minerals, chabazite occurs as pseudo-cubic, rhombohedral crystals, which are often twinned. It can be white, yellowish, pinkish, reddish, greenish, or colorless, with a colorless streak. It is a transparent to translucent mineral, and the luster is vitreous.
• **FORMATION** Forms in cavities in basaltic lavas, and in some limestones. It is associated with many other zeolites, such as harmotome, phillipsite, heulandite, and scolecite, and with quartz and calcite. It can occur in certain metamorphic rocks, such as schists, and forms around hot springs in the crust of minerals deposited from the hot fluids.
• **TESTS** Chabazite gives off water when heated in a closed test tube.

vitreous • luster

rhombohedral chabazite crystal •

TRIGONAL/
HEXAGONAL

uneven fracture •

• basalt groundmass

SG 2.05–2.16	Cleavage Indistinct	Fracture Uneven

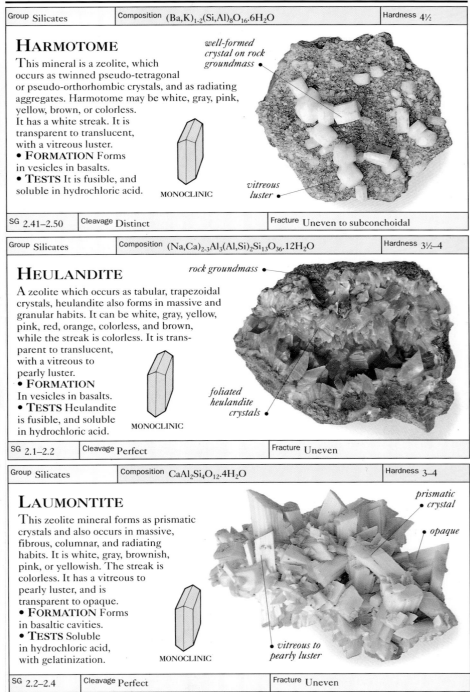

Group Silicates	Composition $(Ba,K)_{1-2}(Si,Al)_8O_{16}.6H_2O$	Hardness 4½

HARMOTOME

This mineral is a zeolite, which occurs as twinned pseudo-tetragonal or pseudo-orthorhombic crystals, and as radiating aggregates. Harmotome may be white, gray, pink, yellow, brown, or colorless. It has a white streak. It is transparent to translucent, with a vitreous luster.
• **FORMATION** Forms in vesicles in basalts.
• **TESTS** It is fusible, and soluble in hydrochloric acid.

well-formed crystal on rock groundmass •

vitreous luster •

MONOCLINIC

SG 2.41–2.50	Cleavage Distinct	Fracture Uneven to subconchoidal

Group Silicates	Composition $(Na,Ca)_{2-3}Al_3(Al,Si)_2Si_{13}O_{36}.12H_2O$	Hardness 3½–4

HEULANDITE

A zeolite which occurs as tabular, trapezoidal crystals, heulandite also forms in massive and granular habits. It can be white, gray, yellow, pink, red, orange, colorless, and brown, while the streak is colorless. It is transparent to translucent, with a vitreous to pearly luster.
• **FORMATION** In vesicles in basalts.
• **TESTS** Heulandite is fusible, and soluble in hydrochloric acid.

rock groundmass •

foliated heulandite crystals •

MONOCLINIC

SG 2.1–2.2	Cleavage Perfect	Fracture Uneven

Group Silicates	Composition $CaAl_2Si_4O_{12}.4H_2O$	Hardness 3–4

LAUMONTITE

This zeolite mineral forms as prismatic crystals and also occurs in massive, fibrous, columnar, and radiating habits. It is white, gray, brownish, pink, or yellowish. The streak is colorless. It has a vitreous to pearly luster, and is transparent to opaque.
• **FORMATION** Forms in basaltic cavities.
• **TESTS** Soluble in hydrochloric acid, with gelatinization.

prismatic crystal •

opaque •

vitreous to pearly luster •

MONOCLINIC

SG 2.2–2.4	Cleavage Perfect	Fracture Uneven

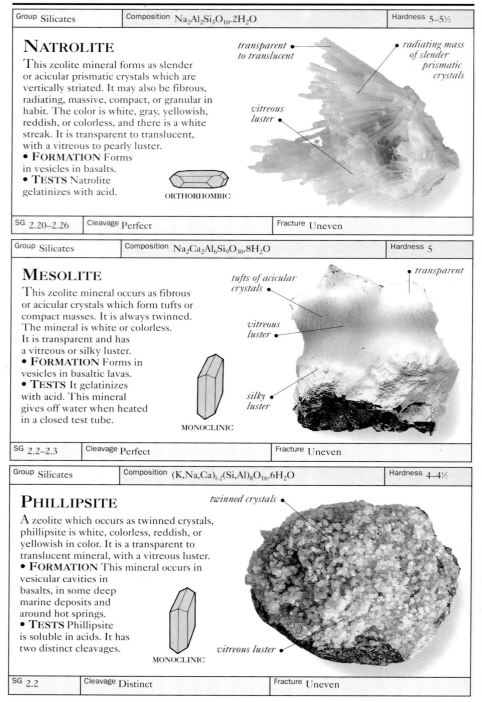

Group Silicates	Composition $Na_2Al_2Si_3O_{10}.2H_2O$	Hardness 5–5½

NATROLITE

This zeolite mineral forms as slender
or acicular prismatic crystals which are
vertically striated. It may also be fibrous,
radiating, massive, compact, or granular in
habit. The color is white, gray, yellowish,
reddish, or colorless, and there is a white
streak. It is transparent to translucent,
with a vitreous to pearly luster.
• **FORMATION** Forms
in vesicles in basalts.
• **TESTS** Natrolite
gelatinizes with acid.

*transparent
to translucent*

*radiating mass
of slender
prismatic
crystals*

*vitreous
luster*

ORTHORHOMBIC

SG 2.20–2.26	Cleavage Perfect	Fracture Uneven

Group Silicates	Composition $Na_2Ca_2Al_6Si_9O_{30}.8H_2O$	Hardness 5

MESOLITE

This zeolite mineral occurs as fibrous
or acicular crystals which form tufts or
compact masses. It is always twinned.
The mineral is white or colorless.
It is transparent and has
a vitreous or silky luster.
• **FORMATION** Forms in
vesicles in basaltic lavas.
• **TESTS** It gelatinizes
with acid. This mineral
gives off water when heated
in a closed test tube.

*tufts of acicular
crystals*

transparent

*vitreous
luster*

*silky
luster*

MONOCLINIC

SG 2.2–2.3	Cleavage Perfect	Fracture Uneven

Group Silicates	Composition $(K,Na,Ca)_{1-2}(Si,Al)_8O_{16}.6H_2O$	Hardness 4–4½

PHILLIPSITE

A zeolite which occurs as twinned crystals,
phillipsite is white, colorless, reddish, or
yellowish in color. It is a transparent to
translucent mineral, with a vitreous luster.
• **FORMATION** This mineral occurs in
vesicular cavities in
basalts, in some deep
marine deposits and
around hot springs.
• **TESTS** Phillipsite
is soluble in acids. It has
two distinct cleavages.

twinned crystals

vitreous luster

MONOCLINIC

SG 2.2	Cleavage Distinct	Fracture Uneven

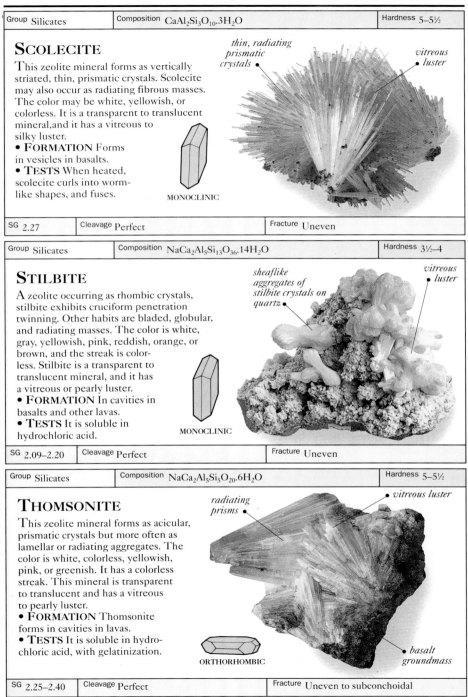

| Group Silicates | Composition CaAl$_2$Si$_3$O$_{10}$·3H$_2$O | Hardness 5–5½ |

SCOLECITE

This zeolite mineral forms as vertically striated, thin, prismatic crystals. Scolecite may also occur as radiating fibrous masses. The color may be white, yellowish, or colorless. It is a transparent to translucent mineral, and it has a vitreous to silky luster.
• **FORMATION** Forms in vesicles in basalts.
• **TESTS** When heated, scolecite curls into worm-like shapes, and fuses.

thin, radiating prismatic crystals

vitreous luster

MONOCLINIC

| SG 2.27 | Cleavage Perfect | Fracture Uneven |

| Group Silicates | Composition NaCa$_2$Al$_5$Si$_{13}$O$_{36}$·14H$_2$O | Hardness 3½–4 |

STILBITE

A zeolite occurring as rhombic crystals, stilbite exhibits cruciform penetration twinning. Other habits are bladed, globular, and radiating masses. The color is white, gray, yellowish, pink, reddish, orange, or brown, and the streak is color-less. Stilbite is a transparent to translucent mineral, and it has a vitreous or pearly luster.
• **FORMATION** In cavities in basalts and other lavas.
• **TESTS** It is soluble in hydrochloric acid.

sheaflike aggregates of stilbite crystals on quartz

vitreous luster

MONOCLINIC

| SG 2.09–2.20 | Cleavage Perfect | Fracture Uneven |

| Group Silicates | Composition NaCa$_2$Al$_5$Si$_5$O$_{20}$·6H$_2$O | Hardness 5–5½ |

THOMSONITE

This zeolite mineral forms as acicular, prismatic crystals but more often as lamellar or radiating aggregates. The color is white, colorless, yellowish, pink, or greenish. It has a colorless streak. This mineral is transparent to translucent and has a vitreous to pearly luster.
• **FORMATION** Thomsonite forms in cavities in lavas.
• **TESTS** It is soluble in hydro-chloric acid, with gelatinization.

radiating prisms

vitreous luster

ORTHORHOMBIC

basalt groundmass

| SG 2.25–2.40 | Cleavage Perfect | Fracture Uneven to subconchoidal |

ROCKS

IGNEOUS ROCKS

I GNEOUS ROCKS form by the crystallization of once molten material. This molten rock is called magma and then lava once it reaches the surface. It is essentially a silicate melt and may contain, as well as silicon and oxygen, other elements, particularly aluminum, iron, calcium, sodium, potassium, and magnesium. These combine, as the magma or lava crystallizes, to form silicate minerals, which in combination make up igneous rocks.

Group Igneous	Origin Intrusive	Grain size Coarse	Crystal shape Anhedral, Euhedral

PINK GRANITE

The commonest of all intrusive igneous rocks, granite is acid. It has a total silica content greater than 65 percent, and a minimum quartz content of 20 percent. K-feldspars (orthoclase and microcline) are dominant over plagioclase (Na-rich) feldspar and are often pink. Mica occurs as dark biotite or as silvery muscovite. Hornblende may be present.
• TEXTURE Granite is a coarse-grained rock, with crystals larger than ³⁄₁₆ inch (5 mm) in diameter.
• ORIGIN Forms at considerable depth in the earth's crust.

biotite mica

gray quartz crystals

pink orthoclase feldspar

Classification Acid	Occurrence Pluton	Color Light

Group Igneous	Origin Intrusive	Grain size Coarse	Crystal shape Anhedral, Euhedral

WHITE GRANITE

A high silica content – over 65 percent total silica, and not less than 20 percent quartz – classifies white granite as an acid rock. K-feldspars (orthoclase and microcline) are dominant, and are white in color. Usually, there is some albitic plagioclase. Dark biotite mica and hornblende give the rock a mottled appearance. Light, glittery muscovite is also common.
• TEXTURE A coarse-grained rock, with euhedral crystals of feldspar and mica and, usually, anhedral quartz.
• ORIGIN In plutonic environments.

white orthoclase feldspar

biotite mica

light gray quartz

Classification Acid	Occurrence Pluton	Color Light

Group Igneous	Origin Intrusive	Grain size Coarse	Crystal shape Anhedral, Euhedral

PORPHYRITIC GRANITE

A granitic rock with more than 65 percent silica, and a minimum of 20 percent quartz. Pink orthoclase feldspar, and white microcline, or albitic feldspar are present. Biotite mica crystals and quartz are visible. Hornblende may add to the speckled appearance.
• TEXTURE Granite may be granular or porphyritic. The phenocrysts are usually of feldspar and may be up to 2½ inch (6 cm) long.
• ORIGIN Forms by magma cooling in two stages at some depth in the earth's crust.

biotite mica crystals

quartz crystals

light phenocrysts of orthoclase feldspar

Classification Acid	Occurrence Pluton	Color Light

Group Igneous	Origin Intrusive	Grain size Coarse	Crystal shape Anhedral, Euhedral

GRAPHIC GRANITE

An acid igneous rock, this granite contains 20 percent quartz, and over 65 percent total silica. It is made up of K-feldspars (orthoclase and microcline) albitic plagioclase, gray quartz, and some dark biotite mica.
• TEXTURE Coarse-grained, with a graphic texture.
• ORIGIN Forms due to the simultaneous crystallization of quartz and K-feldspars.

pink coloring of orthoclase feldspar

gray quartz

Classification Acid	Occurrence Pluton	Color Light

Group Igneous	Origin Intrusive	Grain size Coarse	Crystal shape Anhedral, Euhedral

HORNBLENDE GRANITE

This granitic rock is made up of more than 20 percent quartz and over 65 percent silica. K-feldspars (orthoclase and microcline) are more abundant than plagioclase feldspar. Hornblende occurs as small masses, and as prismatic crystals. Mica is also present in the rock.
• TEXTURE Coarse-grained, with equal-sized crystals, giving an even texture.
• ORIGIN Forms at various depths in the earth's crust.

dark hornblende crystals

pale orthoclase feldspar

Classification Acid	Occurrence Pluton	Color Medium

| Group Igneous | Origin Intrusive | Grain size Coarse | Crystal shape Anhedral, Euhedral |

ADAMELLITE

An acid rock, adamellite has more than 65 percent total silica and over 20 percent quartz. It contains a large quantity of feldspar – equally divided between K-feldspars (orthoclase and microcline) and plagioclase. Biotite mica gives adamellite a speckled appearance. Small gray grains of quartz occur in the matrix.
• **TEXTURE** This is a coarse-grained rock with generally equigranular grains (grains of the same size), though it can be porphyritic. The crystals are large enough to be seen with the naked eye. Most of the crystals in adamellite are euhedral, though some of the quartz is anhedral.
• **ORIGIN** Crystallizes in magmas associated with large plutons.

gray quartz

feldspar crystals over ³/₁₆ inch (5 mm) in diameter

dark biotite mica

pale feldspar

| Classification Acid | Occurrence Pluton | Color Light |

| Group Igneous | Origin Intrusive | Grain size Medium | Crystal shape Anhedral, Euhedral |

WHITE MICROGRANITE

An acid rock with more than 65 percent total silica and over 20 percent quartz. It contains more K-feldspars (orthoclase and microcline) than plagioclase feldspar. There may be dark biotite and/or light muscovite mica. Patches of biotite may give microgranite a darker color.
• **TEXTURE** Medium-grained, with crystals ³/₁₆–¹/₆₄ inch (5–0.5 mm) in diameter. This makes mineral identification difficult. The grains are generally equigranular, but many of the crystals are anhedral, or sometimes porphyritic, because of more rapid cooling.
• **ORIGIN** In the outer margins of pegmatites. Also forms as minor intrusions, such as sills and dikes, from the crystallization of magma at moderate depth.

light orthoclase feldspar

gray quartz

biotite mica gives speckled appearance

| Classification Acid | Occurrence Dike, Sill | Color Light, Medium |

| Group Igneous | Origin Intrusive | Grain size Medium | Crystal shape Anhedral, Euhedral |

PINK MICROGRANITE

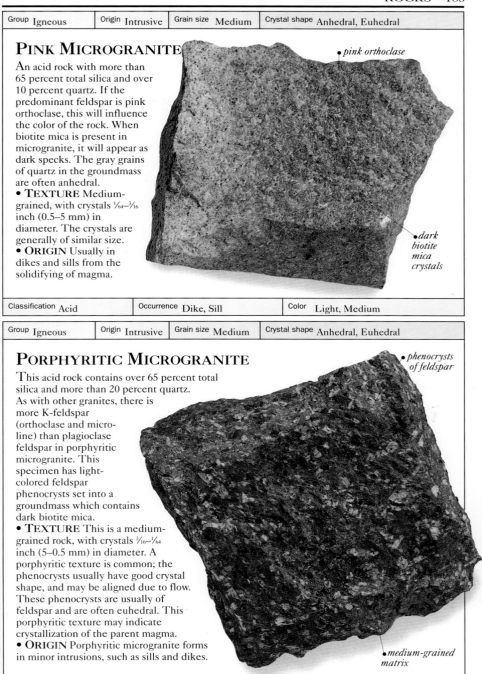

• *pink orthoclase*

An acid rock with more than 65 percent total silica and over 10 percent quartz. If the predominant feldspar is pink orthoclase, this will influence the color of the rock. When biotite mica is present in microgranite, it will appear as dark specks. The gray grains of quartz in the groundmass are often anhedral.
• **TEXTURE** Medium-grained, with crystals ¹⁄₆₄–³⁄₁₆ inch (0.5–5 mm) in diameter. The crystals are generally of similar size.
• **ORIGIN** Usually in dikes and sills from the solidifying of magma.

•*dark biotite mica crystals*

| Classification Acid | Occurrence Dike, Sill | Color Light, Medium |

| Group Igneous | Origin Intrusive | Grain size Medium | Crystal shape Anhedral, Euhedral |

PORPHYRITIC MICROGRANITE

• *phenocrysts of feldspar*

This acid rock contains over 65 percent total silica and more than 20 percent quartz. As with other granites, there is more K-feldspar (orthoclase and micro-line) than plagioclase feldspar in porphyritic microgranite. This specimen has light-colored feldspar phenocrysts set into a groundmass which contains dark biotite mica.
• **TEXTURE** This is a medium-grained rock, with crystals ³⁄₁₆–¹⁄₆₄ inch (5–0.5 mm) in diameter. A porphyritic texture is common; the phenocrysts usually have good crystal shape, and may be aligned due to flow. These phenocrysts are usually of feldspar and are often euhedral. This porphyritic texture may indicate crystallization of the parent magma.
• **ORIGIN** Porphyritic microgranite forms in minor intrusions, such as sills and dikes.

•*medium-grained matrix*

| Classification Acid | Occurrence Dike, Sill | Color Medium |

Group Igneous/Met.	Origin C'try Rock	Grain size Fine	Crystal shape Anhedral, Euhedral

XENOLITH

Xenolith is a term applied to rock fragments that are foreign to the body of igneous rock in which they occur. They are usually engulfed by magma, and partly altered. In some cases, a xenolith may be completely digested and loses its identity. This specimen is a dark mass of lava within pink granite. The granite's feldspar, mica, and quartz contrast noticeably with the dark xenolith.
• **TEXTURE** Xenolith is a medium- to fine-grained rock, with crystals of ¹⁄₆₄ inch (0.5 mm) in diameter. The granite is coarse-grained, with crystals of ³⁄₁₆ inch (5 mm) and over.
• **ORIGIN** Xenoliths occur in many igneous rocks and environments.

granite around margins

coarse grains

xenolith •

Classification Acid to basic	Occurrence Pluton, Volcano	Color Dark

Group Igneous	Origin Intrusive	Grain size Medium	Crystal shape Anhedral, Euhedral

QUARTZ PORPHYRY

An acid rock, with more than 65 percent total silica, and over 10 percent quartz. It contains phenocrysts of quartz and alkali feldspar (usually orthoclase) in a microcrystalline matrix. In quartz porphyry, orthoclase feldspar exceeds plagioclase feldspar. Some patches of hornblende are also visible in this specimen.
• **TEXTURE** This is a medium-grained rock, but with some larger crystals (phenocrysts) of various essential minerals, surrounded by smaller mineral grains. These smaller grains in the matrix are of similiar size. A porphyritic rock, quartz porphyry may have formed in two stages during the cooling of magma.
• **ORIGIN** Quartz porphyry forms in minor intrusive structures, such as sills and dikes, from the intrusion and cooling of magma. It does not usually form at great depth.

phenocrysts in matrix

Classification Acid	Occurrence Dike, Sill	Color Light, Medium

Group Igneous	Origin Intrusive	Grain size Very coarse	Crystal shape Euhedral

FELDSPAR PEGMATITE

This acid rock has the same mineral composition as granite. It contains a high proportion of feldspar (which is usually pink or white), grayish quartz, and dark mica or amphibole. The total silica content is well over 65 percent.

• **TEXTURE** Due to slow cooling, pegmatites are very coarse-grained: some have crystals many feet long. In this specimen, the mass of white feldspar is over 4 inch (10 cm) long. The minerals can be easily identified without a magnifying glass.

• **ORIGIN** Forms in plutonic environments, often in dikes and veins. Pegmatites tend to be concentrated at the margins of granite intrusions.

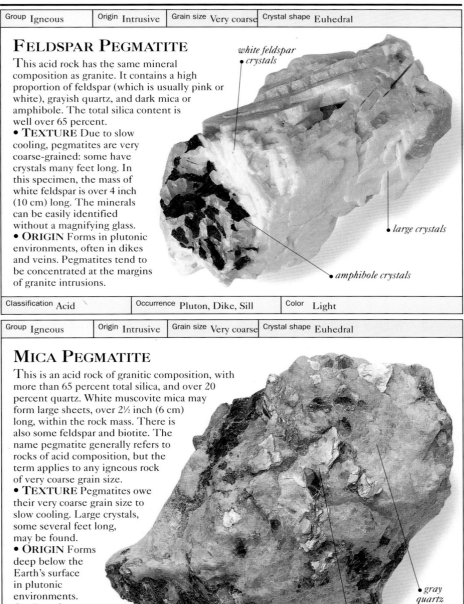

white feldspar crystals

large crystals

amphibole crystals

Classification Acid	Occurrence Pluton, Dike, Sill	Color Light

Group Igneous	Origin Intrusive	Grain size Very coarse	Crystal shape Euhedral

MICA PEGMATITE

This is an acid rock of granitic composition, with more than 65 percent total silica, and over 20 percent quartz. White muscovite mica may form large sheets, over 2½ inch (6 cm) long, within the rock mass. There is also some feldspar and biotite. The name pegmatite generally refers to rocks of acid composition, but the term applies to any igneous rock of very coarse grain size.

• **TEXTURE** Pegmatites owe their very coarse grain size to slow cooling. Large crystals, some several feet long, may be found.

• **ORIGIN** Forms deep below the Earth's surface in plutonic environments. Cooling of magma is slow, and often associated with late-stage fluids, which may carry some of the rarer chemical elements into the rock mass.

gray quartz

large, glittering muscovite mica crystals

Classification Acid	Occurrence Pluton, Dike, Sill	Color Light

Group Igneous	Origin Intrusive	Grain size Very coarse	Crystal shape Euhedral

TOURMALINE PEGMATITE

This rock has an acid composition, similar to that of granite, with well over 20 percent quartz, and more than 65 percent total silica. A high proportion of gray quartz, pink K-feldspars, and dark biotite mica may be present. The dark, prismatic crystals are the borosilicate mineral, tourmaline.

• TEXTURE Consists of very coarse-grained crystals. Some of the larger crystals in this specimen are 2–2½ inch (5–6 cm) long. Most are euhedral (good crystal shape). The tourmaline forms coarse, striated prismatic crystals.

• ORIGIN Tourmaline pegmatite forms in large intrusions, and also in dikes or sills. The rock is created by the slow cooling of magma at a considerable depth in the Earth's crust.

pink orthoclase feldspar

• dark, prismatic tourmaline crystals

Classification Acid	Occurrence Pluton, Dike, Sill	Color Light

Group Igneous	Origin Intrusive	Grain size Medium	Crystal shape Anhedral, Euhedral

GRANOPHYRE

This rock has an acid composition, with more than 20 percent quartz, and a total silica content of over 65 percent. It contains both K-feldspars and plagioclase feldspars, mica, and amphibole. When ferro-magnesian minerals are present in granophyre, they give the rock a darker color.

• TEXTURE This is a medium-grained rock but can be porphyritic, characterized by a texture formed by an intergrowth of feldspars and quartz – called granophyric – and a finer version of graphic texture found in some granites. The texture is best seen with a hand lens, or viewed under a microscope.

• ORIGIN The rock occurs on the margins of large, plutonic intrusive masses, and also in hypabyssal intrusions.

ferro-magnesian minerals give dark color

similar-sized grains

Classification Acid	Occurrence Pluton, Dike	Color Light, Medium

Group Igneous	Origin Intrusive	Grain size Coarse	Crystal shape Anhedral, Euhedral

PINK GRANODIORITE

This is a plutonic rock generally consisting of quartz, plagioclase, and lesser amounts of alkali feldspar. Minor constituents of pink granodiorite may be hornblende, biotite, or pyroxene.
• **TEXTURE** A medium- to coarse-grained rock, with well-formed crystals.
• **ORIGIN** Forms in many types of igneous intrusions. *hornblende* This is probably the common- *crystals* est rock of the granite family.

Classification Intermediate	Occurrence Pluton, Dike	Color Light, Medium

Group Igneous	Origin Intrusive	Grain size Coarse	Crystal shape Anhedral, Euhedral

WHITE GRANODIORITE

The total silica content of this *light feldspar* rock is lower than that of granite, being between 55 and 65 percent. This light form of granodiorite contains a high proportion of gray quartz and white feldspar. Dark mica and hornblende give the rock a speckled appearance.
• **TEXTURE** A coarse-grained rock, white granodiorite has well-formed crystals. Some of the interstitial quartz may be anhedral. *dark*
• **ORIGIN** Forms in many *ferro-magnesian* types of igneous intrusions. *minerals*

Classification Intermediate	Occurrence Pluton	Color Light

Group Igneous	Origin Intrusive	Grain size Coarse	Crystal shape Anhedral, Euhedral

DIORITE

A rock of intermediate composition, diorite has 55 to 65 percent total silica content. Essentially composed of plagioclase feldspar (oligoclase or andesine), and hornblende. Biotite mica and pyroxene may also occur in diorite.
• **TEXTURE** The grain size of diorite is medium to coarse (sometimes pegmatitic). It may be equigranular, or porphyritic with phenocrysts of feldspar or hornblende.
• **ORIGIN** Forms as independent intrusions, such as dikes, but usually comprises parts of major *light plagioclase* granitic masses. *feldspar*

Classification Intermediate	Occurrence Pluton, Dike	Color Medium, Dark

Group Igneous	Origin Intrusive	Grain size Coarse	Crystal shape Euhedral

SYENITE

A coarse-grained plutonic
rock generally lacking quartz
(up to 10 percent quartz in
quartz syenites), syenite is a
light-colored rock, which is often
confused with granite. An intermediate
rock, with total silica between 55 and
65 percent, principally formed of alkali
feldspar, and/or sodic plagioclase,
usually associated with biotite,
amphibole, or pyroxene.
• TEXTURE A coarse-grained
rock, with all minerals visible to
the naked eye, and with grains
generally the same size. It is
sometimes porphyritic – where
larger crystals are enclosed by a
finer-grained matrix. Crystals
are mainly anhedral to euhedral.
• ORIGIN Usually forms in
minor intrusions, dikes, and sills
often associated with granites.

amphibole •

Classification Intermediate	Occurrence Pluton, Dike	Color Light, Dark

Group Igneous	Origin Intrusive	Grain size Coarse	Crystal shape Euhedral

NEPHELINE SYENITE

This rock has the typical intermediate
igneous rock composition of 55 to 65
percent total silica content. It contains a
high proportion of feldspar, amphibole,
and mica. Pyroxene can sometimes be
present. Nepheline syenite contains
the feldspathoid mineral, nepheline,
from which its name is derived. There
is no quartz present in this rock.
• TEXTURE This syenite is coarse-
grained; the minerals can be seen
clearly without a hands lens. The
crystals generally have the same grain
size (equigranular). This rock can
sometimes be pegmatic.
• ORIGIN Nepheline syenite forms from
the crystallization of
magmas that are often   *dark patches of*
associated with highly   *ferro-magnesian •*
alkaline rocks. These are   *minerals*
rocks which contain
minerals rich in sodium   *coarse-grained •*
and potassium.   *texture*

Classification Intermediate	Occurrence Pluton, Dike	Color Light, Dark

Group Igneous	Origin Intrusive	Grain size Coarse	Crystal shape Euhedral

GABBRO

A basic rock in which quartz is very rare. Gabbros are poorer in silica than granites (about 50 percent by weight). Gabbro is composed essentially of calcic plagioclase, pyroxene (usually augite), and olivine and magnetite.
• **TEXTURE** Gabbro is a coarse-grained and equigranular rock.
• **ORIGIN** Forms in major plutonic intrusions, which are commonly layered.

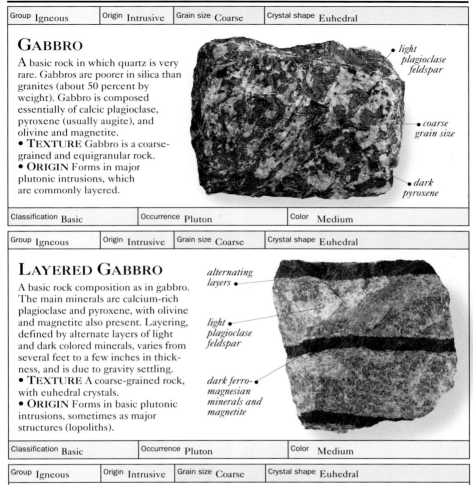

light plagioclase feldspar

coarse grain size

dark pyroxene

Classification Basic	Occurrence Pluton	Color Medium

Group Igneous	Origin Intrusive	Grain size Coarse	Crystal shape Euhedral

LAYERED GABBRO

A basic rock composition as in gabbro. The main minerals are calcium-rich plagioclase and pyroxene, with olivine and magnetite also present. Layering, defined by alternate layers of light and dark colored minerals, varies from several feet to a few inches in thickness, and is due to gravity settling.
• **TEXTURE** A coarse-grained rock, with euhedral crystals.
• **ORIGIN** Forms in basic plutonic intrusions, sometimes as major structures (lopoliths).

alternating layers

light plagioclase feldspar

dark ferro-magnesian minerals and magnetite

Classification Basic	Occurrence Pluton	Color Medium

Group Igneous	Origin Intrusive	Grain size Coarse	Crystal shape Euhedral

LARVIKITE

A variety of augite syenite, larvikite is an intermediate rock consisting of feldspar, pyroxene (usually Ti – augite), mica, and amphibole. It contains minor amounts of nepheline and olivine. Pale to dark gray in coloration, the feldspars usually display a distinctive schiller.
• **TEXTURE** This is a coarse-grained rock. In this specimen, the mafic minerals are seen to form in clots.
• **ORIGIN** Forms in relatively small intrusions, such as sills.

coarse-grained rock

mass of grayish feldspar crystals with ferro-magnesian minerals in between

Classification Intermediate	Occurrence Pluton	Color Light, Dark

Group Igneous	Origin Intrusive	Grain size Coarse	Crystal shape Anhedral, Euhedral

OLIVINE GABBRO

This rock has a basic composition, with a total silica content of less than 55 percent. Quartz occurs only rarely. The high content of ferro-magnesian minerals gives the rock a dark coloring. It is of higher density than the granitic rocks. Olivine gabbro contains plagioclase feldspar (a calcium-rich variety), pyroxene, and olivine. Magnetite is generally present in small amounts.

• TEXTURE A coarse-grained rock, the crystals, which are mostly euhedral, are over ³⁄₁₆ inch (5 mm) and easy to see with the naked eye. The grains are all of similar size, though gabbros can be porphyritic – having larger crystals surrounded by a finer matrix.

• ORIGIN Forms in plutonic environments, often in stocks, sills, and other sheet-like intrusions.

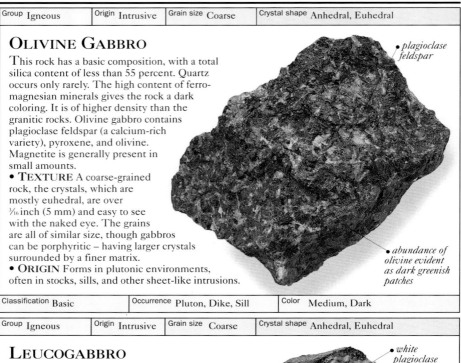

plagioclase feldspar

abundance of olivine evident as dark greenish patches

Classification Basic	Occurrence Pluton, Dike, Sill	Color Medium, Dark

Group Igneous	Origin Intrusive	Grain size Coarse	Crystal shape Anhedral, Euhedral

LEUCOGABBRO

Basic in composition, leucogabbro has a total silica content of less than 55 percent. It is lighter than other gabbros, because of a high percentage of plagioclase feld-spar. This is usually associated with the clinopyroxene, augite. Olivine and magnetite can also sometimes be present.

• TEXTURE This is a coarse-grained rock. The crystals are over ³⁄₁₆ inch (5 mm) in diameter, and can easily be seen with the naked eye.

• ORIGIN This rock forms in plutonic environments, often in major intrusions. During crystal-lization, crystals and liquid may be separated under the influence of gravity. The tapping off of the liquid fraction can lead to the formation of a variety of rock types, a process known as fractional crystallization.

white plagioclase feldspar

dark pyroxene, equal in quantity to feldspar

Classification Basic	Occurrence Pluton	Color Medium, Light

Group Igneous	Origin Intrusive	Grain size Coarse	Crystal shape Anhedral, Euhedral

BOJITE

A plutonic rock consisting of plagioclase feldspar (labradorite), brown hornblende, minor augite, and biotite. The brown hornblende is thought to be primary. A common accessory mineral is iron oxide (magnetite). Bojite is often visually striking, with patches and streaks and a layering of mafic minerals.
• TEXTURE Coarse-grained, with crystals greater than ³/₁₆ inch (5 mm) in diameter. Grains are of the same size, but dark minerals tend to be in patches and layers.
• ORIGIN Forms in plutonic environments, at considerable depth in the Earth's crust.

recognizable patches of different colored minerals •

• coarse-grained texture

• patches of iron-rich alteration

Classification Basic	Occurrence Pluton	Color Dark

Group Igneous	Origin Intrusive	Grain size Coarse	Crystal shape Anhedral, Euhedral

ANORTHOSITE

A rock of basic composition, the total silica content is less than 55 percent, and quartz is virtually absent. Anorthosite comprises at least 90 percent plagioclase feldspar (labradorite-bytownite). Other minerals in the rock include olivine, pyroxene, and iron oxides. Garnet sometimes forms in reaction rims around pyroxene.
• TEXTURE Generally coarse-grained, granular, and light in color, these rocks may have a parallel alignment of dark minerals.
• ORIGIN Forms in plutonic environments, in stocks, dikes, and sheet-shaped intrusions. It is often associated with gabbros in layered sequences, and has been shown to form part of the moon's surface.

mass of light plagioclase feldspar • crystals

• ferro-magnesian minerals

• coarse grain size

Classification Basic	Occurrence Pluton	Color Light

Group Igneous	Origin Intrusive	Grain size Medium	Crystal shape Anhedral, Euhedral

DOLERITE

A rock of basic composition, with
a total silica content of less
than 55 percent; the quartz
content is usually lower than
10 percent. Dolerite consists
of calcium-rich plagioclase
feldspar, and pyroxene – often
augite – with some quartz, and
sometimes magnetite and olivine.
(If olivine is present it is known as
olivine dolerite; if quartz is present
it is called quartz dolerite).
• TEXTURE A medium-grained
rock, with crystals between ¹⁄₆₄–³⁄₁₆ inch
(0.5–5 mm) in diameter. Euhedral or
subhedral crystals of plagioclase are
embedded in pyroxene crystals.
• ORIGIN This rock usually forms as
dikes and sills in basaltic provinces. It
may also occur as dike or sill swarms –
hundreds of individual intrusions
associated with a single igneous center.

plagioclase
•feldspar

• pyroxene

Classification Basic	Occurrence Dike, Sill	Color Dark

Group Igneous	Origin Intrusive	Grain size Medium	Crystal shape Anhedral, Euhedral

NORITE

Similar to gabbro, this is a rock of basic
composition with less than 55 percent total
silica. Norite is composed of plagioclase
feldspar and pyroxene. Importantly, it is a
variety of gabbro, in which orthopyroxene is
dominant over clinopyroxene. Olivine may
be present in some varieties of the rock.
Biotite mica, hornblende, and
cordierite can sometimes also
occur in this rock.
• TEXTURE A coarse-grained rock,
which is granular in texture, norite
often shows a layered structure.
• ORIGIN Forms by the freezing
of magma in a plutonic environment. Norite is associated with
larger basic igneous bodies,
and is often found in layered
igneous intrusions; different
rock types may form within one
intrusion by a separation of their
mineral content, often due to the
effects of gravity settling.

• pale plagioclase
feldspar

• dark
ferro-
magnesian
minerals

Classification Basic	Occurrence Pluton	Color Dark

Group Igneous	Origin Intrusive	Grain size Medium	Crystal shape Anhedral, Euhedral

TROCTOLITE

A variety of gabbro, troctolite has a total silica content of less than 55 percent. It is composed essentially of highly calcic plagioclase and olivine, with virtually no pyroxene. The olivine is often altered to serpentine. Troctolite is generally dark gray, often with a mottled appearance.
• **TEXTURE** This is a medium- to coarse-grained rock, with many crystals about ¹⁄₁₆ inch (5 mm) in diameter. The grains are generally of a similar size.
• **ORIGIN** Troctolite forms in a plutonic environment, where the magma cools slowly. It is usually associated with gabbros or anorthosite, sometimes in layered complexes.

gray-colored• plagioclase feldspar

mottled appearance •

Classification Basic	Occurrence Pluton	Color Dark

Group Igneous	Origin Intrusive	Grain size Medium	Crystal shape Euhedral

DUNITE

greenish coloring from olivine •

A rock of ultrabasic composition, dunite contains less than 45 percent total silica and no quartz. It is made up almost entirely of olivine, which gives the rock its recognizable greenish or brownish coloring. The alternative name, olivinite, refers to its mineral composition. Chromite occurs in this rock as an accessory mineral.
• **TEXTURE** A medium-grained rock, with crystals ¹⁄₆₄–¹⁄₁₆ inch (0.5–5 mm) in diameter. The texture of dunite is granular and sugary.
• **ORIGIN** Forms in a plutonic environment. Small volumes of ultra-basic rocks are often formed as cumulates during the differentiation of basic rocks. Minerals in some dunites are often crushed, and they may have been emplaced in a near solid state due to earth movements. This can produce a mass of ultrabasic rock from a magma that is otherwise of basic composition.

• typical sugary texture

Classification Ultrabasic	Occurrence Pluton	Color Dark, Medium

Group Igneous	Origin Intrusive	Grain size Coarse	Crystal shape Anhedral, Euhedral

SERPENTINITE

This is a plutonic rock with an ultrabasic composition, with less than 45 percent total silica. It is composed almost entirely of serpentine minerals, such as antigorite and chrysotile. Relics of olivine are often present. Other ferro-magnesian minerals such as garnet, pyroxene, hornblende, and mica are also commonly found, as are chromite or chrome spinels. It is dark in color, with areas of black, green, or red.

• **TEXTURE** A coarse- to medium-grained rock in which most crystals are easy to see with the naked eye. This is a compact, often banded rock, commonly veined by fibrous serpentine.

• **ORIGIN** Occurs as dikes, stocks, and lenses. Serpentinites are formed by the serpentinization of other rocks, principally peridotite. It commonly occurs in folded metamorphic rocks, probably from altered olivine-rich intrusions.

easily seen, coarse-grain crystals

dark coloring

patches of different color

Classification Ultrabasic	Occurrence Orogenic belts	Color Dark

Group Igneous	Origin Intrusive	Grain size Coarse	Crystal shape Anhedral, Euhedral

PYROXENITE

This is an ultramafic, plutonic rock with less than 45 percent total silica. As the name suggests, it is composed almost entirely of one or more pyroxenes. Some biotite, hornblende, olivine, and iron oxide may also be present. The light-colored crystals in pyroxenite are of feldspar in very small amounts.

• **TEXTURE** Pyroxenite is a coarse- to medium-grained rock. It has a granular texture, with well-formed crystals sometimes forming layers. The texture can easily be seen with the naked eye.

• **ORIGIN** Pyroxenite forms in small, independent intrusions that are usually associated with gabbros or other types of ultrabasic rock.

dark coloring

granular texture

pyroxene minerals

Classification Ultrabasic	Occurrence Pluton	Color Dark

Group Igneous	Origin Intrusive	Grain size Coarse	Crystal shape Euhedral

KIMBERLITE

An ultrabasic rock consisting of major amounts of serpentinized olivine. It is associated with phlogopite, ortho- or clino-pyroxene, carbonate, and chromite. Pyrope garnet, rutile, and perovskite may also be present. Kimberlite is dark in color.
• TEXTURE This is a coarse-grained rock, often with a porphyritic texture. Kimberlite often has a brecciated appearance.
• ORIGIN Forms in pipes and other igneous bodies which are steep-sided and intrusive. The pipes are usually less than three-fifths of a mile in diameter. Kimberlite pipes are the primary source of diamonds, and are mined, especially in South Africa, for their high diamond content.

crystals of ferro-magnesian minerals

dark groundmass

Classification Ultrabasic	Occurrence Hypabyssal, Plutonic	Color Dark

Group Igneous	Origin Intrusive	Grain size Coarse	Crystal shape Anhedral, Euhedral

GARNET PERIDOTITE

A rock with less than 45 percent total silica content, garnet peridotite is composed only of dark minerals: feldspar is virtually absent. Olivine is essential, as is garnet. Pyroxene and/or hornblende are often present.
• TEXTURE A coarse- or medium-grained rock, with garnets set into a granular groundmass. The garnets may vary in size from very small grains to larger patches over ³⁄₁₆ inch (5 mm) in diameter.
• ORIGIN Garnet peridotite forms in intrusive dikes, sills, and stocks, and is sometimes associated with large masses of gabbro, pyroxenite, and anorthosite. It is found in basalts and as xenoliths in high-grade metamorphic rocks. It is possible for garnet peridotite to have been derived from the Earth's mantle.

smaller patches of red garnet

typical greenish color produced by olivine

Classification Ultrabasic	Occurrence Pluton, Dike, Sill	Color Dark

Group Igneous	Origin Extrusive	Grain size Fine	Crystal shape Anhedral

RHYOLITE

These are extrusive rocks with the same general composition as granite. Like granites, these rocks are often rich in quartz and alkali feldspars. Unlike granites, glass is often one of the major components in rhyolite. Biotite mica is usually present.

• TEXTURE A fine-grained acid, volcanic rock which may have phenocrysts giving a porphyritic texture. The matrix crystals are too small to be seen with the naked eye, and the rapid cooling of the lava causes glass to be formed. Rhyolite may also have vesicles and amygdales.

• ORIGIN These rocks erupt from volcanoes with explosive violence, and are the result of the cooling of viscous lava. These lavas may plug the volcano's vent, causing a buildup of gaseous pressure.

porphyritic texture

phenocrysts include quartz

Classification Acid	Occurrence Volcano	Color Light

Group Igneous	Origin Extrusive	Grain size Fine	Crystal shape Anhedral

BANDED RHYOLITE

A group of rocks similar in composition to granites. Quartz, feldspar, and mica, along with glass, are the major components of banded rhyolite, while hornblende may also be present.

• TEXTURE A fine- or very fine-grained rock, in which the minerals are too small to be seen with the naked eye. Flow banding, common in rhyolites, is defined by swirling layers of different color and texture. These rocks may also have a spheroidal texture formed by radial aggregates of needles composed of quartz and feldspar.

• ORIGIN Formed by the rapid cooling of lava, leading to the formation of minute crystals or glass. The magma is highly viscous.

bands of different colors

hard, flinty appearance

Classification Acid	Occurrence Volcano	Color Light, Medium

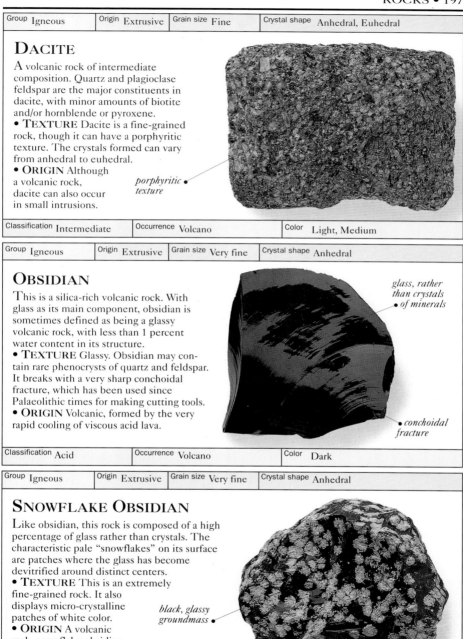

Group Igneous	Origin Extrusive	Grain size Fine	Crystal shape Anhedral, Euhedral

DACITE

A volcanic rock of intermediate
composition. Quartz and plagioclase
feldspar are the major constituents in
dacite, with minor amounts of biotite
and/or hornblende or pyroxene.
• **TEXTURE** Dacite is a fine-grained
rock, though it can have a porphyritic
texture. The crystals formed can vary
from anhedral to euhedral.
• **ORIGIN** Although
a volcanic rock,
dacite can also occur
in small intrusions.

porphyritic
texture

Classification Intermediate	Occurrence Volcano	Color Light, Medium

Group Igneous	Origin Extrusive	Grain size Very fine	Crystal shape Anhedral

OBSIDIAN

This is a silica-rich volcanic rock. With
glass as its main component, obsidian is
sometimes defined as being a glassy
volcanic rock, with less than 1 percent
water content in its structure.
• **TEXTURE** Glassy. Obsidian may contain rare phenocrysts of quartz and feldspar.
It breaks with a very sharp conchoidal
fracture, which has been used since
Palaeolithic times for making cutting tools.
• **ORIGIN** Volcanic, formed by the very
rapid cooling of viscous acid lava.

glass, rather
than crystals
of minerals

conchoidal
fracture

Classification Acid	Occurrence Volcano	Color Dark

Group Igneous	Origin Extrusive	Grain size Very fine	Crystal shape Anhedral

SNOWFLAKE OBSIDIAN

Like obsidian, this rock is composed of a high
percentage of glass rather than crystals. The
characteristic pale "snowflakes" on its surface
are patches where the glass has become
devitrified around distinct centers.
• **TEXTURE** This is an extremely
fine-grained rock. It also
displays micro-crystalline
patches of white color.
• **ORIGIN** A volcanic
rock, snowflake obsidian
is formed from lava that
has cooled rapidly.

black, glassy
groundmass

white
"snowflakes"

Classification Acid	Occurrence Volcano	Color Dark

Group Igneous	Origin Extrusive	Grain size Very fine	Crystal shape Anhedral

PITCHSTONE

This rock has a composition equivalent to
a wide range of other volcanic rocks. It is
essentially a volcanic glass, and it contains a
few phenocrysts. Pitchstone is usually
very dark in color, and has a luster similar
to that of tar or pitch.
• TEXTURE Although the
proportion of glass content
in pitchstone is very high, it   *tarlike*
contains more crystalline   *surface* •
material than obsidian. It
may also be spotted or flow-   *fine-grained*
banded. Even under   *crystals* •
microscopic examination,
the crystals in pitchstone
appear to be poorly formed.
• ORIGIN The rock forms as the result of
very sudden solidification of lava, especially
in dikes and flows. The large quantity of
glass contained in pitchstone is a result of
its rapid cooling history.

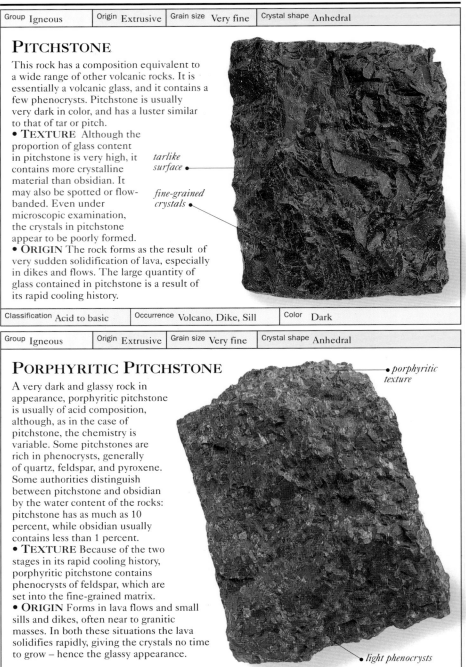

Classification Acid to basic	Occurrence Volcano, Dike, Sill	Color Dark

Group Igneous	Origin Extrusive	Grain size Very fine	Crystal shape Anhedral

PORPHYRITIC PITCHSTONE

*porphyritic
texture*

A very dark and glassy rock in
appearance, porphyritic pitchstone
is usually of acid composition,
although, as in the case of
pitchstone, the chemistry is
variable. Some pitchstones are
rich in phenocrysts, generally
of quartz, feldspar, and pyroxene.
Some authorities distinguish
between pitchstone and obsidian
by the water content of the rocks:
pitchstone has as much as 10
percent, while obsidian usually
contains less than 1 percent.
• TEXTURE Because of the two
stages in its rapid cooling history,
porphyritic pitchstone contains
phenocrysts of feldspar, which are
set into the fine-grained matrix.
• ORIGIN Forms in lava flows and small
sills and dikes, often near to granitic
masses. In both these situations the lava
solidifies rapidly, giving the crystals no time
to grow – hence the glassy appearance.

light phenocrysts

Classification Acid to basic	Occurrence Volcano, Dike, Sill	Color Dark

Group Igneous	Origin Extrusive	Grain size Medium	Crystal shape Anhedral, Euhedral

LAMPROPHYRE

A group of rocks of variable composition. They are characterized by being strongly porphyritic in mafic minerals, typically biotite, amphibole, and pyroxene – any feldspar (whether alkali or plagioclase feldspar) is confined to the matrix. Accessory minerals include hornblende, calcite, sphene, and magnetite.

• TEXTURE Medium-grained, this group of rocks is typically porphyritic. Both biotite and hornblende phenocrysts give the rocks a distinctive appearance.

• ORIGIN Forms in minor intrusions, and in dikes and sills. The rocks often show signs of hydrothermal alteration. They can be associated with a variety of other igneous rocks, such as granites, syenites, and diorites.

• porphyritic texture

Classification Acid to basic	Occurrence Dike, Sill	Color Medium

Group Igneous	Origin Extrusive	Grain size Fine	Crystal shape Anhedral, Euhedral

ANDESITE

An intermediate volcanic rock, andesite usually has 55 to 65 percent total silica content. Plagioclase feldspar (andesine or oligoclase) is the most significant constituent, along with pyroxene, amphibole, and biotite mica.

• TEXTURE A fine-grained, often porphyritic rock. The phenocrysts set into the matrix are usually white tabular feldspar crystals, or biotite, hornblende, or augite.

• ORIGIN This rock forms as lava flows from andesitic volcanoes, which are second only in abundance to basalt. Andesitic volcanoes are often associated with sub-duction zones, as in the Andes mountains of South America.

• phenocrysts of light plagioclase feldspar

• fine-grained matrix

Classification Intermediate	Occurrence Volcano	Color Medium

Group Igneous	Origin Extrusive	Grain size Fine	Crystal shape Anhedral, Euhedral

AMYGDALOIDAL ANDESITE

This is an intermediate volcanic rock which is usually porphyritic. Amygdaloidal andesite consists of plagioclase feldspar (frequently zoned labradorite-oligoclase), pyroxene, and/or biotite. The rock matrix tends to be a medium-colored gray, rather than the black of basalt.
• TEXTURE This rock has a fine-grained matrix although it may often be porphyritic. Many small, rounded vesicles are visible on the rock surface. These vesicles are left after gas bubbles have escaped from the lava. Infilled vesicles are known as amygdales, and are commonly infilled by the zeolite group of minerals. The cavities are widened by the growth of minerals.
• ORIGIN Amygdaloidal andesite forms from the rapid cooling of lava that has been erupted from a gas-rich volcanic eruption.

small gas bubble cavities, infilled with minerals

fine-grained matrix

Classification Intermediate	Occurrence Volcano	Color Medium

Group Igneous	Origin Extrusive	Grain size Fine	Crystal shape Anhedral, Euhedral

PORPHYRITIC ANDESITE

This rock has the same composition as andesite. It is an intermediate rock with 55 to 65 percent total silica. Plagioclase feldspar is an important constituent, as are pyroxene, amphibole, and biotite mica. Andesite is usually a darker-colored volcanic rock than rhyolite, though it is lighter than basalt.
• TEXTURE The matrix is fine-grained, and the crystals can be studied in detail only under a microscope. Larger phenocrysts of feldspar and pyroxene are set into the matrix. This texture indicates that some crystals grew in the magma below the Earth's surface, and that, on eruption, the lava solidified rapidly.
• ORIGIN Porphyritic andesite forms as lava flows, usually associated with andesitic volcanoes.

fine-grained matrix

euhedral phenocrysts set into the matrix

Classification Intermediate	Occurrence Volcano	Color Medium

Group Igneous	Origin Extrusive	Grain size Fine	Crystal shape Anhedral, Euhedral

TRACHYTE

These are volcanic rocks with a total silica content of between 55 to 60 percent. Trachytes are rich in alkali feldspar and also carry either nepheline or small amounts of quartz (less than 10 percent). Dark minerals, such as the pyroxene, aegerine, are present in small amounts, though trachytes are usually light in color.
• TEXTURE A fine-grained rock, usually porphyritic. Feldspar micro-crystals exhibit flow structure.

minute crystals in matrix

• ORIGIN Trachytes form as lava flows and narrow dikes and sills.

small phenocrysts

Classification Intermediate	Occurrence Volcano	Color Medium

Group Igneous	Origin Extrusive	Grain size Fine	Crystal shape Anhedral, Euhedral

PORPHYRITIC TRACHYTE

This rock has a similar composition to trachyte, and has 55 to 65 percent total silica. Dominantly composed of alkali feldspar, some quartz and oligoclase feldspar may be present, as well as pyroxene, hornblende, and biotite mica.
• TEXTURE This rock has a fine-grained matrix. Euhedral phenocrysts are common, giving this rock a porphyritic texture.
• ORIGIN Formed by the cooling of lava.

black phenocrysts, give a porphyritic texture

Classification Intermediate	Occurrence Volcano	Color Medium

Group Igneous	Origin Extrusive	Grain size Medium	Crystal shape Euhedral

RHOMB PORPHYRY

A rock of intermediate chemistry, rhomb porphyry is often called microsyenite. It has 55 to 65 percent total silica content, and up to 10 percent quartz. The main minerals are alkali feldspar with hornblende, pyroxene, and biotite mica.
• TEXTURE This rock derives its name from the distinctive rhombic shape of the cross section of its feldspar phenocrysts.

plagioclase feldspar phenocrysts

• ORIGIN Occurs as lava flows and dikes.

medium-grained matrix

Classification Intermediate	Occurrence Dike, Sill	Color Medium

Group Igneous	Origin Extrusive	Grain size Fine	Crystal shape Anhedral, Euhedral

BASALT

A basic volcanic rock consisting of calcic-plagioclase feldspar and pyroxene, basalt is the most abundant of all lava types. Apatite and magnetite are nearly always present, while olivine may also occur.
• TEXTURE A fine-grained rock, basalt has crystals which are both euhedral and anhedral. The crystals, however, are not easy to see, even with a hand lens.
• ORIGIN Forms by the cooling of highly-mobile basaltic lavas. Because of their fluidity, they may form very thick lava sheets. Basalt occurs widely in continental areas, and is the principal rock of the ocean floor. One of the best studied active basaltic volcanoes, Mauna Loa, forms much of the island of Hawaii.

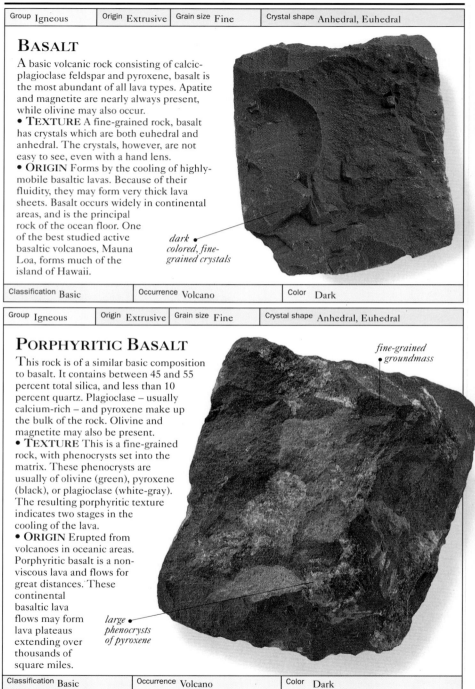

dark colored, fine-grained crystals

Classification Basic	Occurrence Volcano	Color Dark

Group Igneous	Origin Extrusive	Grain size Fine	Crystal shape Anhedral, Euhedral

PORPHYRITIC BASALT

This rock is of a similar basic composition to basalt. It contains between 45 and 55 percent total silica, and less than 10 percent quartz. Plagioclase – usually calcium-rich – and pyroxene make up the bulk of the rock. Olivine and magnetite may also be present.
• TEXTURE This is a fine-grained rock, with phenocrysts set into the matrix. These phenocrysts are usually of olivine (green), pyroxene (black), or plagioclase (white-gray). The resulting porphyritic texture indicates two stages in the cooling of the lava.
• ORIGIN Erupted from volcanoes in oceanic areas. Porphyritic basalt is a non-viscous lava and flows for great distances. These continental basaltic lava flows may form lava plateaus extending over thousands of square miles.

fine-grained groundmass

large phenocrysts of pyroxene

Classification Basic	Occurrence Volcano	Color Dark

Group Igneous	Origin Extrusive	Grain size Fine	Crystal shape Anhedral

AMYGDALOIDAL BASALT

A basic volcanic rock with a total silica content of 45 to 55 percent. Calcium-rich plagioclase feldspar and pyroxene are the main minerals. Olivine and magnetite are other minerals that are frequently associated with amygdaloidal basalt.
• **TEXTURE** Numerous amygdales (small, rounded gas-bubble cavities infilled with minerals) are characteristic of some basalts. Zeolites and quartz – often in the form of agate – are common minerals.
• **ORIGIN** This rock is formed by the cooling of lava.

numerous rounded amygdales

rusty weathering of iron minerals

Classification Basic	Occurrence Volcano	Color Dark

Group Igneous	Origin Extrusive	Grain size Fine	Crystal shape Anhedral, Euhedral

VESICULAR BASALT

This rock has a very similar composition to that of basalt, with calcic-plagioclase feldspar and pyroxene being the essential minerals. Olivine and magnetite are also usually present in vesicular basalt.
• **TEXTURE** The surface may be covered with empty, gas-bubble cavities called vesicles. The matrix is fine-grained, often porphyritic. If the cavities are infilled with minerals, vesicular basalt becomes an amygdaloidal basalt.
• **ORIGIN** Forms from the cooling of basaltic lava.

many small, rounded cavities

Classification Basic	Occurrence Volcano	Color Dark

Group Igneous	Origin Extrusive	Grain size Fine	Crystal shape Anhedral, Euhedral

SPILITE

A basic rock with a silica content averaging 40 percent, spilite occurs as pillow lavas. A distinctive feature of this rock is that the plagioclase feldspar is albite (Na-rich). The pyroxene content in spilite is often altered to chlorite, although augite may sometimes remain.
• **TEXTURE** A fine-grained rock with infilled gas-bubble cavities. Amygdales are sometimes visible, set in the matrix.
• **ORIGIN** Found in underwater lava flows and in pillow lava, formed on the ocean floor.

pale green amygdales, set in fine-grained matrix

Classification Basic	Occurrence Volcano	Color Dark

Group Igneous	Origin Pyroclast	Grain size Coarse	Crystal shape Fragments

AGGLOMERATE

A consolidated or unconsolidated, coarse, pyroclastic rock material, agglomerate may be composed of both volcanic and country rock fragments that are completely unsorted.
• **TEXTURE** The size of the particles varies considerably: the rock texture often consists of angular to sub-rounded fragments set into a finer-grained matrix. The lava particles are vesicular, sometimes spindle-shaped.
• **ORIGIN** This rock generally accumulates in volcanic craters or on the flanks of a volcano. Agglomerate consists of lava fragments and blocks of country rock that have been caught up with the volcanic activity, and have erupted with the lava through a volcanic vent. Usually associated with other extrusive deposits such as tuff.

many rock fragments held together in fine groundmass

Classification Acid to basic	Occurrence Volcano	Color Medium

Group Igneous	Origin Pyroclast	Grain size Fine	Crystal shape Fragments

LITHIC TUFF

This is a pyroclastic rock (tuff) in which lithic fragments are more abundant then either crystal or vitric (glassy) fragments.
• **TEXTURE** A fine-grained rock, tuff consists of consolidated volcanic fragments usually less than ⅓ inch (2 mm) in diameter, and also layered. Lithic tuff contains crystalline rock fragments which may be of rhyolitic, trachytic, or andesitic composition.
• **ORIGIN** This rock forms as a deposit from volcanic ash blown into the atmosphere. Lithic tuff sometimes accumulates underwater, when strata may develop. Grading of these layers may take place, and the tuff can have a variety of structures associated with sedimentation, including layering and banding. From very explosive eruptions, ash is often carried many miles into the atmosphere. Wind systems then carry the ash to settle a long way from the original volcano. When this happens, the dust particles, blown high into the atmosphere, may cause beautiful sunsets.

small fragments of lava and ash cemented together

fine-grained matrix

Classification Acid to basic	Occurrence Volcano	Color Medium

Group Igneous	Origin Extrusive	Grain size Fine	Crystal shape Anhedral, Euhedral

CRYSTAL TUFF

This is a variety of tuff in which crystal fragments are more abundant than either lithic or vitric fragments. Most tuffs are mixtures of lithic, vitric, or crystal fractions. The minerals present in crystal tuff usually include feldspars, and pyroxenes, as well as amphiboles.
• TEXTURE This is a fine- to medium-grained rock, with masses of crystals set into an ash matrix. The crystals are often euhedral.
• ORIGIN Forms when ashes are blown out from volcanoes during eruption. Previously formed crystals are separated from lava, and may accumulate on land or underwater. When underwater deposition occurs, tuff becomes stratified and takes on the features of a sedimentary rock.

mass of fine crystals

dark color due to ferro-magnesian mineral content

Classification Acid to basic	Occurrence Volcano	Color Medium

Group Igneous	Origin Lava, Ash	Grain size Fine	Crystal shape Anhedral

PUMICE

This is a light, porous rock with the composition of rhyolite. It may contain a variety of minute crystals of silicate minerals, such as feldspar and ferro-magnesians, and also has a considerable amount of glass.
• TEXTURE Pumice usually tends to be used as a textural term – applied to vesiculated lavas that may resemble froth or foam. This rock has a highly scoriaceous texture, with many hollows and cavities. The vesicles may join to form elongated passages and tubes throughout the rock. Zeolites may fill these cavities. The density of pumice is so low that it can easily float in water.
• ORIGIN Forms as frothy lavas associated with rhyolitic volcanic eruptions. When erupted into the sea, patches may drift for great distances. Pumice can also be formed by land-bound volcanic eruptions.

typically elongated vesicles

hollow, gas-bubble cavities or vesicles

Classification Acid to basic	Occurrence Volcano	Color Medium

Group Igneous	Origin Extrusive	Grain size Fine	Crystal shape Anhedral

IGNIMBRITE

This is a hard, volcanic tuff consisting of crystal and rock fragments in a matrix of glass shards which are usually welded together. This welding, in some cases, may lead to the original texture, shown by the glass shards, being lost. Ignimbrite has a similar composition to rhyolite.
• **TEXTURE** It is often a fine-grained rock with a banded structure. In the field, you may see wavy flow banding through the outcrop. The glass shards in the rock are often curved where they have formed around gas bubbles in the original frothy flow of ash, tuff, and lava droplets.
• **ORIGIN** Forms as a deposit from a rapidly moving, turbulent, ignited cloud of gas called a *nuée ardente*. Associated with especially violent eruptions, producing clouds of incandescent gas and lava drops. These flow from volcanic eruptions at great speed, close to the ground.

•shard glass

• light-colored acid rock with darker patches

Classification Acid	Occurrence Volcano	Color Light, Medium

Group Igneous	Origin Extrusive	Grain size Fine	Crystal shape Anhedral

BREADCRUST VOLCANIC BOMB

• rough surface texture

Volcanic bombs usually have the composition of the lava erupted by a particular volcano. The lava clots have a high silica content with a high proportion of quartz. Clots from intermediate composition lavas have a silica content of 55 to 65 percent. Basic volcanoes are mainly nonexplosive, and bombs are less likely to form.
• **TEXTURE** Breadcrust volcanic bombs have a fine-grained crust and may show coarser crystals within. The crust may be marked and cracked because of the force of impact with the ground. They may contain small fragments of country rock, torn from around the volcanic pipe.
• **ORIGIN** Volcanic bombs are small to large molten lava clots that have been ejected from a volcano by violent eruption, and have landed on the Earth. The lava clots are usually made of viscous lava, which cools on the outside during flight, forming a skin that cracks on impact of landing to produce the "breadcrust" surface. The bombs may sometimes measure over 3 feet (0.9 m) in diameter. When they land in volcanic ash, these bombs will often form a crater.

fine-grained • crystals

Classification Acid to basic	Occurrence Volcano	Color Dark

Group		Origin		Grain size		Crystal shape	
Igneous		Extrusive		Fine		Anhedral	

ROUNDED SPINDLE BOMB

Spindle bombs usually have the composition of the lava erupted by a particular volcano, whether it be andesite or basaltic. However, they also tend to be associated with acidic and other intermediate lava volcanoes. These rocks are often rich in silica, and contain minerals such as quartz, feldspar, mica, and some ferro-magnesian minerals, such as hornblende.

• **TEXTURE** These rocks are composed of fine-grained crystals, which need microscopic examination. The shape results from the molten lava clot twisting during flight.

• **ORIGIN** Rounded spindle bombs form as molten lava clots thrown from violently erupting volcanoes.

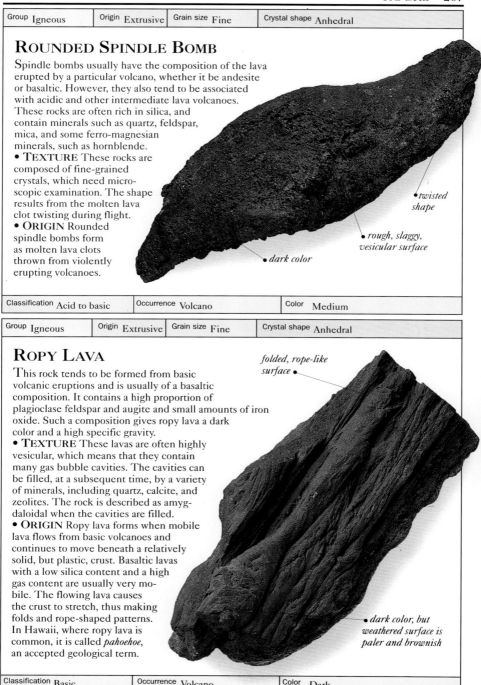

twisted shape

rough, slaggy, vesicular surface

dark color

Classification		Occurrence			Color	
Acid to basic		Volcano			Medium	

Group		Origin		Grain size		Crystal shape	
Igneous		Extrusive		Fine		Anhedral	

ROPY LAVA

folded, rope-like surface

This rock tends to be formed from basic volcanic eruptions and is usually of a basaltic composition. It contains a high proportion of plagioclase feldspar and augite and small amounts of iron oxide. Such a composition gives ropy lava a dark color and a high specific gravity.

• **TEXTURE** These lavas are often highly vesicular, which means that they contain many gas bubble cavities. The cavities can be filled, at a subsequent time, by a variety of minerals, including quartz, calcite, and zeolites. The rock is described as amygdaloidal when the cavities are filled.

• **ORIGIN** Ropy lava forms when mobile lava flows from basic volcanoes and continues to move beneath a relatively solid, but plastic, crust. Basaltic lavas with a low silica content and a high gas content are usually very mobile. The flowing lava causes the crust to stretch, thus making folds and rope-shaped patterns. In Hawaii, where ropy lava is common, it is called *pahoehoe*, an accepted geological term.

dark color, but weathered surface is paler and brownish

Classification		Occurrence			Color	
Basic		Volcano			Dark	

METAMORPHIC ROCKS

METAMORPHIC ROCKS form from the alteration of a pre-existing rock. Contact metamorphism is caused by direct heat, and the resulting rock is usually crystalline. Regional metamorphism is due to heat and pressure, and produces foliation, or cleavage, in rocks where the minerals have been aligned due to pressure and recrystallization. Dynamic metamorphism is associated with the alteration of rocks along major thrust zones (fault planes).

Group Metamorphic	Origin Mountain ranges	Grain size Fine	Classification Regional

GREEN SLATE

A low-grade metamorphic rock, slate is derived from clay (shale) pelitic rocks. Green slate is formed from quartz and some feldspar, mica. The presence of chlorite gives this slate its green color.
- **TEXTURE** Fine-grained with grains of a similar size. The grain size is too fine to be seen without a microscope.
- **ORIGIN** Forms when fine-grained sediments, such as clay or volcanic ash, undergo regional metamorphism. Minerals like mica and chlorite become aligned, giving a perfect, or slaty, cleavage.

many small, dark patches of carbon and pyrite

greenish color across cleavage surface

Pressure Low	Temperature Low	Structure Foliated

Group Metamorphic	Origin Mountain ranges	Grain size Fine	Classification Regional

BLACK SLATE

This rock is formed from pelitic sediments – clays, mudstones, shales, and fine-grained tuff. It contains clay minerals, quartz, mica, and feldspar. Organic matter such as graphite and pyrite give black slate its dark color.
- **TEXTURE** This is a fine-grained rock. It has the characteristic perfect, slaty cleavage produced by the alignment of flaky minerals, such as mica, which makes it easy to split into parallel-sided slabs.
- **ORIGIN** Forms when fine-grained, pelitic sediments, such as mudstones or shales, undergo regional metamorphism at low temperatures and low pressures.

dark color

small, raised pyrite porphyroblasts

fine grain size

Pressure Low	Temperature Low	Structure Foliated

Group Metamorphic	Origin Mountain ranges	Grain size Fine	Classification Regional

SLATE WITH PYRITE

Formed from pelitic sediments, as with
other slates this rock is composed of
quartz, clay minerals, chlorite, mica, and
feldspar. As its name suggests, there is also
pyrite present. The pyrite can be either
finely disseminated small crystals, or larger
porphyroblasts (distinct crystals) set in a
fine-grained matrix. The pyrite is often in
the form of cubic crystals.
• **TEXTURE** This slate is fine-grained,
with only the pyrite porphyroblasts visible to
the naked eye. The fine-grained matrix can
be studied in detail only under a microscope.
As with other slates, this rock is characterized
by its perfect, slaty, cleavage, which has
resulted from the alignment of flaky minerals
due to pressure conditions.
• **ORIGIN** This rock forms
under low temperature
and low pressure
conditions. The distinct
pyrite crystals grow in
response to this regional
metamorphism.

*small pyrite
crystal set in
the surface*

*fine-grained
matrix*

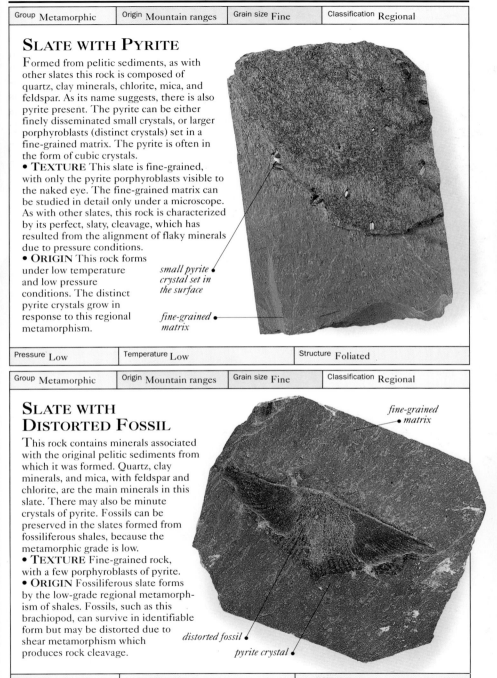

Pressure Low	Temperature Low	Structure Foliated

Group Metamorphic	Origin Mountain ranges	Grain size Fine	Classification Regional

SLATE WITH DISTORTED FOSSIL

This rock contains minerals associated
with the original pelitic sediments from
which it was formed. Quartz, clay
minerals, and mica, with feldspar and
chlorite, are the main minerals in this
slate. There may also be minute
crystals of pyrite. Fossils can be
preserved in the slates formed from
fossiliferous shales, because the
metamorphic grade is low.
• **TEXTURE** Fine-grained rock,
with a few porphyroblasts of pyrite.
• **ORIGIN** Fossiliferous slate forms
by the low-grade regional metamorphism of shales. Fossils, such as this
brachiopod, can survive in identifiable
form but may be distorted due to
shear metamorphism which
produces rock cleavage.

*fine-grained
matrix*

distorted fossil

pyrite crystal

Pressure Low	Temperature Low	Structure Foliated

Group Metamorphic	Origin Mountain ranges	Grain size Medium	Classification Regional

PHYLLITE

pale grayish green coloring •

Derived from low-grade metamorphosed sediments, phyllites are comparable with slates but are not restricted in premetamorphic terms to very fine clays. Quartz and feldspars are more abundant than in shales. Mica and chlorite are essential constituents, imparting a characteristic sheen, and a gray or green color.

• **TEXTURE** This is a foliated rock of fine to medium grain size. Phyllite may have small, distinct crystals (porphyroblasts) of garnet set into the wavy foliation. This foliation results from the alignment of mica and chlorite under low to moderate pressure. Phyllites often show small-scale folding.

• **ORIGINS** Forms from pelitic sediments, during low to moderate pressure, and low temperature regional metamorphism.

• *sheen on surfaces, due to high mica and chlorite content*

Pressure Low, Moderate	Temperature Low	Structure Foliated

Group Metamorphic	Origin Mountain ranges	Grain size Medium	Classification Regional

GARNET SCHIST

• *dark colored rock*
• *wavy foliation*

The group of rocks known as schist are characterized by the presence of visible flaky or tabular minerals aligned in a cleavage. Garnet schist is rich in the micas, biotite, and muscovite, with quartz and feldspar also present. The usually well-shaped crystals of garnet are about 3/16 inch (5 mm) in diameter, and have grown in the rock during pressure and temperature changes. The garnet is usually the reddish variety (almandine).

• **TEXTURE** A medium- to coarse-grained rock. A schistosity is always well-developed due to the parallel alignment of micas. The rock may often show small-scale folding.

• **ORIGIN** Forms in conditions of medium-grade, regional metamorphism, at deeper levels than phyllite. The pressure is moderately high, and temperature has been influential in changing the rock's original character.

red garnet • *porphyroblasts*

• *mica gives glittery, silvery sheen*

Pressure Moderate	Temperature Low to moderate	Structure Foliated

Group Metamorphic	Origin Mountain ranges	Grain size Medium	Classification Regional

FOLDED SCHIST

This rock contains quartz, feldspar, biotite, and muscovite mica. Folded schist is characterized by small-scale folds accentuated by glittering mica crystals.

• **TEXTURE** A medium-grained rock, the constituent minerals are often segregated into distinct bands. Schistosity, a wavy foliation caused by the rock splitting along planes of weakness, is emphasized by the mica crystals.

• **ORIGIN** Formed by moderate pressures and low to moderate temperatures very deep in the crust within fold mountain belts. Folded schist is typical of mountain-forming belts.

dark biotite

light muscovite

wavy folds picked out by mineral bands

Pressure Moderate	Temperature Low to moderate	Structure Foliated

Group Metamorphic	Origin Mountain ranges	Grain size Medium	Classification Regional

MUSCOVITE SCHIST

This rock is rich in silvery muscovite mica. The mica is aligned on the planes of wavy foliation within the rock. Muscovite schist also contains quartz, feldspar, and some biotite mica. Garnet and chlorite minerals may also be present.

• **TEXTURE** A medium-grained rock with mica crystals $\frac{1}{16}$–$\frac{1}{8}$ in (2–3 mm) in size. The schistosity, or wavy foliation, may be emphasized by bands rich and poor in muscovite.

• **ORIGIN** Muscovite schists form from pelitic rocks under conditions of medium-grade regional metamorphism, where pressures are moderate, and temperature influences low to moderate. Such conditions typically lead to the alteration of mud- and clay-based rocks. Other rocks are also affected by this metamorphism, but these tend to show less foliation.

silvery mica on foliation

Pressure Moderate	Temperature Low to moderate	Structure Foliated

| Group Metamorphic | Origin Mountain ranges | Grain size Medium | Classification Regional |

BIOTITE SCHIST

This rock contains a high proportion of mica, along with quartz and feldspar. It is especially rich in biotite mica, which gives it a darkish coloring. Compositionally, biotite schist is very similar to the pelitic sediments from which it developed during metamorphism.

• **TEXTURE** A medium-grained rock, with crystals that are visible to the naked eye. Biotite schist is, however, best studied with a hand lens. This specimen shows the dark flakes of mica aligned with the foliation.

• **ORIGIN** Forms during medium-grade regional metamorphism of pelitic sediments, and other rocks, but these may not become foliated.

quartz

high proportion of mica

wavy foliation from alignment of flaky minerals

| Pressure Moderate | Temperature Low to moderate | Structure Foliated |

| Group Metamorphic | Origin Mountain ranges | Grain size Medium | Classification Regional |

KYANITE SCHIST

The bulk of this rock is composed of quartz, feldspar, and mica, though it is characterized by the mineral kyanite. Kyanite forms sky-blue porphyroblasts of bladed habit which lie parallel to the foliation, or as clusters of crystals. It is often folded. Other minerals can be garnet and staurolite. The overall color is grayish, but may be darker.

• **TEXTURE** A medium- to coarse-grained rock, the crystals are easy to see with the naked eye. These are always schistose but may also be gneissose.

• **ORIGIN** Found in the central high-grade part of metamorphic belts, under moderate to high pressure and temperate regimes. This rock is associated with sillimanite and staurolite schists. Kyanite is one of the minerals used by geologists to map metamorphic zones. Each zone is defined according to a mineral formed under certain pressure-temperature conditions.

gray rock with foliated structure

dark mica

gray

blue-bladed kyanite

medium- to coarse-grained

| Pressure Moderate | Temperature Moderate to high | Structure Foliated |

Group Metamorphic	Origin Mountain ranges	Grain size Coarse	Classification Regional

GNEISS

• dark and light-colored foliated bands

A metamorphic rock characterized by compositional banding of metamorphic origin is known as gneiss. Feldspar and quartz are abundant, while muscovite, biotite, and hornblende are also commonly present. Other rocks characteristic of high-grade regional metamorphism, such as pyroxene and garnet, may also occur.

• pale feldspar

• **TEXTURE** A medium- to coarse-grained rock, characterized by discontinuous, alternating light and dark layers. The presence of quartz and feldspar help to form the lighter layers which tend to have a granular texture. The darker layers of ferromagnesian minerals tend to be foliated.

• **ORIGIN** This rock forms from the high-grade regional metamorphism of any pre-formed rock. The minerals are segregated into bands as a result of high temperatures and pressures. Gneisses may either be meta-sediments or meta-igneous rocks, and occur in association with migmatites and granites. Gneiss is thought to comprise much of the lower continental crust.

dark mica •

Pressure High	Temperature High	Structure Foliated, Crystalline

Group Metamorphic	Origin Mountain ranges	Grain size Coarse	Classification Regional

FOLDED GNEISS

As with other gneisses, this rock is composed of segregated bands: the lighter bands are rich in quartz and feldspar; the dark bands are made up of ferro-magnesian minerals, such as hornblende and biotite mica. In folded gneiss these bands are often very obvious. The composition may be very similar to that of granite.

• **TEXTURE** A coarse-grained rock, with all the minerals easy to see with the naked eye. The folded structure is emphasized by the segregation of the minerals, and gives the impression that parts of the rock had been plastic when formed.

• **ORIGIN** Folded gneiss is formed under conditions of high-grade regional metamorphism. All rock types, such as sediments, sandstones and shales, and igneous rocks, including dolerite and granite, may become gneisses under these conditions.

• pale quartz and feldspar

• dark hornblende and biotite mica

• folded, separate bands of pale and dark minerals

Pressure High	Temperature High	Structure Foliated, Crystalline

Group Metamorphic	Origin Mountain ranges	Grain size Coarse	Classification Regional

AUGEN GNEISS

These are metamorphic rocks of granite composition that contain large lens-shaped crystals ("eyes" or "augen") of feldspar in a banded matrix of quartz, feldspar, and micas.
• TEXTURE A coarse-grained rock, the gneissose banding is somewhat displaced by the augen structure.
• ORIGIN Augen gneiss forms in the highest temperature and pressure zones of regional meta- morphism.

dark and light banding

larger eye-shaped patches of feldspar

Pressure High	Temperature High	Structure Foliated, Crystalline

Group Metamorphic	Origin Mountain ranges	Grain size Coarse	Classification Regional

GRANULAR GNEISS

High proportions of light gray quartz, white and pink feldspar, and light and dark mica make up this rock. Amphibole and pyroxene may be present. The composition is often granitic.
• TEXTURE The crystals are streaked out into typical gneissose banding, with dark and light bands. The texture is granular with interlocking crystals.
• ORIGIN Forms in very high-grade metamorphic environments deep in the earth's crust.

alternating bands of dark and light minerals

Pressure High	Temperature High	Structure Foliated, Crystalline

Group Metamorphic	Origin Mountain ranges	Grain size Coarse	Classification Regional

MIGMATITE

This is a mixed metamorphic rock consisting of a schist or gneissose component, and a granitic component forming as layers or pods. Migmatite may approach granite in composition.
• TEXTURE A coarse-grained rock with a granular texture, it often shows banding like gneiss.
• ORIGIN Forms on a regional scale in areas of high-grade metamorphism, particularly in ancient continental shields.

small-scale folds

light mineral band

dark and light-colored components

dark basic material

Pressure High	Temperature High	Structure Foliated, Crystalline

Group Metamorphic	Origin Base of crust	Grain size Coarse	Classification Regional

ECLOGITE

A rock predominantly composed of pyroxene (green variety, omphacite) and red garnet. Kyanite crystals may sometimes occur in eclogite.
• **TEXTURE** A medium- to coarse-grained rock which may be banded.
• **ORIGIN** Formed under highest temperature and pressure conditions, at considerable depth in the earth's crust. Found in association with perditites and serpentinites.

greenish pyroxene

red garnet

foliated texture

Pressure High	Temperature High		Structure Foliated, Crystalline

Group Metamorphic	Origin Base of crust	Grain size Coarse	Classification Regional

GRANULITE

This rock has a characteristically high content of pyroxene, and either diopside or hypersthene. Garnet, kyanite, biotite, quartz, and feldspar may also be present.
• **TEXTURE** These are tough, massive, coarse-grained rocks which may be banded but are not usually schistose.
• **ORIGIN** Believed to be formed at very high temperatures and pressures. Found in ancient continental shield areas.

light, distinct crystals set in finer matrix

Pressure High	Temperature High		Structure Crystalline

Group Metamorphic	Origin Mountain ranges	Grain size Coarse	Classification Regional

AMPHIBOLITE

This rock is dominantly formed of amphibole, commonly hornblende, but sometimes actinolite or tremolite. Feldspar, pyroxene, chlorite, epidote, and garnet are also often present.
• **TEXTURE** This is a coarse-grained rock. A well-developed foliation or schistosity may be present. Porphyroblasts, particularly of garnet, may also be present.
• **ORIGIN** Medium- to high-grade rocks, amphibolites are formed mostly from the metamorphism of igneous rocks such as dolerites.

amphibole crystals

Pressure High	Temperature High		Structure Foliated, Crystalline

| Group Metamorphic | Origin Contact aureoles | Grain size Coarse–fine | Classification Contact |

GREEN MARBLE

This rock is composed essentially of calcite, derived from the original limestone, but may contain lesser amounts of dolomite. Other minerals formed from impurities in the limestone may include brucite, olivine, tremolite, and serpentine – all of which can give the otherwise whitish rock a greenish coloring.

• **TEXTURE** This is a crystalline rock which, when looked at through a hand lens, but especially under a microscope, is seen to have a mosaic of interlocking and fused crystals of calcite. The original limestone would probably have contained fossils, but these will have been lost during the metamorphic recrystallization.

• **ORIGIN** This rock results from the thermal metamorphism of limestone around igneous intrusions.

green veins of calc-silicate minerals

crystalline texture

| Pressure Low | Temperature High | Structure Crystalline |

| Group Metamorphic | Origin Contact aureoles | Grain size Coarse–fine | Classification Contact |

BLUE MARBLE

Composed essentially of calcite, which forms the original limestone, but may contain lesser amounts of dolomite. If the limestone is impure, new minerals develop when the rock is recrystallized due to thermal metamorphism. The new minerals can include forsterite, wollastonite, serpentine, brucite, diopside, and tremolite. The blue coloring which makes this marble attractive is due mainly to the diopside in its composition.

• **TEXTURE** A crystalline rock, with a mosaic of fused calcite crystals, just visible with a hand lens. Other minerals are set into the matrix.

• **ORIGIN** Forms when limestone is intruded by igneous rock. The heat from such events causes recrystallization of the calcite, thus destroying original structures in the limestone, and leading to the formation of new minerals.

pale-colored calcite

blue patches from diopside

crystalline texture

| Pressure Low | Temperature High | Structure Crystalline |

Group Metamorphic	Origin Contact aureoles	Grain size Coarse–fine	Classification Contact

GRAY MARBLE

Unlike other marbles, this rock forms from relatively pure limestones, and therefore few calc-silicate minerals develop. Gray marble is a calcite-rich rock which, when studied under a microscope, is seen to contain a small amount of wollastonite, brucite, tremolite, serpentine, or diopside.
• **TEXTURE** This is a crystalline rock, with interlocking calcite crystals, forming a pale, soft rock. The sugary surface can be scratched easily with a knife blade. Marbles will effervesce in a weak hydrochloric acid solution – this is a very useful test.
• **ORIGIN** Forms in the metamorphic aureoles of igneous rocks, where limestone has been heated and recrystallized, especially near granite intrusions.

crystalline texture

Pressure Low	Temperature High	Structure Crystalline

Group Metamorphic	Origin Contact aureoles	Grain size Coarse–fine	Classification Contact

OLIVINE MARBLE

individual crystals of olivine

This rock contains a very high percentage of calcite, which is recrystallised from the original pre-metamorphic limestone. Other minerals are produced as a result of metamorphic conditions, the most important of which is olivine. This mineral occurs in the marble as greenish-brown granular crystals in the matrix.
• **TEXTURE** A rock with a crystalline texture, olivine marble is formed from an interlocking mass of calcite crystals. It differs from the original limestone, in which the calcite grains may have pore spaces between them. Fossils occur only rarely in marble, because the calcite is recrystallized. The olivine crystals are granular in texture.
• **ORIGIN** This rock is formed when limestone is thermally metamorphosed by the intrusion of igneous rock.

greenish-brown olivine

calcite matrix

Pressure Low	Temperature High	Structure Crystalline

Group Metamorphic	Origin Contact aureoles	Grain size Fine	Classification Contact

CORDIERITE HORNFELS

A rock that contains a variety of minerals, the final assemblage depends on the composition of the original rock, and on the temperature conditions of metamorphism. Cordierite hornfels is usually a dark-colored rock, and contains quartz, mica, and cordierite, which develops during metamorphism.

• **TEXTURE** A fine- to medium-grained crystalline rock, it contains porphyroblasts of cordierite, which are often several inches in diameter. Without foliation, the original sedimentary structures are usually destroyed by metamorphic recrystallization. The equi-granular composition of the rock causes it to be tough and splintery in texture.

• **ORIGIN** Forms in contact metamorphic aureoles, which occur in rocks close to large igneous (often granite) intrusions. Contact metamorphic aureoles grade outwards into lower grade rocks such as spotted slate.

dark gray, fine-grained rock

Pressure Low	Temperature High	Structure Crystalline

Group Metamorphic	Origin Contact aureoles	Grain size Fine	Classification Contact

PYROXENE HORNFELS

Tough, fine grained, dark-colored rock essentially composed of quartz, mica and pyroxene. Pyroxene in the hornfels often occurs as porphyroblasts. Some of the other minerals may not be visible to the naked eye, as all primary sedimentary structures are destroyed by recrystallization. Hornfels lacks planar structures and its coloration can also be grayish, greenish, or black.

• **TEXTURE** This is a fine- to medium-grained rock, with an even grain size. Porphyroblasts of pyroxene, cordierite or andulusite are often developed. The high degree of recrystallization that has occured removes any original sedimentary structures.

• **ORIGIN** Pyroxene hornfels forms in the innermost part of contact metamorphic aureoles, where the temp-erature is highest. These are formed by thermal metamorphosis following granite intrusion.

dark-colored pyroxene crystals

Pressure Low	Temperature High	Structure Crystalline

Group Metamorphic	Origin Contact aureoles	Grain size Fine	Classification Contact

GARNET HORNFELS

This is generally a dark-colored rock. Garnet hornfels has reddish patches and crystals of garnet set in the matrix. It also contains quartz, mica, and feldspar, and metamorphic minerals, such as cordierite and andalusite.

• **TEXTURE** This is a fine- to medium-grained rock, with a tough, splintery texture. The distinct garnet crystals give garnet hornfels a porphyroblastic texture.

• **ORIGIN** Forms in the contact aureoles of large igneous intrusions. These can be formed of granite, syenite, and gabbro.

red garnet porphyroblasts

flinty texture

Pressure Low	Temperature High	Structure Crystalline

Group Metamorphic	Origin Contact aureoles	Grain size Fine	Classification Contact

SPOTTED SLATE

This is a black, greenish or gray rock with dark spots. The spots may be metamorphic minerals, such as cordierite or andalusite. This rock also has in its composition many of the original non-metamorphic minerals, such as quartz and mica.

• **TEXTURE** Same structures as slate with a good cleavage. This rock is characterized by the presence of spots, which are often indistinct.

• **ORIGIN** Forms in the perimeter zones of contact aureoles, often grading into hornfels.

dark grayish cordierite crystals

small, dark spots

Pressure Low	Temperature High to moderate	Structure Crystalline

Group Metamorphic	Origin Contact aureoles	Grain size Fine	Classification Contact

CHIASTOLITE HORNFELS

A gray or brownish rock, this hornfels contains minerals such as quartz and mica, with andalusite and cordierite. The thin-bladed crystals that stand out from the matrix are of chiastolite, a variety of andalusite.

• **TEXTURE** This rock consists of fine-grained crystals of even size. Porphyroblasts of andalusite sometimes form, with fine dark-grained inclusions known as chiastolite, which is cross shaped in section.

• **ORIGIN** Forms close to the igneous intrusion that provides the heat for metamorphism.

bladed chiastolite

rhombic chiastolite

Pressure Low	Temperature Moderate to high	Structure Crystalline

Group Metamorphic	Origin Contact aureoles	Grain size Medium	Classification Contact

METAQUARTZITE

This rock contains well over 90 percent
quartz, giving it a pale, almost sugary,
appearance. It is formed from quartz-
rich sandstones. At high magnification,
minerals such as mica and feldspar,
along with iron oxides, may be seen.
• TEXTURE A fine- to medium-grained
rock, its texture is very even, with the quartz
crystals fused to form a tough crystalline rock.
The texture is thus very different from that of
the original arenaceous (sandy) sediment, in
which there would have been pore spaces
between the grains.
• ORIGIN Metaquartzite
forms both by contact
metamorphism of sand-   *crystalline texture* •
stone near a large igneous
intrusion, and by regional   *very high*
metamorphism.   *percentage of quartz* •

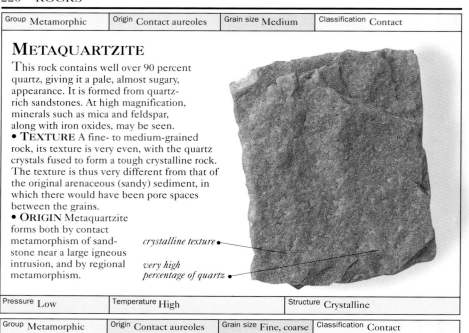

Pressure Low	Temperature High		Structure Crystalline

Group Metamorphic	Origin Contact aureoles	Grain size Fine, coarse	Classification Contact

SKARN

While containing a variety of minerals, skarn
is essentially calcite-rich. Skarn may contain
olivine, periclase, wollastonite, diopside, garnet,
serpentine, tremolite, and other minerals that
are typical of metamorphosed limestones. The
garnet is commonly grossular. Ore minerals
may also be present such as pyrite,
sphalerite, galena, and chalcopyrite.
• TEXTURE With a grain size that is fine to
medium to coarse, skarn has euhedral crystals
of a number of minerals. The associated
minerals may often concentrate into
patches and nodules in the rock.
• ORIGIN The complex mineral
assemblages found in skarns are the
result of its formation from the contact
metamorphism of limestone, usually by
granite or syenite intrusions. Impurities
in the limestone, as well as fluids from
intrusions, cause the formation of
various minerals. Ore deposits,
including copper, manganese,
and molybdenum, which are of   *much pale calcite* •
sufficient size to be of economic
use, are often found in skarns.   *dark mineral bands* •

*• typical veined
and banded
structure*

Pressure Low	Temperature High		Structure Crystalline

Group Metamorphic	Origin Contact aureoles	Grain size Fine	Classification Contact

HALLEFLINTA

This is a rock containing a variety of minerals related to its original pre-metamorphosed composition as a volcanic tuff. Halleflinta, therefore, contains quartz, and has been enriched with silica during metamorphism. It is frequently pale-colored, and can vary from brown to pink, green, gray, or yellowish brown.
• **TEXTURE** Halleflinta is a fine-grained rock – a microscope is needed to study its mineral composition. Texture is even, with a flinty, crystalline appearance. This rock breaks with a sharp, splintery fracture. It may show a layered structure related to the original stratification of the volcanic tuff. Porphyroblastic textures with large, isolated crystals are sometimes found.
• **ORIGIN** Forms by the contact metamorphism of tuffs, which have usually been impregnated by secondary silica. It is often associated with hornfels.

brownish, flinty rock

splintery fracture

high proportion of quartz

Pressure Low	Temperature High	Structure Crystalline

Group Metamorphic	Origin Thrust zones	Grain size Fine	Classification Dynamic

MYLONITE

The minerals contained in mylonite vary depending on the rocks being subjected to metamorphic alteration. Mylonite contains two main groups of material: one is derived from fragments of rock, called "rock flour," and the other consists of minerals that have crystallized at, or soon after, metamorphism. The rock can be dark or light-colored.
• **TEXTURE** This is a rock that has been destroyed by deformation, and the particles streaked out into small lenses and patches. It tends to be fine-grained. However, in some coarser specimens, the streaked-out structure may be visible, and the surfaces may have lineations on them.
• **ORIGIN** Forms when large-scale thrust faults develop. The rocks near the thrust plane suffer great shearing stress and are fragmented and drawn out in the direction of thrust movement. This occurs during earth movements associated with mountain formation.

foliation

pale mylonite with small scale contortions

Pressure Shearing stress	Temperature Low	Structure Streaked out

SEDIMENTARY ROCKS

SEDIMENTARY rocks are formed from the erosion, transportation and subsequent deposition of pre-existing rocks. This book classifies sediments into three broad categories: detrital, organic, and chemical. Detrital sediments result from the erosion and subsequent transportation of a pre-existing rock; organic sediments form from biological activity; chemical sediments form by primary precipitation in shallow marine environments.

Group Sedimentary	Origin Marine, Freshwater	Grain size Very coarse

QUARTZ CONGLOMERATE

This rock contains many light-colored quartz fragments set in a much finer matrix. The matrix usually comprises sand or silt, small rock fragments, and iron oxides, often cemented by silica or calcite.
• **TEXTURE** The large grains are rounded; the matrix may be angular or rounded. Quartz conglomerates rarely contain fossils because of their coarse nature, and the often turbulent conditions associated with their formation. Bedding structures are seldom seen in small samples.
• **ORIGIN** Forms where there is sufficient energy to move large fragments of material. This includes beaches and river systems.

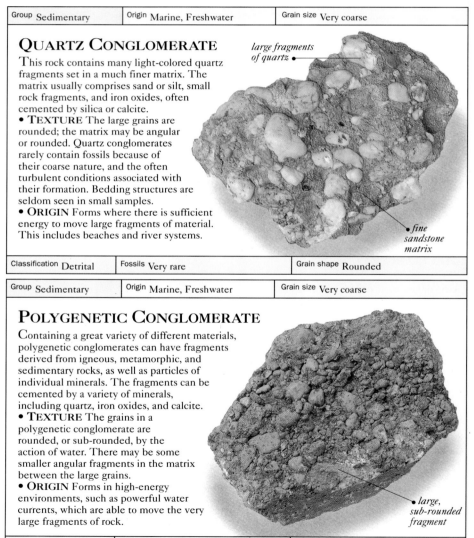

large fragments of quartz

fine sandstone matrix

Classification Detrital	Fossils Very rare	Grain shape Rounded

Group Sedimentary	Origin Marine, Freshwater	Grain size Very coarse

POLYGENETIC CONGLOMERATE

Containing a great variety of different materials, polygenetic conglomerates can have fragments derived from igneous, metamorphic, and sedimentary rocks, as well as particles of individual minerals. The fragments can be cemented by a variety of minerals, including quartz, iron oxides, and calcite.
• **TEXTURE** The grains in a polygenetic conglomerate are rounded, or sub-rounded, by the action of water. There may be some smaller angular fragments in the matrix between the large grains.
• **ORIGIN** Forms in high-energy environments, such as powerful water currents, which are able to move the very large fragments of rock.

large, sub-rounded fragment

Classification Detrital	Fossils Very rare	Grain shape Rounded

Group Sedimentary	Origin Transitional, Water	Grain size Very coarse

LIMESTONE BRECCIA

This is a rock that contains fragments of limestone, usually set in a fine-grained matrix cemented with calcite. Other minerals such as quartz may be present in limestone breccia, as may fragments of other rocks.
• **TEXTURE** The grains are large and angular in contrast to the rounded fragments in conglomerate. The individual fragments in limestone breccia may contain fossils.
• **ORIGIN** Found in transitional environments near continental margins. Limestone breccia may form as deposits at the base of cliffs. As water seeps through the cliff and the accumulated scree, it deposits lime which cements together the fragments.

dark, angular fragments of limestone

finer matrix

Classification Detrital	Fossils Invertebrates	Grain shape Angular

Group Sedimentary	Origin Transitional, Water	Grain size Very coarse

BRECCIA

Fragments of breccia are angular, and may be of any type of igneous, metamorphic and sedimentary rocks. These fragments are set together in a fine- to medium-grained matrix of salt or sand.
• **TEXTURE** Bedding structures are usually visible only on a large scale in the field. Fossils are uncommon in such rocks. The large fragments of rocks and minerals in breccia are angular, and the surrounding matrix material is also angular.
• **ORIGIN** Forms as scree at the base of cliffs. Breccia has a similar origin to limestone breccia, but the fragments in it are not calcareous. The accumulation of the large, angular fragments can take place in a number of environments, especially where mechanical weathering is active.

angular fragments showing no preferred orientation

gray siliceous fragments

yellowish matrix

Classification Detrital	Fossils Uncommon	Grain shape Angular

Group Sedimentary	Origin Glacier, Ice sheet	Grain size Fine

BOULDER CLAY

This rock consists of angular and some rounded pebbles, varying in size, and set in a fine, unconsolidated matrix. The rock types may be of any size, set together in a clay or sandy matrix. The glacial fragments included in the boulder clay are called glacial erratics. These are fragments carried away from their place of origin by the glacier. Fragments of breccia can be of some assistance to geologists in helping them to work out the general direction of ice movement.

• **TEXTURE** The fragments in boulder clay are mainly angular. The rock is made up of various unsorted materials, ranging from clay size to boulder size.

• **ORIGIN** Boulder clay usually forms as a deposit from melting glaciers and ice sheets.

angular rock fragment

brown, fine-grained clay

Classification Detrital	Fossils Rare	Grain shape Angular

Group Sedimentary	Origin Continental	Grain size Fine

LOESS

This is a yellowish or brownish clay made up of very small angular particles of quartz, feldspar, calcite, and other minerals and rock fragments.

• **TEXTURE** Loess is a fine-grained Aeolian clay, and it is porous and earthy. It is poorly cemented, which makes it crumbly. The grains may be rounded because of wind action, and bedding is difficult to determine.

• **ORIGIN** Forms by the winds blowing out from glaciated regions. Loess is deposited by the wind, and the material is probably derived from foliated regions. Wind-deposited loess is found in thick layers, especially in China, but also in areas of Western Europe.

yellowish coloring due to presence of limonite

powdery texture

Classification Detrital	Fossils Rare	Grain shape Rounded, Angular

Group Sedimentary	Origin Marine, Freshwater, Cont.	Grain size Medium

SANDSTONE

These are rocks predominantly made up of quartz grains, but often accompanied by feldspar, mica or other minerals. Grains may be cemented by silica, calcite, or iron oxides.
• **TEXTURE** Sandstone is a medium-grained rock. The grains are usually well-sorted grains all of a similar size. The grains can either be angular (gritstone) or rounded (sandstone).
• **ORIGIN** Sandstones are extremely common rocks which form in a great variety of geological situations. The majority of sandstones, however, are accumulated in either water, usually marine, or as windblown deposits in arid continental areas.

numerous grains of quartz make up the matrix

fine stratification

Classification Detrital	Fossils Invertebrates, Vertebrates, Plants	Grain shape Angular, Rounded

Group Sedimentary	Origin Marine	Grain size Medium

GREENSAND

This is a quartz sandstone which contains a few percent of the glauconite (a green-colored mineral which forms only under marine conditions). Small quantities of detrital mica, feldspar and rock fragments are usually cemented by calcite. The glauconite may well have formed in place (authigenic), and occurs as flaky grains.
• **TEXTURE** Greensand is a medium-grained rock, with the majority of the grains being angular. The sediment is well-sorted.
• **ORIGIN** Greensand forms in a marine environment. The constituent mineral glauconite, a potassium iron silicate, may be used to help in radiometric age-dating.

glauconite gives green coloring

Classification Detrital	Fossils Invertebrates, Vertebrates, Plants	Grain shape Angular

Group Sedimentary	Origin Continental, Marine	Grain size Medium

RED SANDSTONE

These are rocks predominantly formed by quartz grains but also accompanied by some mica and feldspar. The red coloration is due to coatings of hematite over the sand grains. Hematite is an iron oxide, derived by the oxidation of iron-rich minerals swept in from a source area.

• **TEXTURE** This is a well-sorted sediment, and the grains may be angular or rounded. Red sandstone often displays sedimentary structures including cross-bedding, ripple marks, and desiccation cracks.

• **ORIGIN** Forms as continental deposits, where iron may be oxidized. Red sandstone also commonly forms in shallow marine environments.

rounded grains

iron oxide gives red color

well-sorted sediment

Classification Detrital	Fossils Invertebrates, Vertebrates, Plants	Grain shape Angular, Rounded

Group Sedimentary	Origin Continental	Grain size Medium

MILLET-SEED SANDSTONE

A quartz sandstone with conspicuous rounding of the grains, producing what is known as a millet-seed texture. The rock may also contain some feldspar and rock fragments, but mica is usually absent. There is often a thin coating of iron oxides to the grains.

• **TEXTURE** This is a very well-sorted sediment, with the quartz grains all the same size. The grains are rounded, and are of medium size. Fossils are very rare.

• **ORIGINS** Millet-seed sandstone forms in arid environments. The quartz sand grains are rounded by the action of the wind. In the field, large-scale dune bedding may be a feature of this rock, indicating continental deposition.

iron oxide gives brown coloring

medium-sized grains of rounded quartz

Classification Detrital	Fossils Rare	Grain shape Rounded

Group Sedimentary	Origin Marine, Freshwater	Grain size Medium

MICACEOUS SANDSTONE

A rock containing abundant quartz, but also considerable amounts of mica. It may also contain detrital feldspar and rock fragments. On the bedding planes, the surfaces where the sand is deposited, there are many small, glittering, flakes of mica. These can be muscovite, biotite mica, or both.
• **TEXTURE** This rock is well-sorted and medium-grained. The majority of the grains are angular, the mica occurring typically as flakes.
• **ORIGIN** Mica is a rare mineral in continental, wind-deposited sandstones, because its flaky habit causes it to be blown away. Its presence in micaceous sandstone suggests water deposition, in either lakes and rivers, or the sea.

patches of iron oxide on surface

many small mica flakes

Classification Detrital	Fossils Invertebrates, Vertebrates, Plants	Grain shape Angular, Flattened

Group Sedimentary	Origin Marine, Freshwater	Grain size Medium

LIMONITIC SANDSTONE

angular grains cemented with limonite

dark brown coloring due to limonite

Rich in quartz grains, limonitic sandstone may contain small rock fragments, and minerals such as feldspar and mica. The presence of the iron mineral "limonite" – from which the rock gets its name – may give it a yellowish or dark brownish coloring.
• **TEXTURE** This is a well-sorted sediment, with most of the grains the same size. The fragments are angular and coated with limonite, which acts as a cement. As with other sandstones, bedding surfaces may be discernible, although this may not be particularly obvious in a hand specimen.
• **ORIGIN** Limonitic sandstone can form in a number of different environments, including marine and freshwater.

well-sorted sediment

Classification Detrital	Fossils Invertebrates, Vertebrates, Plants	Grain shape Angular

Group Sedimentary	Origin Marine, Freshwater	Grain size Medium

PINK ORTHOQUARTZITE

As with all orthoquartzites, this rock is a sandstone with a quartz content greater than 95 percent. The rocks are composed almost entirely of quartz grains with a silica cement. With a hand lens other minerals may occasionally be visible, including some feldspar or rock fragments. Fossils in ortho-quartzite are very rare.
• TEXTURE This is a medium-grained, well-sorted rock with a crystalline appearance.
• ORIGIN As orthoquartzites contain very little feldspar, they are said to be mature rocks. This is because the long-term processes of weathering, erosion, and deposition have removed virtually all the less resistant materials from the source rocks, and quartz becomes the dominant mineral.

• crystalline appearance

high quartz • content

Classification Detrital	Fossils Rare, Invertebrates	Grain shape Angular

Group Sedimentary	Origin Marine, Freshwater	Grain size Medium

GRAY ORTHOQUARTZITE

Compositionally the same as pink orthoquartzite, the gray coloring of this rock comes from the constituent quartz grains. It contains over 95 percent quartz. The cement is also quartz, and this binds the grains very firmly. Orthoquartzite may be difficult to distinguish from metaquartzite (metamorphosed quartz sandstones), though the occasional presence of fossils can help in identification. There are also stratification and other sedimentary structures, such as cross or graded bedding in orthoquartzite. These are not usually evident in metaquartzite.
• TEXTURE This is a rock of medium-grain size, and it is usually well-sorted.
• ORIGIN This rock forms in marine and freshwater environments and is subject to much erosion and weathering. With so much quartz present this, as with other ortho-quartzites, is known as a mature sediment.

• medium-grained quartz

Classification Detrital	Fossils Rare, Invertebrates	Grain shape Angular

Group Sedimentary	Origin Marine	Grain size Medium, Fine

GRAYWACKE

This rock contains abundant quartz-feldspar, and rock fragments. The matrix is of clay, chlorite, quartz, and pyrite, but the minerals are too small to be seen with the naked eye.
• **TEXTURE** Individual units of graywacke have a poorly sorted nature, with a great variety of different grain sizes apparent. Larger fragments typically contain sharply angular grains in a finer-grained matrix.
• **ORIGIN** These rocks are marine sediments. They may form from a slurry of sediment deposited in deep ocean environments from fast-moving currents. When this is the case, the rocks may exhibit a variety of sedimentary features.

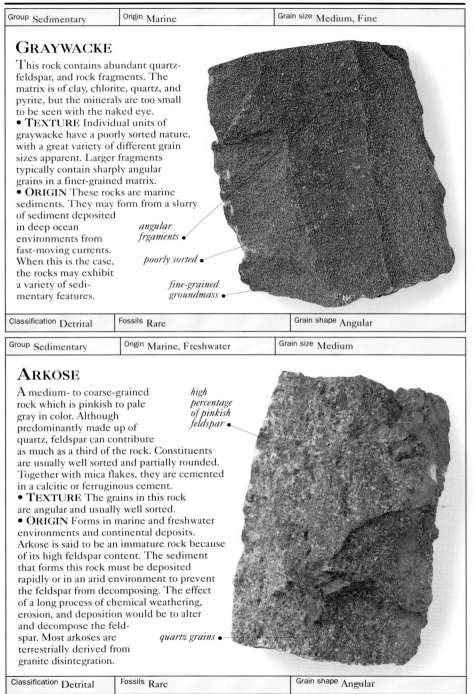

angular frgaments

poorly sorted

fine-grained groundmass

Classification Detrital	Fossils Rare	Grain shape Angular

Group Sedimentary	Origin Marine, Freshwater	Grain size Medium

ARKOSE

A medium- to coarse-grained rock which is pinkish to pale gray in color. Although predominantly made up of quartz, feldspar can contribute as much as a third of the rock. Constituents are usually well sorted and partially rounded. Together with mica flakes, they are cemented in a calcitic or ferruginous cement.
• **TEXTURE** The grains in this rock are angular and usually well sorted.
• **ORIGIN** Forms in marine and freshwater environments and continental deposits. Arkose is said to be an immature rock because of its high feldspar content. The sediment that forms this rock must be deposited rapidly or in an arid environment to prevent the feldspar from decomposing. The effect of a long process of chemical weathering, erosion, and deposition would be to alter and decompose the feldspar. Most arkoses are terrestrially derived from granite disintegration.

high percentage of pinkish feldspar

quartz grains

Classification Detrital	Fossils Rare	Grain shape Angular

Group Sedimentary	Origin Marine, Freshwater, Cont.	Grain size Coarse, Medium

QUARTZ GRITSTONE

This rock contains over 75 percent quartz, and some feldspar and mica. There can also be small rock fragments of varying types, depending on the rocks in the source area from which the sediment is derived. The cementing mineral may be quartz, and a yellowish coating of limonite on the grains might be evident.
• **TEXTURE** This is a coarse- to medium-grained rock. The grains are fairly well sorted, and angular in shape. Gritstones are sometimes poorly cemented, and the individual grains can often be rubbed off with the fingers.
• **ORIGIN** Forms in a number of different environments, ranging from marine and freshwater to continental. Most gritstones are formed in water, often in river systems and deltas. In all these places, a reasonable amount of energy is needed to carry the coarse particles.

well-sorted sediment

high percentage of quartz

Classification Detrital	Fossils Invertebrates, Vertebrates, Plants	Grain shape Angular

Group Sedimentary	Origin Marine, Continental	Grain size Coarse, Medium

FELDSPATHIC GRITSTONE

This rock contains a high percentage of quartz, but also has as much as 25 percent feldspar. Mica is present, and there are small rock fragments derived from the source area. Feldspathic gritstone has a similar composition to arkose, which is its fine-grained equivalent. It is a brownish-colored rock, and may take on a pinkish tinge when pink orthoclase feldspar is present. A cement of quartz or iron oxide may bind the grains together.
• **TEXTURE** This is a coarse- to medium-grained rock. The grains are angular, although the feldspar may have flattened faces where it has broken along cleavage planes. It is well sorted and most of the grains are of the same size.
• **ORIGIN** Forms by rapid deposition in transitional environments. Feldspar decomposes during protracted weathering.

medium grain size

feldspar grains visible

Classification Detrital	Fossils Invertebrates, Vertebrates, Plants	Grain shape Angular

Group Sedimentary	Origin Marine	Grain size Fine

BLACK SHALE

This, and other shales, consists of a mixture of clay minerals together with detrital quartz, feldspar, and mica. Black shales are rich in carbonaceous matter, and pyrite and gypsum commonly occur. The pyrite content may result from the rock forming under reducing conditions in deep, still water. This mineral may occur as cubic crystals on bedding planes, and fossils in black shale are often replaced by pyrite.
• **TEXTURE** This is a very fine-grained rock, with mineral grains invisible, except under a microscope. It is finely laminated, and splits easily along the bedding planes, sometimes revealing flattened fossils.
• **ORIGIN** Forms as a clay deposit in deep marine environments. The fossils in black shale are often marine creatures, such as mollusks.

fine laminations

cracks due to shrinkage

Classification Detrital	Fossils Invertebrates, Vertebrates, Plants	Grain shape Angular

Group Sedimentary	Origin Marine, Freshwater	Grain size Fine

FOSSILIFEROUS SHALE

many fossil brachiopods

Compositionally similar to other shales, fossiliferous shale may also have a high calcite content derived from the fossils it contains. As well as complete fossils, it will also have detrital fossil fragments.
• **TEXTURE** Because of its fine grain size, shale can preserve a variety of fossils with very fine detail. Fossil brachiopods may be present. Fossils commonly found in shales include mollusks, such as ammonoids, bivalves and gastropods. There are also arthropods such as trilobites, and graptolites – delicate structures which are not found in coarser rocks. Plants and vertebrates may also be present.
• **ORIGIN** Usually forms under relatively shallow marine conditions. Fossiliferous shale can also be found under freshwater conditions. The nature of the fossils found in the rock are usually a good indicator of the environment in which the rock was formed.

shale matrix

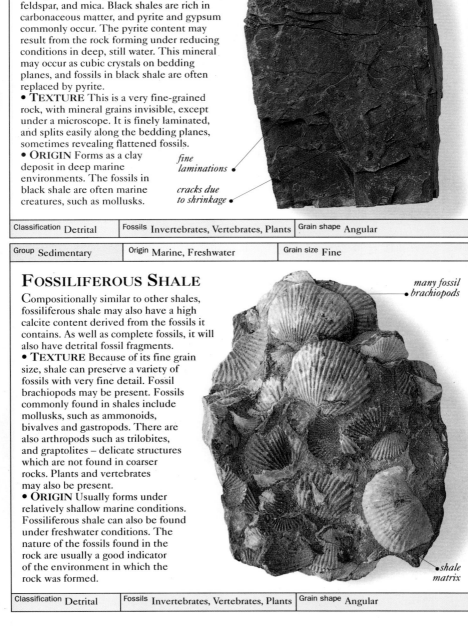

Classification Detrital	Fossils Invertebrates, Vertebrates, Plants	Grain shape Angular

Group Sedimentary	Origin Marine, Freshwater	Grain size Fine

SILTSTONE

This rock contains more quartz than either mudstones or shales. Siltstones are commonly laminated, due to variations in grain size, organic content, or amounts of calcium carbonate.

• **TEXTURE** This is a fine-grained sediment. The individual rock fragments and mineral grains in siltstone are too small to be visible to the naked eye.

• **ORIGIN** Siltstone forms by the compaction of sediment of silt grade which may have accumulated in a variety of environments, both marine and freshwater. The fossil content may be a guide to the precise environment of deposition. Because of the presence of feldspar and other minerals besides quartz, siltstone is said to be immature. A long-term weathering process would decompose feldspar and other material, leaving the quartz grains.

• uneven fracture

• fine-grained sediment

Classification Detrital	Fossils Invertebrates, Vertebrates, Plants	Grain shape Angular

Group Sedimentary	Origin Marine, Freshwater	Grain size Fine

MUDSTONE

• fine-grained rock

• curved fracture

This rock consists of a mixture of clay minerals together with detrital quartz, feldspar, and mica. Iron oxides are also often present.

• **TEXTURE** Mudstone is a very fine-grained rock, and the grains cannot be seen with the naked eye. It shares many characteristics with shale and may contain fossils, though it has less well-defined lamination compared to shale.

• **ORIGIN** Mudstone forms in a variety of environments resulting from the deposition of mud in, for example, oceans and freshwater lakes. Studying the fossils contained in a specimen of mudstone, and comparing them with the lifestyles of related modern organisms, can help to identify the type of environment in which the rock was formed.

Classification Detrital	Fossils Invertebrates, Plants	Grain shape Angular

Group Sedimentary	Origin Marine, Freshwater	Grain size Fine

CALCAREOUS MUDSTONE

As its name suggests, this rock is similar to mudstone, but it also has a high calcite content. Detrital quartz, feldspar and quartz may also be present. Fossils are not uncommon. It is often light colored.
• **TEXTURE** A very fine-grained rock, in which the particles cannot be seen with the naked eye. The grains are much the same size, but recrystallization may change their original shape. The rock may break in a distinctive way, with a subconchoidal fracture. Because of the high calcite content, it will effervesce when tested with cold hydrochloric acid.
• **ORIGIN** Forms in marine and freshwater conditions. Being very fine-grained, calcareous mudstone is easily transported by water into sea and lakes, where it may accumulate with some sand, silt, and other calcerous organisms.

calcite vein •

curved •
fracture

Classification Detrital	Fossils Invertebrates, Plants	Grain shape Angular

Group Sedimentary	Origin Marine, Freshwater, Cont.	Grain size Fine

CLAY

This rock is very rich in clay minerals (from where it gets its name), together with detrital quartz, mica, and feldspar.
• **TEXTURE** The grain size is so fine that the individual minerals cannot be seen, except with very powerful microscopes. Clays often have a characteristic smell, and the grains absorb water to become plastic.
• **ORIGIN** Clay forms in many different environments. It can occur in deep and shallow marine conditions (fossils of oysters are evident in clays from marine environments), in lakes, and as a continental sediment. Glacial clays develop from the powdering of rock by ice action. Clay minerals are formed by the decay and alteration of certain silicate minerals, such as feldspars, under chemical weathering. Fossils are often well preserved in clay because of its very fine grain size.

very fine grains •

these mollusk shells suggest •
a marine environment

Classification Detrital	Fossils Invertebrates, Vertebrates, Plants	Grain shape Angular

Group Sedimentary	Origin Marine, Freshwater	Grain size Fine

RED MARL

This rock is a sediment intermediate between clay and limestones, and includes gradations between calcareous clays and muddy limestones. The calcareous matter should range between 40–60 percent, with detrital quartz, clay, and silt particles. The red coloring is due to the presence of iron oxide.
• **TEXTURE** Because marl is such a fine-grained rock, it can be examined in detail only under a microscope. The grains are well formed and may be cemented by calcite.
• **ORIGIN** Marls are often found in shallow lakes with much vegetation. They are also associated with evaporite deposits formed in saline basins. In this case they may be interbedded with gypsum and rock salt.

curved fracture •

fine-grained rock •

• *reddish-brown color*

Classification Detrital	Fossils Invertebrates, Vertebrates, Plants	Grain shape Angular

Group Sedimentary	Origin Marine, Freshwater	Grain size Fine

GREEN MARL

As with its red counterpart, green marl is an intermediate sediment between the clays and the limestones. It differs only in color, with the greenish coloring due to the presence of minerals such as glauconite and chlorite. Green marl also has a high calcite content.
• **TEXTURE** Green marl is a fine-grained rock. The individual particles can be seen only under a microscope. The calcite present causes the rock to effervesce when it is tested with cold dilute hydrochloric acid.
• **ORIGIN** This rock forms in marine and freshwater conditions. When glauconite is present in green marl, it indicates that the rock would have formed in a marine environment.

fine-grained • *sediment*

Classification Detrital	Fossils Invertebrates, Vertebrates, Plants	Grain shape Angular

Group Sedimentary	Origin Marine, Evaporites	Grain size Crystalline

ROCK SALT

This rock is essentially composed of halite, together with impurities of clay minerals and iron oxides. The rock is often colored reddish brown when iron oxides are present.
• **TEXTURE** Rock salt is usually massive and coarsely crystalline, sometimes forming as distinct cubic crystals. Under pressure, the rock salt may be caused to flow, forming salt plugs that intrude other strata.
• **ORIGIN** Forms from saline waters, such as salt lakes, in a sequence which includes other evaporites – minerals such as dolomite and gypsum.

orange-brown crystals •

Classification Chemical	Fossils None	Grain shape Crystalline

Group Sedimentary	Origin Marine, Salt lakes	Grain size Crystalline

ROCK GYPSUM

• crystalline rock

This rock normally occurs as massive gypsum (hydrated calcium sulphate).
• **TEXTURE** Coarse to fine in texture, this crystalline rock shows a fibrous habit. It may also show bedding which is often strongly distorted. Rock gypsum is usually interbedded with sandstones, marls, and limestones. A soft rock, it can be scratched easily with a fingernail.
• **ORIGIN** Forms in evaporite rock sequences in association with dolomite rocks and marl, and the minerals anhydrate, halite, and calcite.

• vitreous luster

• uneven fracture

Classification Chemical	Fossils None	Grain shape Crystalline

Group Sedimentary	Origin Marine, Evaporites	Grain size Crystalline

POTASH ROCK

This rock is a mixture of sylvite and halite. The crystalline sylvite is light gray color when pure, while orange-red sylvite gets its color from iron oxide staining.
• **TEXTURE** This is a crystalline rock. Potash occurs with other minerals in strata containing rock salt, gypsum, and dolomite.
• **ORIGIN** Deposited from saline waters, potash rock forms in a sequence that includes evaporites such as dolomite, marl, and mudstone.

rough, partly dissolved surface •

iron impurities give reddish coloring •

Classification Chemical	Fossils None	Grain shape Crystalline

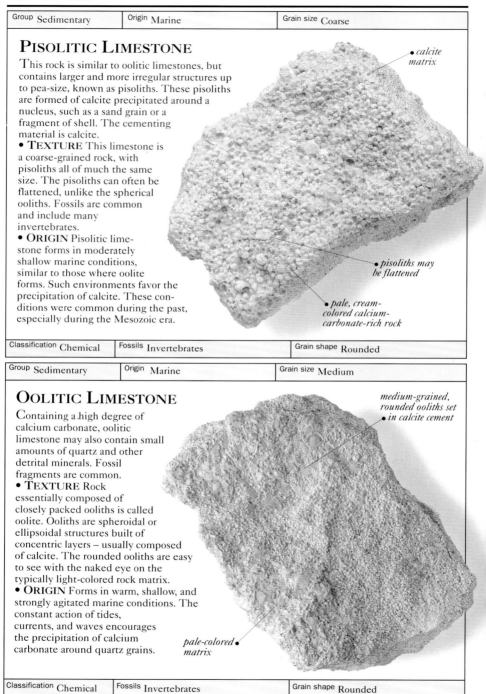

Group Sedimentary	Origin Marine		Grain size Coarse

PISOLITIC LIMESTONE

This rock is similar to oolitic limestones, but contains larger and more irregular structures up to pea-size, known as pisoliths. These pisoliths are formed of calcite precipitated around a nucleus, such as a sand grain or a fragment of shell. The cementing material is calcite.

• **TEXTURE** This limestone is a coarse-grained rock, with pisoliths all of much the same size. The pisoliths can often be flattened, unlike the spherical ooliths. Fossils are common and include many invertebrates.

• **ORIGIN** Pisolitic limestone forms in moderately shallow marine conditions, similar to those where oolite forms. Such environments favor the precipitation of calcite. These conditions were common during the past, especially during the Mesozoic era.

• calcite matrix

• pisoliths may be flattened

• pale, cream-colored calcium-carbonate-rich rock

Classification Chemical	Fossils Invertebrates		Grain shape Rounded

Group Sedimentary	Origin Marine		Grain size Medium

OOLITIC LIMESTONE

Containing a high degree of calcium carbonate, oolitic limestone may also contain small amounts of quartz and other detrital minerals. Fossil fragments are common.

• **TEXTURE** Rock essentially composed of closely packed ooliths is called oolite. Ooliths are spheroidal or ellipsoidal structures built of concentric layers – usually composed of calcite. The rounded ooliths are easy to see with the naked eye on the typically light-colored rock matrix.

• **ORIGIN** Forms in warm, shallow, and strongly agitated marine conditions. The constant action of tides, currents, and waves encourages the precipitation of calcium carbonate around quartz grains.

medium-grained, rounded ooliths set • in calcite cement

pale-colored • matrix

Classification Chemical	Fossils Invertebrates		Grain shape Rounded

Group Sedimentary	Origin Marine	Grain size Fine

CHALK

This is a very pure limestone formed of calcite, and containing only small amounts of silt or mud. It consists mainly of the tests of microorganisms, such as coccoliths and foraminifera, which cannot be seen without the aid of a microscope. Macrofossils, which can be seen with the naked eye, are often present, and these include mollusks, such as ammonites and bivalves, brachiopods, and echinoderms. Chalk may contain detrital material, mainly quartz, as well as other mineral fragments.
• TEXTURE A very fine-grained, powdery, soft rock. It effervesces strongly when in contact with cold, dilute hydrochloric acid.
• ORIGIN Formed in marine conditions during the Cretaceous period. During this period, the continental shelves, where the chalk was deposited, were below a much greater depth of sea water than today. The small amount of detrital material suggests that nearby continental areas were low-lying and arid.

soft, white powdery texture

almost pure calcite rock composed of microfossils

Classification Organic	Fossils Invertebrates, Vertebrates	Grain shape Rounded, Angular

Group Sedimentary	Origin Marine	Grain size Fine

RED CHALK

A fine-grained calcareous rock, red chalk gets its color from a detrital component of iron oxide (hematite). It may also contain scattered quartz pebbles. Many of the minute grains in red chalk are microfossils, such as coccoliths. Macrofossils, including belemnites, ammonites, bivalves, and echinoderms, are frequently present in red chalk.
• TEXTURE The grain size is small, and the individual particles are too minute to be detected, except with a microscope.
• ORIGIN Thought to be formed under slow marine deposition, the red coloring agent hematite may be derived from a nearly lateritic land surface. A study of the fossils in red chalk will give a much more detailed indication of the environment of deposition.

reddish coloring due to iron oxide

calcite grains

small veins and patches of calcite

Classification Organic	Fossils Invertebrates	Grain shape Rounded

Group Sedimentary	Origin Marine	Grain size Coarse

CRINOIDAL LIMESTONE

This rock is essentially formed of calcite as fine or larger crystals. These may have been derived from animal skeletons such as crinoid plates. Ossicles of crinoid stems are conspicuous ingredients of this rock.

- **TEXTURE** The large fragments in the rock are the broken stems of crinoids. These may be long, cylindrical pieces, as well as single, rounded ossicles. They are bound in a groundmass of massive calcite, with a calcite cement.
- **ORIGIN** This limestone is formed in marine conditions, and takes its name from crinoids – a group of sea-dwelling creatures related to starfish and sea urchins. The presence of crinoids in coral limestone suggests that they inhabited shallow marine environments. Crinoids are not the only fossils that are commonly found in crinoidal limestone; it can be rich in brachiopods, mollusks, and corals.

pale grayish pink rock with much fragmented calcite

mass of broken crinoid stems

Classification Organic	Fossils Invertebrates	Grain shape Angular, Rounded

Group Sedimentary	Origin Marine	Grain size Fine

CORAL LIMESTONE

This limestone is almost entirely formed from the calcareous remains of fossil coral. The individual structures are called corallites, and they are held in a matrix of lime-rich mud. As well as a high proportion of calcite, this mud, now limestone, contains small amounts of detrital material such as clay and quartz.

- **TEXTURE** The texture is determined by the type of coral preserved in the rock. The matrix of this limestone is fine-grained.
- **ORIGIN** These rocks form in marine conditions, and by studying the individual corals it may be possible to give more precise details of the environment. Most coral limestone forms on the continental shelf. Though these rocks are rich in coral, they can also contain other shallow water marine invertebrates, including brachiopods, cephalopods, gastropods, and bryozoans.

overall pink-gray color of calcite

mass of coral held in lime mud matrix

Classification Organic	Fossils Invertebrates	Grain shape Angular

| Group Sedimentary | Origin Marine, Freshwater | Grain size Medium, Fine |

SHELLY LIMESTONE

A general name for calcareous rocks containing a high proportion of fossil shells. This limestone can contain a great variety of brachiopod and bivalve shells. The rock matrix is usually cemented by calcite. Any brownish coloring the rock exhibits may be due to detrital minerals and iron oxides.
• **TEXTURE** The matrix of this rock is medium- or fine-grained, and has angular fragments.
• **ORIGIN** These limestones are essentially of marine origin although a very few of them may also form in freshwater environments. As with many of the rocks that contain fossils, it is often possible to discover the actual environment in which a specimen formed by a careful study of the fossils found within the shelly limestone.

many gray calcite brachiopod shells

brownish coloring from iron oxides

shells set in calcite-rich matrix

| Classification Organic | Fossils Invertebrates | Grain shape Angular |

| Group Sedimentary | Origin Marine | Grain size Fine |

BRYOZOAN LIMESTONE

The percentage of calcite in bryozoan limestone is very high. This rock also contains a very small amount of detrital material, such as quartz and clay. These detrital materials may give the rock a coloring that is darker than the pale gray of purer limestone. Essentially, bryozoan limestone is lime mud characterized by the netlike structures of fossil bryozoans.
• **TEXTURE** The lime mud that forms the groundmass is fine-grained and even-textured.
• **ORIGIN** This rock forms in marine conditions. It commonly originates in calcareous reef deposits, where the bryozoans, such as *Fenestella*, help to bind the mounds of reef sediment. Besides bryozoans, the reef environment also supports a wealth of other organisms, and these limestones are rich in mollusks, brachiopods, and other marine invertebrates.

high percentage of calcium carbonate

small, net-like bryozoans within a lime mud

| Classification Organic | Fossils Invertebrates | Grain shape Angular |

Group Sedimentary	Origin Freshwater	Grain size Medium, Fine

FRESHWATER LIMESTONE

lime mud matrix •

Less common than marine limestone, the freshwater variety is distinguished by the nature of its contained fossils which are connected freshwater environments. As with other limestones, this rock has a high proportion of calcium carbonate and it can also contain detrital quartz and clay.

• **TEXTURE** The calcareous matrix is crystalline and binds the rock together. This rock consists essentially of a calcareous mud, with a number of coiled gastropod shells. The chief way to determine if a limestone is marine or freshwater is by identifying the fossils. The high calcite content causes the rock to effervesce when it comes into contact with cold, dilute hydrochloric acid.

• **ORIGIN** This limestone forms in freshwater lakes with a high lime content, and is unusual in the stratigraphic record.

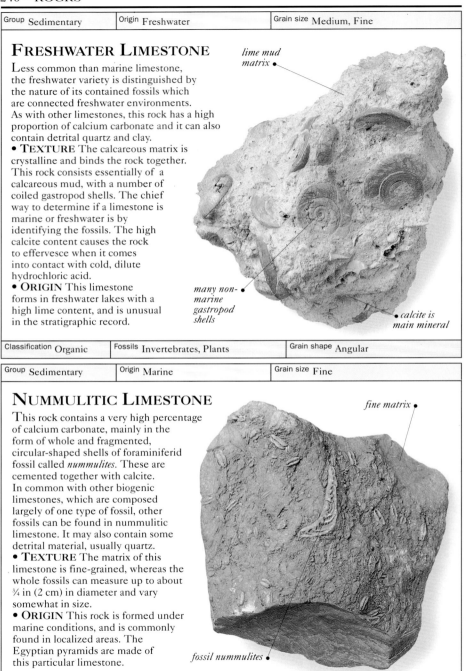

many non-marine gastropod shells •

• *calcite is main mineral*

Classification Organic	Fossils Invertebrates, Plants	Grain shape Angular

Group Sedimentary	Origin Marine	Grain size Fine

NUMMULITIC LIMESTONE

fine matrix •

This rock contains a very high percentage of calcium carbonate, mainly in the form of whole and fragmented, circular-shaped shells of foraminiferid fossil called *nummulites*. These are cemented together with calcite. In common with other biogenic limestones, which are composed largely of one type of fossil, other fossils can be found in nummulitic limestone. It may also contain some detrital material, usually quartz.

• **TEXTURE** The matrix of this limestone is fine-grained, whereas the whole fossils can measure up to about ¾ in (2 cm) in diameter and vary somewhat in size.

• **ORIGIN** This rock is formed under marine conditions, and is commonly found in localized areas. The Egyptian pyramids are made of this particular limestone.

fossil nummulites •

Classification Organic	Fossils Invertebrates	Grain shape Crystalline

Group Sedimentary	Origin Marine	Grain size Medium, Fine

DOLOMITE

The name of a rock and also a mineral, the rock contains a high proportion of dolomite from which it gets its name. Detrital minerals and secondary silica (chert) are also present. While the mineral dolomite is magnesium carbonate, dolomite rocks are usually darker than other limestones (often creamy brown). Dolomites also tend to be less fossiliferous than other limestones, possibly because of the recrystallization that has often taken place during their formation.
• **TEXTURE** It has an even crystalline texture. Dolomite masses are often compact and earthy.
• **ORIGIN** These rocks form in marine environments. Most dolomites are believed to be of secondary origin, replacing original limestones.

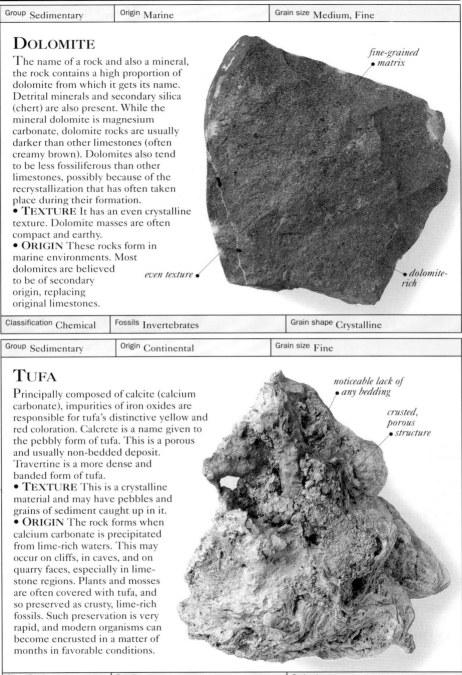

fine-grained matrix

even texture

dolomite-rich

Classification Chemical	Fossils Invertebrates	Grain shape Crystalline

Group Sedimentary	Origin Continental	Grain size Fine

TUFA

Principally composed of calcite (calcium carbonate), impurities of iron oxides are responsible for tufa's distinctive yellow and red coloration. Calcrete is a name given to the pebbly form of tufa. This is a porous and usually non-bedded deposit. Travertine is a more dense and banded form of tufa.
• **TEXTURE** This is a crystalline material and may have pebbles and grains of sediment caught up in it.
• **ORIGIN** The rock forms when calcium carbonate is precipitated from lime-rich waters. This may occur on cliffs, in caves, and on quarry faces, especially in limestone regions. Plants and mosses are often covered with tufa, and so preserved as crusty, lime-rich fossils. Such preservation is very rapid, and modern organisms can become encrusted in a matter of months in favorable conditions.

noticeable lack of any bedding

crusted, porous structure

Classification Chemical	Fossils Plants, Invertebrates	Grain shape Crystalline

| Group Sedimentary | Origin Continental | Grain size Crystalline |

TRAVERTINE

Consisting of almost pure calcium carbonate, travertine may also contain some detrital quartz and clay. Fossil material is virtually absent. Travertine is a very light-colored rock, unless it contains iron compounds or other impurities, which can give it coloring. Travertine deposits are rounded, botryoidal (resembling a grape structure), and often banded structures.
• **TEXTURE** This rock is formed of small crystals of calcite which bind together other sediment particles. In many situations travertine occurs in strata. The rock is often bedded.
• **ORIGIN** Travertine is frequently associated with springs rising from deep-seated sources. This results in many hot springs, especially in volcanic regions, giving rise to travertine by the deposition of solid calcium carbonate.

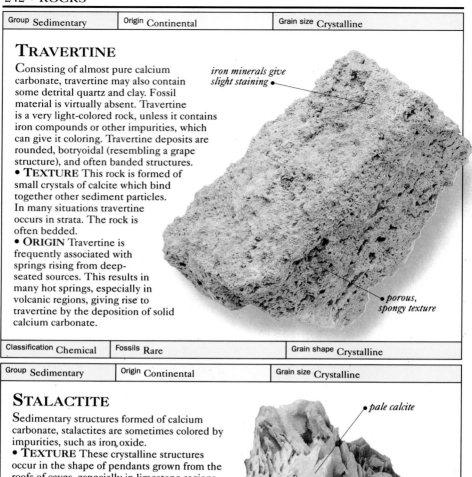

iron minerals give slight staining

porous, spongy texture

| Classification Chemical | Fossils Rare | Grain shape Crystalline |

| Group Sedimentary | Origin Continental | Grain size Crystalline |

STALACTITE

Sedimentary structures formed of calcium carbonate, stalactites are sometimes colored by impurities, such as iron oxide.
• **TEXTURE** These crystalline structures occur in the shape of pendants grown from the roofs of caves, especially in limestone regions. While stalactites are long, slender forms, the corresponding structures - stalagmites - that grow up from the cave floor are stumpy and shorter. The two sometimes join together to form calcite columns.
• **ORIGIN** These structures form by inorganic precipitation of calcium carbonate, from waters seeping through fractures in the roofs of caves. When carbon dioxide is released and the lime-rich waters meet, the air lime is deposited, while evaporation of the water speeds up the process. Lime-rich water, dropping from the end of a stalactite, results in the formation of a stalagmite.

pale calcite

pendant-shaped

| Classification Chemical | Fossils None | Grain shape Crystalline |

Group Sedimentary	Origin Continental	Grain size Medium, Fine

BANDED IRONSTONE

These rocks, ferruginous cherts, show a marked banded structure. The banding mainly consists of alternate layers of chert and siderite or hematite in which considerable recrystallization has taken place. Magnetite and pyrite may also occur in the iron-rich bands of the rock.

• **TEXTURE** Banded ironstones are fine- to medium-grained rocks.

• **ORIGIN** Mostly formed in the Precambrian, between 2000 and 3000 million years ago. It is open to interpretation whether or not banded ironstones were deposited by precipitation in enclosed lakes or basins. They do, however, occur in many sedimentary environments, from shallow and intertidal to deep water situations. There is evidence from some areas that these rocks formed in marshes and waterlogged mud flats, and some geologists suggest that organic activity was important in helping the carbonate and sulphide association to be precipitated. The possibility of organic involvement is of considerable interest, because at the time of formation only very primitive organisms existed on the earth.

alternating gray and red layers of chert and iron-rich material

prominent banding

Classification Chemical	Fossils None	Grain shape Crystalline

Group Sedimentary	Origin Marine	Grain size Medium

OOLITIC IRONSTONE

This rock consists of closely packed ooliths variably replaced by siderite and other iron minerals. Quartz, feldspar, and other detrital minerals may be present. The rock may have originally been lime-rich, and replacement has converted the lime to iron minerals. The ooliths, which give the rock its name, are small and rounded as they are in oolitic limestone.

• **TEXTURE** Detrital grains in the rock may be angular. Calcite is a common cement between the ooliths.

• **ORIGIN** Forms in marine environments; the rock may undergo change shortly after deposition, or it may be deposited already rich in iron.

dark-red, iron-rich coloring

rounded ooliths form body of rock

Classification Chemical	Fossils Invertebrates	Grain shape Rounded, Angular

Group Sedimentary	Origin Continental	Grain size Medium, Fine

BITUMINOUS COAL

shiny patches •

The action of pressure on the rock lignite leads to the formation of bituminous or "household" coal. It is hard, brittle, and has a high carbon content. This rock has alternating shiny and dull layers, and may contain some recognizable plant material. It is dirty to handle.
• **TEXTURE** It is even-textured, with the appearance of being fused material. Bituminous coal breaks into cubelike fragments due to its structure – two sets of joints at right angles.
• **ORIGIN** It forms by the accumulation of peat and subsequent changes due to pressure and heat burial – water being driven off.

dull
patches •

Classification Organic	Fossils Plants	Grain shape None

Group Sedimentary	Origin Continental	Grain size Medium, Fine

ANTHRACITE

uneven
• surfaces

conchoidal
• fracture

This differs from other coals because of its extremely high content of carbon with a correspondingly low proportion of volatile matter. Normally an unbanded type of coal.
• **TEXTURE** It is more glassy in appearance, and cleaner to handle than bituminous coal. Anthracite ignites at much higher temperatures than other coals.
• **ORIGIN** Forms by accumulation of peat. It is suggested that the increase of pressure and especially heat has caused volatiles to be driven off – thus forming a higher grade of coal.

dark, shiny •
matrix

Classification Organic	Fossils Plants	Grain shape None

Group Sedimentary	Origin Continental	Grain size Medium, Fine

LIGNITE

This is a brown-colored coal, having a carbon content that is between peat and bituminous coal. Lignite still has a large amount of visible plant material in its structure and is friable.
• **TEXTURE** Less compact than other coals, lignite has a high moisture content and is crumbly. It also contains more volatiles and impurities.
• **ORIGIN** A type of low-rank coal most commonly found in Tertiary and Mesozoic strata where changes have not occured to the vegetable matter. Lignite also occasionally results from shallow burial of peat.

plant fragments •

crumbly surface •

Classification Organic	Fossils Plants	Grain shape None

Group Sedimentary	Origin Continental·	Grain size Medium, Fine

PEAT

This rock represents the initial stage in the modification of plant material to lignite and bituminous coal. Peat is dark brown to black in color, and contains about 50 percent carbon, as well as much volatile material. It is crumbly and can easily be broken by hand.

• **TEXTURE** There are many plant fragments visible in peat, often including large roots. It is frequently high in water, and breaks unevenly when dry. Peat is a soft rock.

• **ORIGIN** Forms from the deposition of plant debris on forest floors, in fens, or on moorland. The large deposits of coal, now used for fuel, were originally forest peat. Much of the vegetable matter in the peat that accumulates today is mosses, rushes, and sedges. The deposits may be many feet thick. By decay and reconstruction, the bottom layers of peat banks become compacted, darkened and hardened, while the carbon content increases.

• plant fragments

• crumbly surface

Classification Organic	Fossils Plants, Invertebrates	Grain shape None

Group Sedimentary	Origin Marine	Grain size Medium, Fine

JET

Due to its high carbon content, jet is classified as a type of coal. It is a compact substance found in bituminous shales, and it produces a brown streak. Jet has a conchoidal fracture and it is hard enough to take a good polish. It rarely forms in geographically extensive seams.

• **TEXTURE** When examined in close detail, jet shows woody tissue structures. It has a vitreous luster, which has been exploited for making ornaments and jewelry.

• **ORIGIN** The formation of jet has been open to debate. It is generally believed that this black, coallike rock developed in marine strata from logs and other drifting plant material which then became waterlogged and sank into the mud of the seabed. Jet is found in rocks of marine origin; unlike other forms of coal which form from plant matter accumulated on the land surface.

• bedded structure

vitreous luster •

Classification Organic	Fossils Plants	Grain shape None

Group Sedimentary	Origin Marine	Grain size Fine

CHERT

This occurs as siliceous nodules or sheets, especially in sedimentary rocks such as limestone and among lavas. Chert is usually grayish in coloring.
• **TEXTURE** It is composed of cryptocrystalline silca, and its components can be seen only under a microscope. Chert breaks with an uneven to subconchoidal fracture. It is a hard rock that cannot be scratched with a knife.
• **ORIGIN** Chert is formed from the accumulation of silica, possibly in a colloidal form on seabeds. The silica may well come from organic sources.

fine grain size

subconchoidal fracture

Classification Chemical	Fossils Invertebrates, Plants	Grain shape Crystalline

Group Sedimentary	Origin Marine	Grain size Fine

FLINT

The term flint is used principally for siliceous nodules in the Chalk of western Europe. It is a hard, compact substance with an homogenous appearance and breaks with a conchoidal fracture. Its flakes were used as tools by primitive peoples.
• **TEXTURE** Consists entirely of silica. Cryptocrystalline silica in flint appears to be derived from organic opal in the contained sponge spicules.
• **ORIGIN** Occurs as bands and nodular masses in fine-grained limestones, especially Chalk. Flint frequently contains fossils.

sharp edges

conchoidal fracture

Classification Chemical	Fossils Invertebrates	Grain shape Crystalline

Group Sedimentary	Origin Continental	Grain size Crystalline

AMBER

This rock is the fossil resin of extinct coniferous trees. Amber is soft and has a resinous or subvitreous luster. It varies from transparent to translucent. Insects and small vertebrates which were trapped in the original sticky resin are sometimes found fossilized in amber. Amber is frequently used to make jewelry.
• **TEXTURE** When broken, amber has a conchoidal fracture.
• **ORIGIN** Forms from the resin of coniferous trees, and is found in sedimentary deposits.

conchoidal fracture

resinous luster

Classification Organic	Fossils Vertebrates, Invertebrates	Grain shape None

Group Sedimentary	Origin Post-depositional	Grain size Crystalline

SEPTARIAN CONCRETION

Concretions are often formed of the same material as the host sediment, but are cemented (concreted) together by silica, carbonate minerals, or iron oxides. Septarian concretions have radiating and polygonal internal patterns of veins – usually of calcite.
• **TEXTURE** The structure is one of radiating and concentric cracks, in a tough outer shell. When opened, this internal veined structure is apparent.
• **ORIGIN** It may form by the segregation of minerals during diagenesis: that is, all the processes that turn soft, muddy material into rock, and their concentration around a nucleus. This may be a grain of sediment or even a fossil. After formation of the concretion, the cracks, known as septa, may develop during shrinkage.

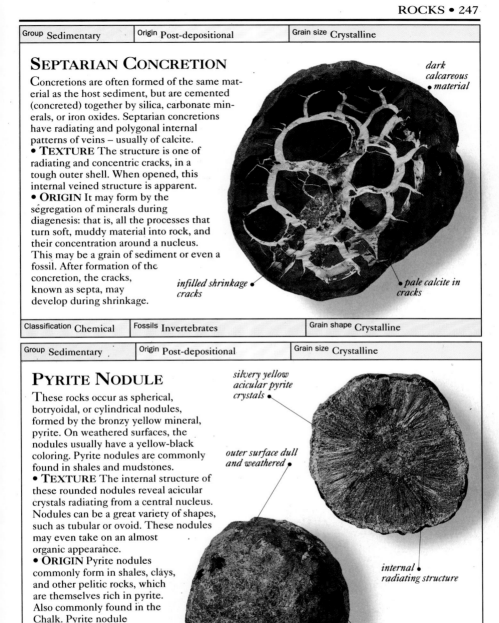

dark calcareous material

infilled shrinkage cracks

pale calcite in cracks

Classification Chemical	Fossils Invertebrates	Grain shape Crystalline

Group Sedimentary	Origin Post-depositional	Grain size Crystalline

PYRITE NODULE

These rocks occur as spherical, botryoidal, or cylindrical nodules, formed by the bronzy yellow mineral, pyrite. On weathered surfaces, the nodules usually have a yellow-black coloring. Pyrite nodules are commonly found in shales and mudstones.
• **TEXTURE** The internal structure of these rounded nodules reveal acicular crystals radiating from a central nucleus. Nodules can be a great variety of shapes, such as tubular or ovoid. These nodules may even take on an almost organic appearance.
• **ORIGIN** Pyrite nodules commonly form in shales, clays, and other pelitic rocks, which are themselves rich in pyrite. Also commonly found in the Chalk. Pyrite nodule formation is not fully understood, but precipitation of pyrite around a central nucleus seems a highly possible explanation.

silvery yellow acicular pyrite crystals

outer surface dull and weathered

internal radiating structure

brownish coating

Classification Chemical	Fossils Rare	Grain shape Crystalline

Group Meteorite	Origin Extra-terrestrial	Grain size/Crystalline Crystalline

STONY IRON

Stony iron meteorites are composed of about 50 percent metal, and 50 percent silicate material. The metallic content is nickel-iron alloy. The silicate components are minerals recognized in many of the rocks on earth, and include olivine, pyroxene, and plagioclase feldspar.

• **TEXTURE** These are rocklike objects and have a surface showing various components, including crystals. The silicate minerals, such as olivine, may be removed by weathering, giving the surface a pitted appearance.

• **ORIGIN** These are rare meteorites and only about 4 percent of known meteorites are in this group. Stony iron meteorites help geologists to understand how certain elements combine with iron or silica during the process of melting and vein formation. They give an insight into planets with an iron-rich core and a silicate outer shell.

rough surface with some alteration due to ablation

cavities on surface

Classification Stony Iron	Shape Angular, Rounded	Composition Silicate, Metal

Group Meteorite	Origin Terrestrial	Grain size/Crystalline Glass

TEKTITE

These are silica-rich glass objects that were once believed to be meteorites. However, their distribution on the earth, and their chemistry, have now led scientists to suggest that they may not in fact have an extra-terrestrial origin. Tektites actually have a composition not unlike that of some volcanic rocks. These rocks have a high silica content, and are also rich in oxides of potassium, calcium and aluminum.

• **TEXTURE** The rocks are small in size, usually about 7–10 oz (200 to 300 g) in weight, and have a disk or ovoid shape. Their surface may be smooth or rough.

• **ORIGIN** A matter of debate, but tektites may result from the melting of terrestrial rocks on the impact of a meteorite. It seems unlikely that these rocks were fired toward the earth from a large volcano on the moon, as has been suggested in the past.

typical rounded shape

smooth surface

indentations

Classification Tektite	Shape Rounded	Composition Silicate

Group Meteorite	Origin Extra-terrestrial	Grain size/Crystalline Crystalline

CHONDRITE

These rocks form the largest group of meterorites classified as stones. Chondrites contain silicate minerals, mostly pyroxene and olivine, and small amounts of plagioclase feldspar. There is also a small proportion of nickel-iron.
• **TEXTURE** These meteorites have a structure consisting of chondrules, which are small, spherical grains. The overall shape of chondrite varies, but many are rounded or even dome-shaped. Angular specimens are those that have fragmented on impact.
• **ORIGIN** How chondrites form is not certain, but their chemistry seems to represent the mantle material of planet-forming bodies, planetesimals. This type of meteorite gives the oldest radiometric date yet obtained from rocky material – 4600 million years – a figure generally accepted as the date of the formation of the Solar system.

crystalline, rocky texture

crust around edges showing features of melting on entry into the earth's atmosphere

Classification Chondrite	Shape Rounded	Composition Silicate, Metal

Group Meteorite	Origin Extra-terrestrial	Grain size/Crystalline Crystalline

ACHONDRITE

rough surface

These rocks vary from chondrites in both structure and composition. Achondrites contain a high proportion of silicate material, similar to that found in rocks on the earth. This includes pyroxene and olivine, as well as plagioclase feldspar. However, the composition of achondrites is more variable than that of chondrites, and they generally contain very little metallic iron.
• **TEXTURE** The structure is coarser-grained than chondrites, and they lack chondrules.
• **ORIGIN** As achondrites resemble the rocks found in the mantle and basaltic crust of the Earth, their origin may possibly be volcanic. These rocks also could have originated on planet-forming bodies, called planetesimals.

medium to coarse grains

much silicate material including pyroxene and olivine

Classification Achondrite	Shape Angular	Composition Silicate

GLOSSARY

TECHNICAL EXPRESSIONS have been avoided wherever possible, but a limited use of them is essential in a book of this nature. The terms listed below, many of them peculiar to minerals and rocks, are defined in a concise manner. Some definitions have been simplified and generalized in order to avoid obscure language, and involved examples have been left out. Words that appear in bold type in the definitions are explained elsewhere in the glossary. Many key words are also fully explained with color photographs in the introduction section of the book.

• **ACCESSORY MINERAL**
The mineral constituents of a rock that occur in such small amounts that they are disregarded in the definition and chemistry.

• **ACICULAR**
Needle-shaped mineral habit.

• **ACID ROCK**
Igneous rock with over 65% total silica and over 20% quartz.

• **ADAMANTINE**
Very bright mineral **luster** similar to that of diamond.

• **AEOLIAN**
Term applied to deposits arranged by the wind. Some features of sedimentary rocks, such as dune bedding, are aeolian structures.

• **AMPHIBOLE GROUP**
Group of common rock-forming minerals, often with complex composition but mostly **ferromagnesian** silicates.

• **AMYGDALE**
Secondary infilling of a **vesicle** in an igneous rock. Minerals that occur as amygdales include quartz, calcite, and the zeolite group.

• **ANHEDRAL**
Poorly formed crystal.

• **ARENACEOUS**
Sedimentary rocks that have either been derived from sand or that contain sand.

• **AUREOLE**
Area around an igneous **intrusion**, where contact metamorphism of the original **country rock** has occurred.

• **BASAL CLEAVAGE**
Cleavage that is parallel to the basal crystal plane of a mineral.

• **BASIC ROCK**
Igneous rock that contains between 45% and 55% total silica. These have less than 10% quartz and are rich in **ferro-magnesian minerals**.

• **BATHOLITH**
Very large, irregularly-shaped mass of igneous rock formed from the **intrusion** of magma at great depth.

• **BEDDING**
Layering of sedimentary rocks. Beds or strata are divided by bedding planes.

• **BLADED**
Blade-shaped habit in minerals.

• **CLAY MINERALS**
Alumino-silicate group of minerals, common in sedimentary rocks.

• **CLEAVAGE**
The way certain minerals break along planes related to their internal atomic structure.

• **CONCORDANT**
Following existing rock structures.

• **CONCHOIDAL**
Curved or shell-like fracture in many minerals and some rocks.

• **CONCRETION**
Commonly discrete, rounded nodular rock masses formed and found in beds of shale or clay.

• **COUNTRY ROCK**
Rock surrounding an igneous **intrusion** or below a lava flow.

• **CRYPTOCRYSTALLINE**
Crystalline, but very fine-grained. Individual components need to be viewed under a microscope.

• **DENDRITIC**
Having a treelike habit.

• **DETRITAL**
Group of sedimentary rocks formed essentially of fragments and grains derived from pre-existing rocks.

• **DISCORDANT**
Cuts across existing rock structures.

• **DULL LUSTER**
Luster with little reflectiveness.

• **DIKE**
Sheet-shaped igneous **intrusion**. Cuts across existing rock structures.

• **EARTHY**
Nonreflective, mineral **luster**.

• **ESSENTIAL MINERAL**
The mineral constituents of a rock that are necessary to classification and name.

• **EUHEDRAL**
Crystal that shows good faces.

• **EVAPORITE**
Mineral or rock formed by the evaporation of saline water.

• **FELDSPATHOID MINERAL**
Group of minerals similar in chemistry and structure to the feldspars, but with less silica.

• **FERRO-MAGNESIAN MINERAL**
Mineral rich in iron and magnesium. These are dense, dark-colored silicates, such as the olivines, pyroxenes, and amphiboles.

• **FOLIATED**
Laminated, parallel orientation or segregation of different minerals.

• **FOSSIL**
Any record of past life preserved in the crustal rocks. As well as bones and shells, fossils can be of footprints, excrement, and borings.

• **GLASSY TEXTURE**
In igneous rock, where glass forms because of speed of cooling.

• **GRADED BEDDING**
Sedimentary structure where coarser grains gradually give way to finer grains upward through a bed.

• **GRANULAR**
Having grains, or in grains.

• **GRAPHIC TEXTURE**
Rock texture resulting from the regular intergrowth of quartz and feldspar.

• **GROUNDMASS**
Also called matrix. Mass of rock in which larger crystals may be set.

• **HACKLY**
Mineral fracture that has a rough surface with small protuberances, as on a piece of cast iron.

- **HEMIMORPHIC**
Crystal that has different facial development at each end.
- **HOPPER CRYSTAL**
Crystal with faces that are hollowed as in the "stepped" faces of some halite crystals.
- **HYDROTHERMAL VEIN**
Fracture in rocks in which minerals have been deposited from hot magmatic emanations rich in water.
- **HYPABYSSAL**
Minor intrusions at relatively shallow depths in the earth's crust.
- **INCLUSION**
A crystal or fragment of another substance enclosed in a crystal or rock.
- **INTERMEDIATE ROCK**
Igneous rock with between 65% and 55% total silica.
- **INTRUSION**
A body of igneous rock that invades older rock. This may be by forceful intrusion or by magmatic sloping.
- **LACCOLITH**
Mass of intrusive igneous rock with dome-shaped top; usually flat base.
- **LAMELLAR**
In thin layers or scales, composed of plates or flakes.
- **LUSTER**
The way in which a mineral shines because of reflected light.
- **MAGMA**
Molten rock that may consolidate at depth or be erupted as lava.
- **MASSIVE**
Mineral habit of no definite shape.
- **MATRIX** *see* **Groundmass.**
- **METALLIC LUSTER**
Like that of fresh metal.
- **METASOMATIC**
Process that changes composition of a rock or mineral by the addition or replacement of chemicals.
- **METEORIC WATER**
Water derived from, or in, the atmosphere.
- **MICROCRYSTALLINE**
Small crystal size that is only detectable with a microscope.
- **OOLITH**
Individual, spheroidal sedimentary grains from which oolite rocks are formed. Usually calcareous with a concretic or radial structure.
- **OROGENIC BELT**
Region of the Earth's crust that is, or has been, active, and in which fold mountains are, or were, formed.

- **OSSICLE**
Fragment of the stem of a crinoid, a group of creatures within the phylum *Echinodermata*.
- **PELITIC**
Sediment made of mud or clay.
- **PILLOW LAVA**
Masses of lava formed on seabed, shaped like rounded pillows.
- **PHENOCRYST**
Relatively large crystal set into the **groundmass** of an igneous rock to give a **porphyritic** texture.
- **PISOLITH**
Pea-sized sediment grain with concentric internal structure.
- **PLACER DEPOSIT**
Deposit of minerals often in alluvial conditions, or on a beach, formed because of their high specific gravity or resistance to weathering.
- **PLATY HABIT**
Mineral habit with flat, thin crystals.
- **PLUTON**
Mass of igneous rock that has formed beneath the surface of the Earth by consolidation of magma.
- **PORPHYRITIC**
Igneous rock **texture** with relatively large crystals set in the **matrix**.
- **PORPHYROBLASTIC**
Metamorphic rock **texture** with relatively large crystals set into rock matrix, i.e. garnets in schist.
- **PSEUDOMORPH**
A crystal with the outward form of another species of mineral.
- **PYROCLAST**
Detrital volcanic material that has been ejected from a volcanic vent.
- **RADIOMETRIC DATING**
A variety of methods by which absolute ages for minerals and rocks can be obtained by studying the ratio between stable (or radioactive) daughter products and their parent elements.
- **RECRYSTALLIZATION**
Formation of new mineral grains in a rock while in the solid state.
- **RESINOUS LUSTER**
Having the reflectivity of resin.
- **RETICULATED**
Having a network or netlike structure.
- **ROCK FLOUR**
Very fine-grained rock dust, often the product of glacial action.
- **SALT DOME**
Large intrusive mass of salt.

- **SCHILLERIZATION**
Brilliant play of bright colors, often produced by minute rodlike intrusions of, for example, iron oxide, in certain minerals.
- **SCHISTOSITY**
Variety of foliation that occurs in medium, coarse-grained rocks. Generally the result of **platy** mineral grains.
- **SCORIACEOUS**
Lava or other volcanic material that is heavily pitted with hollows and empty cavities.
- **SCREE**
Mass of unconsolidated rock waste found on a mountain slope or below a cliff face, derived by weathering.
- **SECONDARY MINERAL**
Any mineral that has subsequently formed in a rock due to secondary processes.
- **SILL**
Concordant, sheet-shaped igneous **intrusion.**
- **SLATY CLEAVAGE**
Structure in some regionally metamorphosed rocks, allowing them to be split into thin sheets.
- **TEXTURE**
Size, shape, and relationships between rock grains or crystals.
- **THRUST PLANE**
Type of fault (break in the rocks of the crust) that has a low angle plane of movement, where older rock is pushed over younger rock.
- **TWINNED CRYSTALS**
Crystals that grow together, with a common crystallographic surface.
- **ULTRABASIC ROCK**
Igneous rock having less than 45% total silica.
- **VEIN**
Sheet-shaped mass of mineral material; usually cuts through rock.
- **VESICLE**
Gas-bubble cavity in lava, left as a hole after the lava solidifies.
- **VITREOUS LUSTER**
Having the luster of broken glass.
- **VOLCANIC PIPE**
Fissure through which lava flows.
- **WELL SORTED**
In sedimentary rock, when all the grains are much the same size.
- **ZEOLITE**
Group of hydrous alumino-silicates. Characterized by their easy and reversible loss of water.

INDEX

ACKNOWLEDGEMENTS

The author would like to thank the following people for their help with the production of this book: "My wife, Helen, has worked tirelessly throughout the project. She has checked the factual content and read the proofs with meticulous attention to detail. Without her help and encouragement, the work would have taken many more months to complete. My elder son, Daniel, has been a great help on the occasions when I have not fully understood the workings of my word processor, and Emily, my daughter, provided the photograph for the back flap of the jacket. Adam, my other son, has tried to help me relax now and then with games of indoor cricket and golf. I must also thank Stella Vayne, Gillian Roberts, Mary-Clare Jerram, and James Harrison for their editorial work; Dr. George Rowbotham, of Keele University, for answering numerous mineralogical questions; and Dr. Robert Symes, of the Natural History Museum, for his expert help."

Dorling Kindersley would like to thank: David Preston, Marcus Hardy, Susie Behar, Irene Lyford, Gillian Roberts, and Sophy Roberts for their invaluable editorial work; Arthur Brown, Peter Howlett of Lemon Graphics, and Alastair Wardle for additional design; Michael Allaby for compiling the index; The Right Type for additional text film output.

The author and publisher are greatly indebted to the Natural History Museum for making available for photography most of the rocks and minerals illustrated, and Alan Hart of the Mineralogy department for selecting the specimens.

PICTURE CREDITS
All photographs are by Harry Taylor except for: Chris Pellant *(top right)*, 16 *(bottom left)*, 17 *(bottom)*, 18 *(bottom left and right)*, 19 *(top right and bottom left)*, 30 *(bottom left and right)*, 31 *(bottom left)*, 32 *(bottom left)*, 33 *(top right (3) and middle)*, 34 *(top right)*, 35 *(top right and bottom left)*, 37 *(middle left)*, 38 *(bottom left)*, 39 *(middle left and right)*; Colin Keates *(Natural History Museum)* 17 *(top, right, and middle)*, 24 *(bottom right)*, 25 *(lower middle, bottom left and right)*; C.M. Dixon/ Photosources 26 *(bottom)*. Line illustrations by Chris Lyon; airbrushing by Janos Maffry; color illustrations, 7, 30, and 31 by Andy Farmer; and endpaper illustrations by Caroline Church.